Hands-On Linux Administration on Azure

Explore the essential Linux administration skills you need to deploy and manage Azure-based workloads

Frederik Vos

Pack*t>

BIRMINGHAM - MUMBAI

Hands-On Linux Administration on Azure

Copyright © 2018 Packt Publishing

Commissioning Editor: Vijin Boricha
Acquisition Editor: Rahul Nair
Content Development Editor: Nithin George Varghese
Technical Editor: Komal Karne
Copy Editor: Safis Editing
Project Coordinator: Drashti Panchal
Proofreader: Safis Editing
Indexer: Mariammal Chettiyar
Graphics: Tom Scaria
Production Coordinator: Deepika Naik

First published: August 2018

Production reference: 1310818

Published by Packt Publishing Ltd.
Livery Place
35 Livery Street
Birmingham
B3 2PB, UK.

ISBN 978-1-78913-096-6

www.packtpub.com

Mapt

`mapt.io`

Mapt is an online digital library that gives you full access to over 5,000 books and videos, as well as industry leading tools to help you plan your personal development and advance your career. For more information, please visit our website.

Why subscribe?

- Spend less time learning and more time coding with practical eBooks and Videos from over 4,000 industry professionals

- Improve your learning with Skill Plans built especially for you

- Get a free eBook or video every month

- Mapt is fully searchable

- Copy and paste, print, and bookmark content

PacktPub.com

Did you know that Packt offers eBook versions of every book published, with PDF and ePub files available? You can upgrade to the eBook version at `www.PacktPub.com` and as a print book customer, you are entitled to a discount on the eBook copy. Get in touch with us at `service@packtpub.com` for more details.

At `www.PacktPub.com`, you can also read a collection of free technical articles, sign up for a range of free newsletters, and receive exclusive discounts and offers on Packt books and eBooks.

Contributors

About the author

Frederik Vos, living in Purmerend, a city near Amsterdam in the Netherlands, works as a senior technical trainer of virtualization technologies, such as Citrix XenServer, and VMware vSphere. He specializes in data center infrastructures (hypervisor, network, and storage) and cloud computing (CloudStack, CloudPlatform, OpenStack, and Azure). He is also a Linux trainer and evangelist. He has a lot of knowledge as a teacher and also real-world experience as a system administrator. For the last three years he has been working as a freelance trainer and consultant within the ITGilde Cooperation, delivering many Linux training, such as Linux on Azure training for the Linux Foundation.

I really enjoyed working on this book! However, writing would not have been possible without the help of my wife, Carola Dahmen. During all the hours that I wasn't available, she did the hard job of keeping everything running at home!

I want to thank Packt Publishing, especially Nithin George, Varghese, and Rahul Nair for their patience and for believing me, even with the big delay caused by my move to another city.

Thanks to everyone who supported me in terms of knowledge and ideas, especially Sander van Vugt, Pascal van Dam, and several Microsoft employees.

About the reviewers

Toni Willberg is a Linux on Azure subject matter expert with over 20 years of professional IT experience. His career started in 1997 as software developer and Linux sysadmin. Currently, Toni works with Microsoft as cloud solution architect, specializing in Azure infrastructure services. Prior to Microsoft, he was with Red Hat for eight years, working as solution architect focusing on Red Hat Enterprise Linux and related infrastructure technologies.

Sander van Vugt is a Linux expert and author living in the Netherlands. Sander has published different Linux-related titles and teaches classes for customers around the world. Sander is also the Director of ITGilde Academy.

Pascal van Dam has a bachelor's degree in Computer Science and has had his first experiences with Linux and the open source world as early as 1993. He's a HP-UX, AIX, and Linux Foundation trainer. As a Linux Foundation trainer he has had the honor to bring the Story of Linux and Open Source on Azure to many Microsoft colleagues in the world. Currently, Pascal is the Cloud Linux Architect for ATOS for both the on-premise and the public clouds such as Azure. At home, Pascal has six sons together with his love in lively home full of energy. Pascal strongly believes in having an open mind with an open view in an open world.

Packt is searching for authors like you

If you're interested in becoming an author for Packt, please visit `authors.packtpub.com` and apply today. We have worked with thousands of developers and tech professionals, just like you, to help them share their insight with the global tech community. You can make a general application, apply for a specific hot topic that we are recruiting an author for, or submit your own idea.

Table of Contents

Preface

This book shows how to deploy open source workloads in Microsoft Azure using virtual machines and containers. It provides an introduction to working with Linux in Azure environments, and the reader will get an introduction to working with Azure as well.

An important part of this book contains working with command-line interfaces, which makes it easy to use automation to deploy your workload in Azure.

Last but not least, it will show you how to use configuration management solutions such as Ansible and Salt to manage Linux instances in an Azure cloud environment.

Who this book is for

This book is for Microsoft professionals and Linux administrators and developers that need to deploy and manage their workloads in Azure. Prior knowledge of Linux and Azure is not necessary.

What this book covers

Chapter 1, *Exploring the Azure Cloud*, introduces cloud computing, explaining where it started and covering the meaning of all the terminology and abbreviations that are so common in the cloud.

Chapter 2, *Getting Started with the Azure Cloud*, covers the first steps in Azure: creating your account and getting started in Azure. The chapter introduces the user interfaces, and at the end of the chapter, your first virtual machine is running.

Chapter 3, *Basic Linux Administration*, contains Linux essentials, such as using the bash shell, where to find help, and topics such as user/group management and process management, which you need as a Linux user.

Chapter 4, *Managing Azure*, explains how to work with the Azure components that you need for virtual machines and other services: network and storage. It explains commands already used in more detail, and prepares you for the next chapters.

Chapter 5, *Advanced Linux Administration*, is a deep dive into, or (if you want) a crash course on Linux system administration: network, storage, software, and services. It also covers the recently introduced systemd init system.

Chapter 6, *Managing Linux Security and Identities*, is all about protection for your workload. Starting with some tips for security, the chapter covers Linux security modules (SELinux and Apparmor), Linux firewall (FirewallD), and network ACLs. The last part of this chapter is about integration with Azure Active Directory Services.

Chapter 7, *Deploying Your Virtual Machines*, covers the automation of deployments in Azure. How do you get a reproducible environment, especially if you are a developer? And if a standard image to deploy a virtual machine is not good enough, you'll learn how to build your own.

Chapter 8, *Exploring Continuous Configuration Automation*, explains that automation is very important, especially for the deployment phase. It's not that good at managing configuration or updates, though, during the complete life cycle. Ansible, Salt, and PowerShell DSC to the rescue!

Chapter 9, *Container Virtualization in Azure*, discusses why container virtualization is very popular, what it is exactly, what the available options are, and how to build and run your containers. A great deal in this chapter is about Docker, but other solutions, such as Rkt, are covered as well.

Chapter 10, *Working with the Azure Kubernetes Service*, explains that, like the other workloads, it is not very difficult to automate containers, after that: orchestration is needed. On top of that, Kubernetes provides scalability and availability.

Chapter 11, *Troubleshooting and Monitoring Your Workloads*, the last chapter of this book, covers troubleshooting options. What can you do if you can't access the workload? What do you do if your application doesn't perform as expected? And don't forget: logging is always very important!

To get the most out of this book

This book is written for system administrators and developers that need to know how to deploy and manage their workloads in Azure. This means that you have already day-to-day experience of operational tasks. It helps if you already have some experience of using the command line and writing scripts, but it's not strictly necessary. Hence, the scripting examples in this book are not perfect. A pragmatic approach is taken to help you understand the technology in Azure and get the job done.

To get the most out of the book, it is very important that you use this book as a workbook. Go and sit behind your computer and go through all the examples. This is the only way to really understand the topics covered in this book. The only things you need are as follows:

- A computer with Linux, Windows 10, or macOS installed
- An internet connection so you are able to connect to Azure

I am also a big fan of virtual machines, running in Azure or not. You can play without breaking your daily workstation, and on top of that, you can easily redeploy them or use snapshots to undo or replay the steps you have taken.

Download the example code files

You can download the example code files for this book from your account at www.packtpub.com. If you purchased this book elsewhere, you can visit www.packtpub.com/support and register to have the files emailed directly to you.

You can download the code files by following these steps:

1. Log in or register at www.packtpub.com.
2. Select the **SUPPORT** tab.
3. Click on **Code Downloads & Errata**.
4. Enter the name of the book in the **Search** box and follow the onscreen instructions.

Once the file is downloaded, please make sure that you unzip or extract the folder using the latest version of:

- WinRAR/7-Zip for Windows
- Zipeg/iZip/UnRarX for Mac
- 7-Zip/PeaZip for Linux

The code bundle for the book is also hosted on GitHub at https://github.com/PacktPublishing/Hands-On-Linux-Administration-on-Azure. In case there's an update to the code, it will be updated on the existing GitHub repository.

We also have other code bundles from our rich catalog of books and videos available at https://github.com/PacktPublishing/. Check them out!

Download the color images

We also provide a PDF file that has color images of the screenshots/diagrams used in this book. You can download it here: https://www.packtpub.com/sites/default/files/downloads/HandsOnLinuxAdministrationonAzure_ColorImages.pdf.

Conventions used

There are a number of text conventions used throughout this book.

CodeInText: Indicates code words in text, database table names, folder names, filenames, file extensions, pathnames, dummy URLs, user input, and Twitter handles. Here is an example: "Let's make another change in the sshd_config file."

A block of code is set as follows:

```
[Mount]
What = /dev/sdc1
Where = /home/finance
Type = xfs
Options = defaults
```

When we wish to draw your attention to a particular part of a code block, the relevant lines or items are set in bold:

```
[Mount]
What = /dev/sdc1
Where = /home/finance
Type = xfs
Options = defaults
```

Any command-line input or output is written as follows:

```
sudo cp /etc/ssh/sshd_config /tmp
sudo sed -i 's/#Port 22/Port 22/' /etc/ssh/sshd_config
```

Bold: Indicates a new term, an important word, or words that you see onscreen. For example, words in menus or dialog boxes appear in the text like this. Here is an example: "If you click on **Download template and parameters**, you'll get the next screen."

Warnings or important notes appear like this.

Tips and tricks appear like this.

Get in touch

Feedback from our readers is always welcome.

General feedback: Email feedback@packtpub.com and mention the book title in the subject of your message. If you have questions about any aspect of this book, please email us at questions@packtpub.com.

Errata: Although we have taken every care to ensure the accuracy of our content, mistakes do happen. If you have found a mistake in this book, we would be grateful if you would report this to us. Please visit www.packtpub.com/submit-errata, selecting your book, clicking on the Errata Submission Form link, and entering the details.

Piracy: If you come across any illegal copies of our works in any form on the Internet, we would be grateful if you would provide us with the location address or website name. Please contact us at copyright@packtpub.com with a link to the material.

If you are interested in becoming an author: If there is a topic that you have expertise in and you are interested in either writing or contributing to a book, please visit authors.packtpub.com.

Reviews

Please leave a review. Once you have read and used this book, why not leave a review on the site that you purchased it from? Potential readers can then see and use your unbiased opinion to make purchase decisions, we at Packt can understand what you think about our products, and our authors can see your feedback on their book. Thank you!

For more information about Packt, please visit `packtpub.com`.

Exploring the Azure Cloud

1

In this first chapter, I want to talk about cloud computing. What exactly is the cloud?

Starting with a small history of virtualization, I want to explain how the transformation of physical hardware into hardware components that are build-in software, made it possible to go beyond the borders of the classic data center in many ways.

After that, I'll explain the different terminology used in cloud technology.

Here is a list of topics covered in this chapter:

- Virtualization of compute, network, and storage
- Software Defined Networking, storage, and the data center
- **Service-oriented architecture** (SOA)
- Cloud services
- Cloud types

Fundamentals of cloud computing

If you are starting in a new area of expertise in **Information Technology** (IT), most of the time you'll start studying the concepts, the architecture, and sooner or later you'll start playing around and getting familiar with the topic.

However, in cloud computing, it really helps if you not only understand the concept and the architecture, but also where it comes from. I don't want to give you a lesson in the facts of history, but I want to show you that inventions and ideas in the past are still in use in modern cloud environments. This will give you a better understanding of what the cloud is and how to use it within your organization.

Virtualization

In the early 1970s, IBM was working on some sort of virtualization: each user had their own separated operating system, while still sharing the overall resources of the underlying system.

The main reason to develop this system was the possibility of assigning the resources based on the application needs, to add extra security and reliability: if a virtual machine crashes, the other virtual machines are still running without any problem. Nowadays, this type of virtualization has evolved into container virtualization!

Fast forward to 2001, and another type of virtualization, called hardware virtualization, was introduced by companies such as VMWare. In their product, VMware Workstation, they added a layer on top of an existing operating system that provided a set of standard hardware, build-in software instead of physical elements, to run a virtual machine. This layer become known as a **hypervisor**. Later on, they built their own operating system that specialized in running virtual machines: VMware ESX.

In 2008, Microsoft entered the hardware-virtualization market with the Hyper-V product, as an optional component of Windows 2008.

Hardware virtualization is all about separating software from hardware, breaking the traditional boundaries between hardware and software. The hypervisor is responsible for mapping the virtual resources on physical resources.

This type of virtualization was the enabler for a revolution in data centers:

- Because of the standard set of hardware, every virtual machine can run everywhere
- Because virtual machines are isolated from each other, there is no problem if a virtual machine crashes
- Because a virtual machine is just a set of files, you have new possibilities for backup, moving virtual machines, and so on
- New options possible in **high availability** (**HA**), the migration of running virtual machines
- New deployment options, for example, working with templates
- New options in central management, orchestration, and automation, because it's all software
- Isolation, reservation, and limiting of resources where needed, sharing resources where possible

Software-Defined Datacenter

Of course, if you can transform hardware into software for compute, it's only a matter of time before someone realizes you can do the same for network and storage.

For networking, it all started with the concept of virtual switches. Like every other form of hardware virtualization, it is nothing more than building a network switch in the software instead of hardware.

In 2004, development started on **Software Defined Networking** (**SDN**), to decouple the control plane and the data plane. In 2008, there was the first real switch implementation that achieved this goal using the OpenFlow protocol at Stanford University.

Using SDN, you have similar advantages as in compute virtualization:

- Central management, automation, and orchestration
- More granular security by traffic isolation and providing firewall and security policies
- Shaping and controlling data traffic
- New options available for HA and scalability

In 2009, **Software-Defined Storage** (**SDS**) development started at several companies, such as scality and cleversafe. Again, it's about abstraction: decoupling services (logical volumes and so on) from the physical storage elements.

If you have a look into the concepts of SDS, some vendors added a new feature to the already existing advantages of virtualization. You can add a policy to a virtual machine, defining the options you want: for instance, replication of data or a limit on the number of IOPS. This is transparent for the administrator; there is communication between the hypervisor and the storage layer to provide the functionality. Later on, this concept was also adopted by some SDN vendors.

You can actually see that virtualization slowly changed to a more service-oriented way of thinking.

If you can virtualize every component of the physical data center, you have a **Software-Defined Datacenter** (**SDDC**). The virtualization of networking, storage, and compute function made it possible to go further than the limits of one piece of hardware. SDDC makes it possible, by abstracting the software from the hardware, to go beyond the borders of the physical data center.

In the SDDC environment, everything is virtualized and often fully automated by the software. It totally changes the traditional concept of data centers. It doesn't really matter where the service is hosted or how long it's available (24-7 or on demand), and there are possibilities to monitor the service, maybe even add options such as automatic reporting and billing, which all make the end user happy.

SDDC is not the same as the cloud, not even a private cloud running in your data center, but you can argue that, for instance, Microsoft Azure is a full-scale implementation of SDDC. Azure is by definition software-defined.

SOA

In the same period that hardware virtualization become mainstream in the data center, and the development of SDN and SDS started, something new was coming in the world of software development and implementation for web-based applications' SOA:

- Minimal services that can talk to each other, using a protocol such as SOAP. Together they deliver a complete web-based application.
- The location of the service doesn't matter, the service must be aware of the presence of the other service, and that's about it.
- A service is a sort of black box; the end user doesn't need to know what's inside the box.
- Every service can be replaced.

For the end user, it doesn't matter where the application lives or that it consists of several smaller services. In a way, it's similar to virtualization: what seems to be one physical resource, for instance, a storage LUN, can actually include several physical resources (storage devices) in multiple locations.

The power of virtualization combined with SOA gives you even more options in scalability, reliability, and availability.

There are many similarities between the SOA model and SDDC, but there is a difference: SOA is about interaction between different services; SDDC is more about the delivery of services to the end user.

The modern implementation of SOA is microservices, provided by cloud environments such as Azure, running standalone or running in virtualization containers such as Docker.

Cloud services

here's that magic word: *cloud*. It's not that easy to find out exactly what it means. One way to describe it is that you want to provide a service that:

- Is always available, or available on-demand
- Can be managed by self-service
- Is able to scale up/down, and so is elastic
- Offers rapid deployment
- Can be fully automated and orchestrated

On top of that, you want monitoring and new types of billing options: most of the time, you only pay for what you use.

Cloud technology is about the delivery of a service via the internet, in order to give an organization access to resources such as software, storage, network, and other types of IT infrastructure and components.

The cloud can offer you many service types, here are the most important ones:

- **Infrastructure as a service (IaaS)**: A platform to host your virtual machines
- **Platform as a service (PaaS)**: A platform to develop, build, and run your applications, without the complexity of building and running your own infrastructure
- **Software as a service (SaaS)**: Using an application running in the cloud, such as Office 365

Cloud types

There are several cloud implementations possible:

- **Public cloud**: Running all the services at a service provider. Microsoft's Azure is an implementation of this type.
- **Private cloud**: Running your own cloud in your data center. Microsoft recently developed a special version of Azure for this: Azure Stack.
- **Hybrid cloud**: A combination of a public and private cloud. One example is combining the power of Azure and Azure Stack, but you can also think about new disaster recovery options or moving services from your data center to the cloud and back if more resources are temporarily needed.

The choice for one of these implementations depends on several factors, to name a few:

- **Costs**: Hosting your services in the cloud can be more expensive than hosting them locally, caused by resource usage. On the other hand, it can be cheaper; for example, you don't need to implement complex and costly availability options.
- **Legal restrictions**: Sometimes you are not allowed to host data in a public cloud.
- **Internet connectivity**: There are still countries where the necessary bandwidth or even the stability of the connection is a problem.
- **Complexity**: Hybrid environments can be especially difficult to manage; support for applications and user-management can be challenging.

Understanding the Azure Cloud

Now that you know more about virtualization and cloud computing, it's time to introduce you to the Microsoft implementation of the cloud: Azure.

Starting again with some history, in this chapter, you'll find out about the technology behind Azure and that Azure can be a very good solution for your organization.

A small history of the Azure Cloud

In 2002, Microsoft started a project called Whitehorse, to streamline the development, deployment, and implementation of an application within an SOA model. In this project, there was a focus on delivering small prebuilt web applications and the ability to transform them into a service. This project died silently around 2006.

Many of the lessons learned in this project and the appearance of **Amazon Web Services** (**AWS**) were the drivers for Microsoft to start a project called RedDog in 2006.

After a while, Microsoft added three other development teams to this project:

- **.NET Services**: Services for developers using the SOA model. .NET Services offered Service Bus as a secure, standards-based messaging infrastructure.
- **Live Services and Live Mesh**: A SaaS project to enable PCs and other devices to communicate with each other through the internet.
- **SQL Services**: A SaaS project to deliver Microsoft SQL through the internet.

In 2008, Microsoft announced the start of Azure, and with its public release in 2010, Azure was ready to deliver IaaS and PaaS solutions. The name RedDog survived for a while: the classic portal was also known as **RedDog Front-End** (**RDFE**).

Nowadays, Azure is the Microsoft solution for the public cloud, delivering all kinds of services, such as virtual machines, Web and Mobile Apps, Active Directory, and databases.

It's still growing in its number of features, customers, and availability. Azure is available in more than 36 regions. This is very important for scalability, performance, and redundancy.

Having these many regions also helps compliance with legal rules and security/privacy policies. Microsoft is using the same Online Services Terms (`http://www.microsoftvolumelicensing.com/`) for all their online services, such as Office 365, which includes rulings such as the EU Standard Contractual Clause. Information and documents regarding security, privacy, and compliance are available via Microsoft's Trust Center: `https://www.microsoft.com/en-us/TrustCenter`.

Azure architecture

Microsoft Azure is running on a customized, stripped-down, and hardened version of Hyper-V, also known as the **Azure Hypervisor**.

On top of this hypervisor, there is a cloud layer. This layer or fabric is a cluster of many hosts hosted in Microsoft's data center and is responsible for the deployment, management, and health of the infrastructure.

This layer is managed by the fabric controller, which is responsible for resource management, scalability, reliability, and availability.

This layer also provides the management interface via an API, built on REST, HTTP, and XML. Another way to interact with the fabric controller is provided by the Azure Portal and software such as the Azure CLI via the Azure Resource Manager.

These user-interfacing services will communicate through resource providers to the fabric:

- Compute Resource Provider
- Network Resource Provider
- Storage Resource Provider

These resource providers will create the needed services, such as a virtual machine.

Azure in your organization

Azure can deliver IaaS: it's easy to deploy virtual machines, manually or automated, and use these virtual machines to develop, test, and host your applications. There are many extra services available to make your life as a system engineer easier, such as backup and restore options, adding storage, and availability options. For web applications, it's even possible to deliver the service without creating a virtual machine!

Of course, Azure can also be used for PaaS solutions; like IaaS, PaaS includes all components for your infrastructure but adds support for the complete life cycle of your cloud applications: building, testing, deploying, managing, and updating. There are precoded application components available as well; you can save time transforming these components together with your code into the service you want to deliver. Containers can be another part of your PaaS solution, the Azure Container Service simplifies the deployment, management, and operations on containers using Kubernetes or another orchestrator, such as Mesos.

If you are a company or organization that wants to host an SaaS solution in Azure, this is possible using AppSource. You can even provide integration with other Microsoft products, such as Office 365 and Dynamics.

In 2017, Microsoft announced Azure Stack. You can run Azure now in your own data center or run it in the data center from a service provider of your choice to provide IaaS and PaaS. It will give you the power of Azure in scalability and availability, without worrying about the configuration. You only need to add more physical resources if needed. And if you want, you can use it in a hybrid solution with the public Azure for disaster recovery or consistent workloads in both cloud and on-premises deployments.

Azure Stack is not the only thing you can use for hybrid environments. You can, for instance, connect your local Active Directory with Azure Active Directory, or use the Azure Active Directory application to provide SSO to both local and hosted web applications.

Azure and open source

In 2009, before Azure went public, Microsoft started adding support for open source frameworks, such as PHP, and in 2012, added support for Linux virtual machines, due to requests from many customers.

At that time, Microsoft was not a big friend of the open source community, and it's fair to say that they really didn't like the Linux operating system. This changed around 2014, when Satya Nadella succeeded Steve Ballmer as CEO of Microsoft. In October of that year, he even announced at a Microsoft Conference in San Francisco that *Microsoft loves Linux*!

Since that time, Azure has grown into a very open-source-friendly environment:

- It offers a platform for many open source solutions, such as Linux instances, container technology, and application/development frameworks.
- Integration with open source solutions by providing open and compatible APIs. For instance, the CosmoDB service offers a MongoDB-compatible API.
- Documentation, SDKs, and examples are all Open Source and available on GitHub: `https://github.com/Azure`.
- Microsoft is working together with open source projects and vendors and is also a major contributor of code to many open source projects.

In 2016, Microsoft entered the Linux Foundation organization as a Platinum member to confirm their steadily increasing interest and engagement in open source development.

In October 2017, Microsoft said that more than 40% of all virtual machines in Azure are running the Linux Operating System and Azure is running many containerized workloads. Besides that, the microservices are all using open source programming languages and interfaces.

Microsoft is very serious about open source technology, open source PowerShell, and many other products. Not every Microsoft product in Azure is open source, but at least you can install and run Microsoft SQL on Linux.

Summary

In this chapter, we discussed the history of virtualization, the concept of the cloud, and explained the terminology used in cloud environments.

Some people think that Microsoft was a little bit late entering the world of the clouds, but actually they started researching and developing techniques in 2006, and many parts of that work survived in Azure. Some of the projects died, because it was too early and many people were skeptical about the cloud in those days.

We also covered the architecture of the Azure cloud and the services that Azure can offer your organization.

In the last part of this chapter, I showed you that Azure is a very open-source-friendly environment and that Microsoft puts in a lot of effort to make Azure an open, standard cloud solution with interoperability in mind.

In the next chapter, we'll start using Azure and learn how to deploy and use Linux in Azure.

Questions

1. What components in your physical data center can be transformed into software?
2. What is the difference between container virtualization and hardware virtualization?
3. If you want to host an application in the cloud, which service type is the best solution?
4. Let's say one of your applications needs strict privacy policies. Is it still a good idea to use cloud technology for your organization?
5. Why are there so many regions available in Azure?
6. What is the purpose of Azure Active Directory?

Further reading

If you want to learn more about Hyper-V and how you can use Azure together with Hyper-V for site recovery and protection of your workloads, check out *Windows Server 2016 Hyper-V Cookbook, Second Edition* by Packt.

There are many nice technical articles about the history of virtualization, cloud computing, and their relationship. One I really want to mention is about the *Formal Discussion on Relationship between Virtualization and Cloud Computing* (ISBN 978-1-4244-9110-0).

Don't forget to visit the Microsoft website and GitHub repository as mentioned in this chapter!

Getting Started with the Azure Cloud

2

In the first chapter, I covered the history of, and the ideas behind, virtualization and cloud computing. After that, you read about the Microsoft Azure Cloud. This chapter will help you take your first steps into the world of Azure, get access to Azure, explore the different Linux offerings, and deploy your first Linux virtual machine.

After deployment, you will need access to your virtual machine using SSH with password authentication, or using an SSH key pair.

To take the first steps on your journey into the Azure Cloud, it is important to complete all the exercises and examine the outcome.

> Everything in this chapter is tested on macOS, Windows Subsystem for Linux, and the latest versions of CentOS and openSUSE LEAP.

Technical requirements

If you want to try all the examples in this chapter, you'll need at least a browser. For stability reasons, it's important to use a very recent version of a browser. Microsoft offers a list of supported browsers in the documentation on the Azure documentation website:

- Microsoft Edge (latest version)
- Internet Explorer 11
- Safari (latest version, Mac only)
- Chrome (latest version)
- Firefox (latest version)

Based on personal experience, I recommend using Google Chrome or a browser based on a recent version of its engine, such as Vivaldi.

You can do all the exercises in your browser, even the exercises involving the command line. In daily life, it's a better idea to use a local installation of the software; it's faster, easier to copy and paste code, and you can save history and the output from the commands.

Getting access to Azure

To start in Azure, the first thing you'll need is an account. Go to `https://azure.microsoft.com` and get yourself a free account to get started, or use the corporate account that is already in use. Another possibility is to use Azure with a Visual Studio Dev Essentials subscription, a Visual Studio subscription, or an Enterprise/Dev subscription.

If you are using a free account, you'll get some credits to start, some of the popular services for a limited time, and some services that will stay free forever, such as the container service. You can find the most recent list of free services at `https://azure.microsoft.com/en-us/free`. You won't be charged during the trial period, except for virtual machines that need additional licensing, but you do need a credit card to identify yourself.

Logging in using the Azure portal

Point your browser to `https://azure.microsoft.com` and use your credentials to log in. You are ready to start using Azure, or, in other words, to start using your subscription. In Azure, a subscription grants you access to the Azure Portal with your account, which is also used for accounting and billing, and a subscription gives you access to Azure services.

The Azure portal takes you to a dashboard that you can modify to meet your monitoring needs. You can now do the following:

- Inspect your resources
- Create new resources
- Visit the marketplace
- Get insights into your billing

You can use the web interface, doing everything graphically, or use the Azure Cloud Shell available via the web interface, which provides a Bash or a PowerShell interface.

Getting command-line access to Azure

There are several good reasons to prefer the command line. That's why in this book we'll mostly cover command-line access:

- It can help you to understand the architecture of Azure. In the graphical interface, often you can do many things in one configuration window, without understanding the relationships between the different fields and components.
- It is the first step in automation and orchestration.
- The web interface is still in active development; the web interface can, and will, change over time:
    - Some features and options are not available yet.
    - It is possible that Microsoft will relocate features and options in the web interface.
- The command-line interface, on the other hand, is very stable in syntax and output.

In this book, we will use both the Azure CLI in the Bash shell and PowerShell with the AzureRM cmdlet. Both are well-suited, platform agnostic, and there is, besides one or two exceptions, feature-wise no difference between them. Choose your favorite, because you're already familiar with it, or give both interfaces a try and choose afterward.

Installing the Azure command-line interface

If you use the Bash interface within the Azure Cloud Shell, there is a pretty complete Linux environment available to play with. It also provides Azure-specific commands, such as the `az` command.

You can also install this utility in Windows, macOS, and Linux. A Docker container is available as well. You can find detailed installation instructions for all these platforms at https://docs.microsoft.com/en-us/cli/azure.

Let's use CentOS/RHEL 7 as an example to install the Azure command-line interface:

1. Import the Microsoft repository GPG key:

```
sudo rpm --import https://packages.microsoft.com/keys/microsoft.asc
```

2. Add the repository:

```
sudo yum-config-manager --add-repo\
  https://packages.microsoft.com/yumrepos/azure-cli
```

3. Install the software:

```
sudo yum install azure-cli
```

4. Use the `az -v` command to find out which version is installed, and which components are in use by the Azure CLI.

On macOS, you have to install Homebrew first, a free and open source package management system that simplifies the installation of, mostly, open-source software:

1. Open a Terminal and execute:

```
ruby -e "$(curl -fsSL \
https://raw.githubusercontent.com/Homebrew/install/master/install)"
```

2. Update Homebrew and install the Azure CLI:

```
brew update && brew install azure-cli
```

3. Use the `az -v` command to find out which version is installed, and which components are in use by the Azure CLI.

Logging in with the Azure CLI

Before you can use the CLI, you have to log in:

```
az login
```

This command will prompt you to go to `https://microsoft.com/devicelogin` and enter a code for authorization. This code will be displayed by the command.

To sign in, use a web browser to open `https://microsoft.com/devicelogin` and enter the code to authenticate. If this is successful, it will give you some output in JSON format regarding your subscription, such as your username:

```
[
  {
    "cloudName": "AzureCloud",
      "id": "....",
      "isDefault": true,
      "name": "Pay-As-You-Go",
      "state": "Enabled",
      "tenantId": "....",
      "user": {
        "name": "....",
```

```
      "type": "user"
    }
  }
]
```

Entering the code for authentication will be removed in the near feature.

To get this information again, type the following:

```
az account list
```

You can always format the output in JSON, JSONC, TABLE, or TSV formats, using extra parameters.

The JSON (or JSONC, the colored variant) format is easy to parse in programming and scripting languages:

```
~ >>> az group list --output jsonc
[
  {
    "id": "/subscriptions/88525bff-081c-45ad-ba31-
oud-shell-storage-westeurope",
    "location": "westeurope",
    "managedBy": null,
    "name": "cloud-shell-storage-westeurope",
    "properties": {
      "provisioningState": "Succeeded"
    },
    "tags": null
  }
]
```

TSV, **Tab-Separated Values**, can be a very good idea if the output is a single value, if you want to use text filtering utilities such as AWK, or if you want to export the output to a spreadsheet:

```
~ >>> az group list --output tsv
/subscriptions/88525                                  )e69/resourceGroups/clo
torage-westeurope          westeurope      None    cloud-shell-storage-we
one
```

The table output is very human-readable, but is more limited than the default output:

```
~ >>> az group list --output table
Name                              Location     Status
--------------------------------  ----------   ---------
cloud-shell-storage-westeurope    westeurope   Succeeded
```

```
az account list -o table
```

To make reading the JSON output easier, you can also query for specific fields:

```
az account list -o table --query '[].[user.name]'
```

The `--query` parameter allows you to narrow down the output to just the data I want using a powerful query language called JMESPATH (`http://jmespath.org`). Look at the JSON output of the `az` account listing command again. This query is searching for the field user and the property name. Let's go back to the login procedure. Doing this every time, again and again, is maybe not the most user-friendly procedure. A better way to do it is by creating a service principle, a credential for a specific application:

```
az ad sp create-for-rbac --name <USERNAME> --password <PASSWORD>
```

The output, again in JSON format, will provide an application ID (`appID` parameter):

```
{
    "appID": "....",
    "displayName": "USERNAME",
    "name": "http://USERNAME",
    "password": "PASSWORD",
    "tenant": "...."
}
```

An application represents an object in the Azure tenant. An application that requires access must be represented by a security principle. The security principle defines the access policy and permissions for the user/application in the tenant. This enables authentication of the user/application during sign-in, and role-based authorization during resource access. To summarize, you can use the appID to sign in.

List the role that is assigned to the newly created appID:

```
az role assignment list --assignee <appID> -o table
```

By default, the contributor role is used. This rule has full permissions to read and write to your Azure account.

Now, it's a good idea to test this and log out:

```
az logout
```

Now, log in again using the appID:

```
az login --service-principal --username <appID> --tenant <tenant id>
```

Unfortunately, there is no way to store the username, appID, or tenant ID in a configuration file. Optionally, you can add `--password` to the command.

Instead of typing complete commands using the `az` command, you can also open it in interactive shell mode:

```
az interactive
```

One of the greatest features of this shell is that it splits the terminal into two windows. In the upper screen, you can type your commands; in the lower screen, you'll get all the help while typing the commands. On top of that, there is auto-complete support for commands, parameters, and often parameter values.

PowerShell

You can find detailed instructions on the GitHub repository for PowerShell: `https://github.com/PowerShell`. In this book, we're using Red Hat/CentOS 7 as an example:

1. Import the Microsoft repository GPG key, if not already done, while following the installation procedure for the Azure CLI:

   ```
   sudo rpm --import https://packages.microsoft.com/keys/microsoft.asc
   ```

2. Add the repository:

   ```
   sudo yum-config-manager --add-repo \
     https://packages.microsoft.com/rhel/7/prod/
   ```

3. Install the software:

   ```
   sudo yum install powershell
   ```

4. Use `pwsh -v` to show the installed version.
5. Enter PowerShell:

   ```
   pwsh
   ```

On macOS, you'll need Homebrew and Homebrew Cask. Cask extends Homebrew to install more and bigger applications:

1. Install Homebrew Cask:

   ```
   brew tap caskroom/cask
   ```

2. Install PowerShell:

   ```
   brew cask install powershell
   ```

3. Use `pwsh -v` to show the installed version.
4. Enter PowerShell:

   ```
   pwsh
   ```

It doesn't matter which operating system you want to use PowerShell for Azure on; you'll need to install the Azure for PowerShell modules.

PowerShell has an online repository, **PowerShell Gallery** (**PSGallery**), and an Azure module called `PowerShellGet`.

> In Windows and Linux, you can only install modules if you have enough privileges. In Linux, run `pwsh` as root. In Windows, run PowerShell as administrator.

Install or update this module first:

```
Install-Module PowerShellGet -Force
```

Use this module to install the Azure modules:

```
Install-Module -Name AzureRM.Netcore -AllowClobber
```

`PowerShellGet` will prompt you to trust the repository, select `[A] Yes to All`. Untrusted repository—You are installing the modules from an untrusted repository.

If you trust this repository, change its `InstallationPolicy` value by running the `Set-PSRepository` cmdlet:

```
Are you sure you want to install the modules from 'PSGallery'?
[Y] Yes [A] Yes to All [N] No [L] No to All [S] Suspend [?] Help
(default is "N"): A
```

AzureRM.Netcore only contains a subset of all available cmdlets for Azure, but for the purposes of this book, that's enough. However, if you want all cmdlets, just remove the Netcore part. As with the az command, we'll cover the Azure PowerShell cmdlets often, for the same reasons. Both methods are very powerful; try them both, and use the one you like!

Logging in with PowerShell

After the installation process, import the cmdlet:

```
Import-Module AzureRM.Netcore
```

If you don't create a PowerShell script, but are only executing commands within the PowerShell environment, every time you want to play with Azure, you'll need to execute this command again. But, if you want, you can automatically load the modules.

First, find out where your PowerShell profile is on your filesystem by executing the following:

```
$profile
```

Open or create this file in a text editor, and add a line:

```
Import-Module AzureRM.Netcore
```

It may be necessary to create the directory structure before you can actually create this file.

Now, you can execute all available commands for Azure.

1. Log in using the following cmdlet:

   ```
   Login-AzureRmAccount
   ```

   This cmdlet will prompt you to go to https://microsoft.com/devicelogin and enter a code for authorization.

2. To sign in, use a web browser to open `https://microsoft.com/devicelogin`, and enter the code to authenticate. If login is successful, you will receive information about your account, such as the username and tenant ID:

```
PS /Users/frederik> Login-AzureRmAccount
WARNING: To sign in, use a web browser to open the page https://microsoft.com/de
vicelogin and enter the code B6DSM5FWE to authenticate.


Account           : frederik.vos@linvirt.nl
SubscriptionName  : Pay-As-You-Go
SubscriptionId    : 88                              69
TenantId          : 0491                            01
Environment       : AzureCloud
```

3. Similar to the Azure CLI method, create a service principle. But, before you can do that, convert the password to a secure string. Store this string in a variable named `pass`:

```
$pass = ConvertTo-SecureString "YOURPASS" `
  -AsPlainText -Force
```

4. Now, create the service principle:

```
New-AzureRmADServicePrincipal
  -DisplayName <USERNAME> -Password $pass
```

```
PS /Users/frederik> New-AzureRmADServicePrincipal -DisplayName linvirt1 -Passwor
d $pass


ServicePrincipalNames : {d7d2711b-a1e1-496d-96a6-6faa8f71b12b, http://linvirt1}
ApplicationId         : d7d2711b-a1e1-496d-96a6-6faa8f71b12b
DisplayName           : linvirt1
Id                    : 39b32819-bd7b-4224-85ef-13f928847597
Type                  : ServicePrincipal
```

In the output, please note the `ApplicationId` of the `ServicePrincipal`.

5. Assign the contributor role to this service principle:

```
New-AzureRmRoleAssignment `
  -RoleDefinitionName Contributor `
  -ServicePrincipalName <APP ID>
```

6. Now, you should be able to log in:

```
$cred = New-Object `
System.Management.Automation.PSCredential("<APP ID>",$pass)
```

7. It's a very good idea to save everything to a file:

```
Save-AzureRmContext`
  -Path /home/student/azprofile.json
```

Then, log in automatically:

```
Import-AzureRmContext `
  -Path /home/student/.azprofile.json
```

If you want, you can add this command to your PowerShell profile as well.

Azure Resource Manager

Before you can start the deployment of your first Linux Virtual Machine, it's important to know more about the **Azure Resource Manager** (**ARM**).

Basically, the ARM enables you to work with resources, such as storage and virtual machines. To do so, you have to create one or more Resource Groups, so you can execute life-cycle operations, such as deploy, update and delete all the resources in the Resource Group, in a single operation.

> A Resource Group must be created in a region, also known as a location. Please notice that there can be differences in the services offered in a specific region. To learn more about the differences, please visit https://azure.microsoft.com/en-us/global-infrastructure/services/

First, get a list of locations and execute them in PowerShell:

```
Get-AzureRMLocation | Select-Object "Location"
```

You can also execute them in Bash:

```
az account list-locations --query '[].name'
```

Create a resource group in one of the regions:

```
New-AzureRmResourceGroup -Location westus `
    -Name "MyResource1"
```

Now, verify the result:

```
Get-AzureRmResourceGroup | Format-Table
```

This is the Bash version:

```
az group create --location westus2 --name MyResource2
```

To verify the result of this command, execute the following:

```
az group list -o table
```

Besides working with regions and resource groups, you have to understand the concept of SKU. An SKU refers to replication options. The available SKUs are as follows:

- **Standard_LRS**: Locally Redundant Storage
    - **Premium_LRS**: Same as the LRS, but it supports blobs
    - **Standard_GRS**: Geo Redundant Storage
    - **Standard_RAGRS**: Read-Access Geo-Redundant storage
- **Standard_ZRS**: Zone-Redundant Storage

> More information is available on the Microsoft website: `https://docs.microsoft.com/en-us/azure/storage/common/storage-redundancy`.

Understanding this concept is important because, together with your resource group, a storage account is needed in a region. A storage account provides a unique namespace in Azure to store data (such as diagnostics and the possibility to uses services such as Azure Files). To configure redundancy for this data, you have to specify the SKU:

```
New-AzureRmStorageAccount -Location westus `
    -ResourceGroupName MyResource1`
    -Name "<NAME>" -SkuName Standard_LRS
```

Or do so via the Azure CLI:

```
az storage account create --resource-group MyResource2
  --sku Standard_LRS --name <NAME>
```

You can create one storage account per region, and the name must be unique across Azure.

Linux and Azure

Linux is everywhere, on many different devices, in many different environments. There are many different flavors. Why? The choice is yours, but what do you choose? There are any questions, and many different answers are possible. But one thing's for sure: in corporate environments, support is important.

Linux distributions

There are many different Linux distributions around. There are often discussions on internet forums about this fact. But, there are reasons why there are so many:

- A Linux distribution is a collection of software. Some collections are there for a specific objective. A good example of such a distribution is Kali Linux, which is an advanced penetration testing Linux distribution.
- Linux is not a multi-purpose operating system. You can use Linux on many different devices: from cars to servers, from synthesizers to workstations. Every Linux implementation must be optimized for a specific goal.
- Open source is Darwinist by nature. Sometimes, a project is forked, for instance, because some other developers don't like the goal of the project or think they can do better and patches are not accepted. Only the strongest projects will survive.
- It is a matter of taste. Different people have different tastes and opinions. Some people like the Debian apt package manager; other people may like SUSE's Zypper tool.

Another big difference is that some distributions are collected and supported by vendors such as Red Hat, SUSE, and Canonical, whereas others, such as Debian, are community-driven.

In production environments, support is important:

- Who is responsible for the updates, and what kind of information comes together with the updates?
- Who is responsible for support, and who am I going to call if there is a problem?
- Who is going to advise me if there are legal problems with the software licensing?
- Linux vendors often pay developers to create and maintain software.

Microsoft-endorsed Linux distributions

In the Azure Marketplace, there are Linux images provided by third parties, also called Microsoft Azure Partners. These are Microsoft-endorsed Linux distributions.

Microsoft works together with these partners and the Linux community to make sure that these Linux distributions are working well on Azure.

It is possible to import your own image, even your own Linux distribution, into Azure. Microsoft contributes directly to the Linux kernel, providing the Linux Integration Services for Hyper-V and Azure, and because of this you can run every Linux distribution on Linux as long as support is compiled into the kernel. Also, on every Linux image in the Azure Marketplace, the Azure Linux Agent is installed, but the source code of this agent is available on GitHub as well, so you can install it in your image. Microsoft is even willing to guide you if you have issues with Linux; just buy a support plan!

For some commercial Linux distributions, there are great support options available:

- **Red Hat**: There is full support by the vendor, but extra money is charged. There is an RHEL VM image surcharge.
- **Oracle Linux**: Microsoft offers a support plan; additional commercial support can be bought from Oracle.
- **SUSE**: There are premium images supported by Microsoft; if needed, they will call SUSE for you. This premium image includes all software, updates, and patches.
- **Other vendors**: Microsoft offers a support plan.

> Please visit the Microsoft website for a recent list of endorsed distributions and versions, and details about the support that is available for a distribution.

Deploying a Linux virtual machine

After covering the the available Linux distributions in Azure and the level of support you can get, after setting up an environment where you can create a virtual machine, it's time to deploy our first virtual machine.

Your first virtual machine

The resource group is created, a storage account is created in this resource group, and now you are ready to create your first Linux Virtual Machine in Azure.

In PowerShell use the following command:

```
New-AzureRmVM -Name "UbuntuVM" -Location westus `
  -ResourceGroupName MyResource1 -ImageName UbuntuLTS `
  -Size Standard_B1S
```

The cmdlet will prompt you to provide a username and password:

```
PS /Users/frederik> New-AzureRmVM -Name "UbuntuVM" -Location westus `
>> -ResourceGroupName MyResource1 -ImageName UbuntuLTS `
>> -Size Standard_B1S

cmdlet New-AzureRmVM at command pipeline position 1
Supply values for the following parameters:
Credential
User: student
Password for user student: **********


 Creating Azure resources
    11% |
    [ooooooo                                                    ]

    Creating UbuntuVM virtual machine.
```

In Bash use the following command:

```
az vm create --name UbuntuVM --resource-group MyResource2 \
  --image UbuntuLTS --authentication-type password \
  --admin-username student -size Standard_B1S
```

This was very easy, but if you create a virtual machine instance this way, the number of options you can set is very limited. Many things are automatically created, using default settings, and there are only a few versions of all Linux images available.

Let's dive a little bit further into the details, getting information about the choices made.

Images

In the example, we used an image name. You can choose between several Linux images:

- CentOS
- Debian
- RHEL
- UbuntuLTS
- CoreOS
- openSUSE-Leap SLES

But there are many more images available offered by different vendors, called **Publishers**.

Let's get a list of these publishers, in PowerShell or Bash:

```
Get-AzureRmVMImagePublisher -Location <REGION>

az vm image list-publishers --location <REGION> --output table
```

Now you know the publisher, you can get a list of images provided by this publisher:

```
Get-AzureRmVMImageOffer -Location REGION `
  -PublisherName <PUBLISHER> | select Offer
```

After that, execute the following:

```
az vm image list-offers --location <REGION> `
  --publisher <PUBLISHER> --output table
```

The output is a list of so-called *offers*. An offer is the name of a group of related images created by a publisher.

Query for a specific instance within this offer, an SKU:

```
Get-AzureRmVMImage -Location <REGION>`
 -PublisherName <PUBLISHER> -Offer <OFFER> `
 -Skus <SKU> | select Version -last 1

az vm image list --location <REGION> --publisher <PUBLISHER> \
  --offer <OFFER> --sku SKU --all --query '[].version' \
  --output tsv | tail -1
```

To reduce the output to the latest version, parameters were added to select the last line. The collected information are parameters for the `Set-AzureRmVMSourceImage` cmdlet:

```
Set-AzureRmVMSourceImage -PublisherName <PUBLISHER>`
  -Offer <OFFER> -Skus <SKU> -Version <VERSION>
```

In Bash, the collected information contains parameters for the `az vm create` command:

```
az vm create --location <REGION> --publisher <PUBLISHER> \
  --offer <OFFER> --sku <SKU> --version <VERSION>
```

Note: In both Bash and PowerShell, it's possible to use the word *latest* instead of a specific version.

Image sizing

Another thing you have to take care of is a decision regarding the virtual machine's size, based on your needs and costs. More information on the available sizes is available here: `https://azure.microsoft.com/en-us/pricing/details/virtual-machines/linux` The list on this website, that includes the price of the instances, changes often! You can get a list (without displaying the costs) on the command line:

```
Get-AzureRmVMSize -Location <REGION> | Format-List
```

```
az vm list-sizes --location <REGION>
```

To execute the exercises in this book, a small virtual machine is enough: At the time of writing, this is `Standard_B1S`. But it's a good idea to recheck the virtual machine sizing/pricing list, as mentioned earlier on.

In PowerShell, the `New-AzureRmVM` cmdlet can take the `-size` parameter, or you can use it in the `New-AzureRmVMConfig` cmdlet:

```
New-AzureRmVMConfig -VMName "<VM NAME>" -VMSize <SIZE>
```

In Bash, add the `--size` parameter of the `vm create` command.

Virtual machine networking

Using the command at the beginning of this chapter, several items regarding networking were created automatically:

- Virtual network
- Virtual subnet
- Virtual network interface attached to the virtual machine, and plugged into the virtual network
- Private IP address, configured on the virtual network interface
- Public IP address

The network resources will be covered in a later chapter; for now, it's enough to query the private and public IP addresses of the virtual machines:

```
Get-AzureRmPublicIpAddress -ResourceGroupName <RESOURCE GROUP>`
 | select Name,IpAddress

Get-AzureRmNetworkInterface -ResourceGroupName <RESOURCE GROUP>`
 | Get-AzureRmNetworkInterfaceIpConfig | select Name,PrivateIpAddres

az vm list-ip-addresses --resource <RESOURCE GROUP> --output table
```

The public IP address is the IP address that makes the virtual machine accessible via the internet; incoming traffic on this IP address is undergoing network address translation to the private IP address configured on the network interface inside the Linux virtual machine via DHCP.

Virtual machine information

After the deployment of the virtual machine, all the information attached to the virtual machines is available using PowerShell and Bash, for instance, the state. Querying the state is important; there are several states available:

- Running
- Stopped
- Failed
- Deallocated

If a virtual machine is not deallocated, Microsoft will charge you for this virtual machine. The state *Failed* means that the virtual machine is not able to boot. Query the state:

```
Get-AzureRmVM -Name <VM NAME> -Status -ResourceGroupName <RESOURCE GROUP>
```

In Bash, it is possible to receive the state of the deployed virtual machines, but it's not possible to limit it without using complex queries to a single virtual machine:

```
az vm list --output table
```

To deallocate a virtual machine, first stop it:

```
Stop-AzureRmVM -ResourceGroupName <RESOURCE GROUP> -Name <VM NAME>
```

Now you are able to deallocate it:

```
az vm deallocate --name <VM NAME> --resource-group <RESOURCE GROUP>
```

You can receive much more information about the deployed virtual machines. In PowerShell, it's somewhat difficult to receive the properties of the virtual machine. First, create a variable:

```
$MYVM=Get-AzureRmVM -Name <VM NAME> -ResourceGroupName <RESOURCE GROUP>
```

Now ask for the properties and methods of this MYVM object:

```
$MYVM | Get-Members
```

View the HardwareProfile property to see the size of this instance:

```
$MYVM.HardwareProfile
```

Or to be more precise use the following command:

```
$MYVM.HardwareProfile | Select-Object -ExpandProperty VmSize
```

Try the NetworkProfile, OSProfile, and StorageProfile.ImageReference.

If you want to use the az command in Bash, the first command you maybe want to try is this:

```
az vm list --resource-group <RESOURCE GROUP>
```

The only problem here is that it shows all the information about all the virtual machines in one time; luckily, there is a `show` parameter as well, to reduce the output to a single virtual machine:

```
az vm show --name <VM NAME> --resource-group <RESOURCE GROUP>
```

And it's a good idea to limit the output by using queries:

```
az vm show --name <VM NAME> --resource-group <RESOURCE GROUP>\
  --query 'storageProfile'
```

Connecting to Linux

The virtual machine is running, ready for you to log in remotely using the credentials (username and password) you provided during the deployment of your first virtual machine. Another, more secure method using SSH key pairs is available as well.

Logging in to your Linux VM using password authentication

In the *Virtual machine networking* section, the public IP address of a virtual machine was queried from the information attached to the virtual machine. This IP address is needed to connect to an SSH client to the virtual machine.

SSH, or Secure Shell, is an encrypted protocol used to administer and communicate with servers. Linux, macOS, and the Windows subsystem for Linux comes with the command-line based openSSH client, but there are more advanced clients available, some examples are as follows:

- Windows: Putty, MobaXterm and Bitvise Tunnelier
- Linux: Putty, Remmina and Pac Manager
- Mac OS: Putty, Termius and RBrowser

Using the openSSH command-line client, connect to the virtual machine:

```
ssh <username>@<public ip>
```

Logging in to your Linux VM with an SSH private key

Using a username and password is not the best way to log into a remote machine. It is not a complete insecure operation, but you're still sending your username and password over the connection. It's also difficult to use if you want to execute scripts remotely, perform back-up operations and so forth.

An alternative, and more secure way, to log into your system is by using SSH key pairs. This is a pair of two cryptographically secured keys: a private and a public key.

The private key is retained by the client and should not be copied to any other computer. It should be kept absolutely secret. And it is a good idea, during the creation of the key pair, to protect the private key with a passphrase.

The public key on the other hand can be copied to all the remote computers you want to administer. This public key is used to encrypt the messages that only the private key can decrypt. When you try to log in, the server verifies that the client owns the private key, using this property of working with keys. There is no password sent over the connection.

There are multiple ways to create an SSH key pair; for instance, Putty and MobaXterm both provide tooling to create them. You have to do this from every workstation that needs access to the remote machine. In this book, I am using `ssh-keygen` because it's available for every operating system:

```
ssh-keygen
```

The output of the preceding command should looks as follows:

```
▶~> ssh-keygen
Generating public/private rsa key pair.
Enter file in which to save the key (/Users/frederik/.ssh/id_rsa):
Enter passphrase (empty for no passphrase):
Enter same passphrase again:
Your identification has been saved in /Users/frederik/.ssh/id_rsa.
Your public key has been saved in /Users/frederik/.ssh/id_rsa.pub.
```

Don't forget to enter a passphrase!

Create another virtual machine, and, for the case of simplicity, use the `az` command:

```
az vm create --name UbuntuVM3 --resource-group MyResource2 \
   --admin-username student --generate-ssh-keys --image UbuntuLTS
```

If you want to do it in PowerShell, use the `Add-AzureRmVMSshPublicKey` cmdlet.

After the provisioning of the virtual machine, you should be able to log in:

```
ssh student@<IP ADDRESS>
```

You will be prompted for the passphrase that protects the private key.

Summary

This chapter covered the first steps into the Microsoft Azure Cloud. And the first step always involves creating a new account or using an existing company account. With an account, you're able to log in and start discovering the Azure cloud.

In this chapter, the discovery of the Azure cloud was done within the Azure CLI command `az`, or via PowerShell; example by example, you learned more about the following:

- The log in process into Azure
- Regions
- The storage account
- Images provided by publishers
- The creation of virtual machines
- Query of information attached to a virtual machine
- What Linux is and the support available for Linux virtual machines

Last, but not least: log into your Linux virtual machine, using SSH. The next chapter starts here, with a new journey: the Linux operating system

Questions

1. What are the advantages of the command-line to access Microsoft Azure?
2. What is the purpose of a storage account?
3. Can you think of a reason why you can get the following error message?
   `Code=StorageAccountAlreadyTaken`
   `Message=The storage account named mystorage is already taken.`
4. What is the difference between an offer and an image?
5. What is the difference between a stopped and a de-allocated virtual machine?
6. What is the advantage of using the private SSH key for authentication to your Linux virtual machine?
7. The `az vm create` command has a parameter `—generate-ssh-keys`. Which keys are created, and where are they stored?

Further reading

By no means is this chapter a tutorial on using PowerShell. But if you want a better understanding of the examples or learn more about PowerShell, I can recommend you reading the book *Mastering Windows PowerShell Scripts* (ISBN 9781787126305). I suggest that you start with second chapter *Working with PowerShell* and continue until at least fourth chapter *Working with Objects in PowerShell*.

You can find more then enough online documentation about using SSH. A very good start is the wikibook: `https://en.wikibooks.org/wiki/OpenSSH`.

There is also a very old book, *SSH, The Secure Shell: The Definitive Guide* (ISBN 978-0596008956), which is still a valid source of information, especially for system engineers.

Basic Linux Administration

3

After the deployment of your first Linux **virtual machine** (**VM**), let's log in and discuss some basic Linux commands and learn how to find your way in the Linux environment. This chapter is about the Linux shell: the shell is the user interface from which you access the filesystem, manage processes such as starting and killing programs, and many other things. We'll be going into the widely used Bash shell, the configuration of the Bash shell and how to use it.

The last part of this chapter discusses the **Discretionary Access Control** (**DAC**) model and how to create, manage, and verify users and groups in Linux and get permissions for files and directories based on the username and group membership. It also covers changing file user/group ownership and how to change and verify basic permissions and access control lists.

The Linux shell

A shell is the user interface in which you can do the following:

- Interact with the kernel, filesystem, and processes
- Execute programs, aliases, and shell built-ins

A shell provides extra features such as the following:

- Scripting
- Auto-completion
- History and aliasing

There are many different shells available, such as KornShell, Bash, and the Z-Shell. Bash is the default shell on almost every Linux system. Its development started in 1988 as a replacement for one of the oldest shells: the Bourne Shell. Based on Bourne and lessons learned from other shells such as KornShell and the C-shell, Bash has become the most popular shell and is available on many different operating systems including Windows 10, FreeBSD, macOS, and Linux.

The most important features that were added are as follows:

- Command-line editing
- History support
- Auto-completion
- Integer calculations
- Function declaration
- Here documents (a way of getting text input into a separate file)
- New variables such as `$RANDOM` and `$PPID`

Lately, the Z-Shell has become more popular; the development of this shell started in 1990 and can be seen as an extension to Bash. There is also a compatibility mode with Bash! It comes with even better auto-complete support including spelling correction, more advanced pathname expansion, and can be extended with modules, for example, to get more help with commands. Worth mentioning are Oh-My-ZSH (`https://github.com/robbyrussell/oh-my-zsh`) and Prezto (`https://github.com/sorin-ionescu/prezto`) projects—these provide theming, advanced configuration, and plugin management to make Z Shell very user-friendly. All these nice features come with a price: the Z-Shell is definitely more resource-hungry than Bash.

Executing commands

One of the most important features of a shell is that you can execute commands. A command can be one of the following:

- Shell built-in (a command that is provided by Bash itself)
- Executable on a filesystem
- Alias

To find out what type of command you're executing, there is the `type` command:

```
type echo
```

Adding the −a parameter will show you if there is another version available on the filesystem:

```
alias cp='cp -i'
alias egrep='egrep --color=auto'
alias fgrep='fgrep --color=auto'
alias grep='grep --color=auto'
alias l.='ls -d .* --color=auto'
alias ll='ls -l --color=auto'
alias ls='ls --color=auto'
alias mc='. /usr/libexec/mc/mc-wrapper.sh'
alias mv='mv -i'
alias rm='rm -i'
```

Another example:

```
type ls
```

Here we see that ls is an alias for the ls command with some parameters added. An alias can replace an existing command or create a new one. The alias command without parameters will give you aliases that are already configured:

```
alias cp='cp -i'
alias egrep='egrep --color=auto'
alias fgrep='fgrep --color=auto'
alias grep='grep --color=auto'
alias l.='ls -d .* --color=auto'
alias ll='ls -l --color=auto'
alias ls='ls --color=auto'
alias mc='. /usr/libexec/mc/mc-wrapper.sh'
alias mv='mv -i'
alias rm='rm -i'
```

The ll alias is an example of a newly created command. The mv command is an example of a replacement. Create a new alias with the following:

```
alias <command>='command to execute'
```

For instance, to replace the man command with pinfo:

```
alias man='pinfo -m'
```

The `which` command can help you to identify the location of a program in the `$PATH` variable. This variable contains a list of directories that is used to find an executable. This way you don't have to provide the full path.

```
which passwd
```

The output tells you that it's available in the `/usr/bin` directory.

Command-line editing

In many ways, entering commands in the Bash shell is the same as working in a text editor. That is probably the reason why there are shortcuts for actions such as going to the start of a line, and why the shortcuts are same as in the two most famous, and most commonly used, text editors: Emacs and VI.

By default, Bash is configured to be in Emacs editing mode. The following (very important) shortcuts are as follows:

Shortcut	Use
Ctrl + l	Clear screen
Ctrl + d	Exit
Ctrl + c	Break (interrupt process)
Ctrl + a	Move to beginning of the line
Ctrl + e	Move to end of the line
Ctrl + k	Delete until the end of the line
Ctrl + y	Undo delete
Esc + b	One word backwards
Esc + f	One word forwards
Esc + Del	Delete one word backwards
Esc + d	Delete one word forwards

If you want to use the VI mode, execute the following:

```
set -o vi
```

To switch back to Emacs mode, use the following:

```
set -o emacs
```

The VI editor is covered in the section *Working with text files*. For now, you can use almost every command from command mode, including but not limited to navigation, yank and put, and so on.

The `set` command is a Bash built-in command that toggles attributes specific to Bash. Without parameters, it dumps the environment variables.

Working with history

The Bash shell provides command-line tools to work with the user's command history. Every command that you execute is registered in a history file in the home directory: `~/.bash_history`. To view the content of this history, execute the following command:

history

The output shows a numbered list; you can simply redo a command using the following:

- `!<number>`: Execute the command based on the history list number.
- `!<-number>`: For instance, `!-2`. Execute the command that was executed two commands prior to the last command in the history.
- `!<first characters of the command>`: This will execute the last item that starts with this character.
- `!!`: Redo last command. You can combine this together with other commands. For instance: `sudo !!`.

You can backward-search the history using *Ctrl + R* (Emacs mode) or using the forward slash (VI command mode). Browsing is possible using the arrow keys.

The history file is not written directly after the execution of a command, but at the end of a login session. If you are working in multiple sessions, it can be a good idea to write the history directly. To do so, execute the following:

history -a

To read the just-saved history in an other session, execute:

history -r

To clear the history of the current session:

```
history -c
```

After that, execute the following:

```
history -w
```

So, by saving the cleared history, you emptied the history file.

Another nice feature of working with the history is that you can edit it. Let's say you executed the command ls -alh, but you need ls -ltr. Just type:

```
^alh^ltr
```

This is actually the same as the following:

```
!!:s/ltr/alh/
```

Of course, you can do it for every entry in the history; for instance, for number 6 in the history list:

```
!6:s/string/newstring/
```

Sometimes there is a need for more flexibility, and you want to edit a big line that contains too many typos. That's a use case for the fc command. Fix the command using the following:

```
fc <history number>
```

This opens a text editor (VI by default), and after saving the modification, it will execute the modified command.

Auto-completion

Everyone makes typos; no one can remember every parameter. Autocompletion can prevent many errors and helps you in many ways when you enter commands.

Autocompletion works for the following:

- Executables
- Aliases
- Shell built-ins

- Programs on the filesystem
- Filenames
- Parameters, if the utility supports it and the package bash-completion is installed

If the shell is configured in Emacs mode, use *Ctrl* + i to activate autocomplete; if the shell is configured in VI mode, use *Ctrl* + p.

> If there is more than one possibility, you have to execute *Ctrl* + i or *Ctrl* + p twice.

Globbing

Globbing is expanding a non-specific filename that contains a wildcard into one or more specific filenames. Another common name for globbing is pathname expansion.

The following wildcards are recognized in the Bash shell:

- ?: One single character.
- *: Multiple characters. Please notice that if you use this wildcard as the first character, filenames starting with a dot don't match. Of course, you can use .*.
- [a-z], [abc]: One character from the range.
- {a,b,c}: A or B or C.

The following are some nice examples of using wildcards:

```
echo *

cd /usr/share/doc/wget*

ls /etc/*/*conf

mkdir -p /srv/www/{html,cgi-bin,logs}
```

Redirections

In the early days of Unix, one of the developers, Ken Thompson, defined a Unix philosophy, an approach based on experience to make everything as modular as possible and to reuse code and programs as much as possible. Especially in those days, it was important for performance reasons and to provide a method that allowed for easy maintenance of the code.

In a modified version of this Unix philosophy by Peter H Salus, the aims are as follows:

- Write programs that do one thing and do it well
- Write programs to work together
- Write programs to handle text streams, because that is a universal interface

To make this philosophy possible, programs were developed with support for file descriptors, or, in modern parlance, communication channels. Every program has at least three communication channels:

- Standard input (0)
- Standard output (1)
- Standard error (2)

One of the nice features with this implementation is that you can redirect the channels.

To redirect the standard output to a file, use the following:

```
command > filename
```

You can also append:

```
command >> filename
```

Redirect the standard error and output to a file as follows:

```
command &> filename
```

You can also use:

```
command 2>&1 filename
```

To redirect the standard input, use the following:

```
filename < command
```

Examples include:

```
ls > /tmp/test.list

echo hallo > /tmp/echotest

echo hallo again >> /tmp/echotest

ls -R /proc 2> /tmp/proc-error.test

ls -R /proc &> /tmp>proc-all.test

sort < /etc/services
```

A special version of input redirection is `heredoc.txt`:

```
cat << EOF >> /tmp/heredoc.txt
 this is a line
 this is another line
EOF
```

The `cat` command concatenates the standard output and appends it to the `/tmp/heredoc.txt` file. There is no way to interrupt that, because the keyboard is not the standard input until it encounters a label, in this example `EOF`. This method is often used to create configuration files from scripts.

Another possibility is taking the standard output of one command and redirecting it to the standard input of another command using the `|` symbol:

```
command | other command
```

For example:

```
ls | more
```

Using the `tee` command, you can combine the power of redirection and piping. There are times when you want to make sure the output of `command 1` is written to a file for troubleshooting or logging and at the same time you pipe it to the standard input of another command:

```
<command 1> | tee <file> | <command 2>
```

Appending to a file is also possible, using the `-a` parameter.

Another use case of `tee` is:

```
<command> | sudo tee <file>
```

This way, it is possible to write into a file, without using difficult `su` constructions.

Working with variables

Every command-line interface, even those without the advanced scripting possibilities, has the concept of variables. In Bash, there are two types of variable available:

- Built-in or internal variables that affect the behavior of Bash or give information about Bash. Some examples include: BASH_VERSION, EDITOR, PATH.
- Environment variables that are known to one or more application including built-in variables and user-defined variables.

To list the environment variables for your current shell, you can use the `env` or `printenv` command. The `printenv` is also able to show the content of a specific variable:

```
[linvirt@CentOS-01 ~]$ printenv PATH
/usr/local/bin:/usr/bin:/usr/local/sbin:/usr/sbin:/home/linvirt/.local/bin:/home
/linvirt/bin
```

Another way to view the content of a variable is as follows:

    echo $VARNAME

To declare an environment variable, execute `var=value`. For instance:

    animal=cat

    echo $animal

To add more characters to the value, use:

    animal=$animal,dog

    echo animal

The animal variable is only known to your current shell. If you want to export it to child processes, you need to export the variable:

    export animal

Another feature is putting the output of a command into a variable—a technique called **nesting**:

```
MYDATE=$(date -+%F)

echo $MYDATE
```

Bash is also capable of doing some simple calculations:

```
a=$(( 4 + 2 ))
```

Alternatively:

```
let a=4+2

echo $a
```

Of course, this is just a glimpse of what Bash is capable of, but this should be enough for you to learn how to handle Bash configuration files and modify them for the environment you need, so they behave in the way you like.

Bash configuration files

There are three important system-wide configuration files for the Bash shell: /etc/profile, /etc/bashrc, and /etc/environment.

The /etc/ profile is a script that is executed once if any user logs in to a system. It is not a good idea to modify this file; instead use the snap-in directory /etc/profile.d. Files in this directory are executed in alphabetical order and must have .sh as the filename extension. On a side note, /etc/profile is not only used by the Bash shell but by all available shells for Linux except PowerShell. You can also create a user-specific profile script in the home directory, ~/.bash_profile, which is also Bash-specific.

Some typical content of a profile script is as follows:

```
set -o vi

alias man="pinfo -m"

alias ll="ls -lv --group-directories-first"

shopt -u mailwarn

unset MAILCHECK
```

The `shopt` command changes some default Bash behavior, such as checking for mail or the behavior of globbing and the `history` command. The `unset` command is the opposite of the `set` command. In our example, by default, every minute Bash checks for mail; after executing the `unset MAILCHECK` command, the `MAILCHECK` variable is removed.

The script `/etc/bashrc` is started every time any user invokes a shell or shell script. For performance reasons, keep it as minimal as possible. Instead of the file `/etc/bashrc`, you can use the user-specific file: `~/.bashrc` and the script `~/.bash_logout` is executed if you exit a shell. The `bashrc` configuration files are often used to modify the prompt (`PS1` variable):

```
DARKGRAY='\e[1;30m'
GREEN='\e[32m'
YELLOW='\e[1;33m'
PS1="\n$GREEN[\w] \n$DARKGRAY(\t$DARKGRAY)-(\u$DARKGRAY)-($YELLOW-> \e[m"
```

In the following we explain the changes in the prompt:

- Colors are defined in ANSI color code
- \e: Escape character in ANSI
- \n: Newline
- \w: Current working directory
- \t: Current time
- \u: Username

The `/etc/environment` file (empty by default in Red Hat-based distributions) is the first file that is executed at login. It contains variables for every process, not just the shell. It's not a script, just one variable for each line.

An example of `/etc/environment` is:

```
EDITOR=/usr/bin/vim
BROWSER=/usr/bin/elinks
LANG=en_US.utf-8
LC_ALL=en_US.utf-8
LESSCHARSET=utf-8
SYSTEMD_PAGER=/usr/bin/more
```

The `EDITOR` variable is an important one. Many programs can invoke an editor; sometimes it's by default VI, sometimes it's not. Setting a default ensures that you can always use your favorite editor.

> If you don't want to log out and log in again, you can use the source command. This way, the variables will be read into your current shell. For instance: `source /etc/environment`.

Getting help

Whether you are new to Linux or a long-time user, from time to time, you'll need help. It's impossible to remember all available commands and their parameters. Almost every command has a `--help` parameter, and there is sometimes documentation installed in the `/usr/share/doc` directories, but the most important sources of information are the information documents and man-pages.

Using the man-pages

There is a saying, **Read The Fine Manual** (**RTFM**), and sometimes people replace the word *fine* with another less friendly word. Almost every command has a manual: a man-page provides you with all the information you need. And yes, not all man-pages, especially older ones, are easy to read, but if you use the man-pages frequently you'll get used to it, and you'll be able to find the information you need quickly enough. Normally, man-pages are installed on your system, and they are available online: `http://man7.org/linux/man-pages`.

> The man-pages are removed in the Azure images for OpenSUSE LEAP and SUSE Linux Enterprise. You have to reinstall every package to make them available again:
> `sudo zypper refresh`
> `for package in $(rpm -qa); do sudo zypper install --force --no-confirm $package; done`

Man-pages are installed in the `/usr/share/man` directory in GZIP compressed archives. Man-pages are special formatted text files that you can read with the `man` command or `pinfo`. The `pinfo` utility acts as a text browser, very similar to a text-based web browser. It adds hyperlink support and the possibility to navigate between different man-pages using the arrow keys.

If you want to replace the `man` command with `pinfo`, it is a good idea to create an alias using the `alias man="pinfo -m"` command.

Man-pages are always formatted in the same way:

- **Name**: Also with a description.
- **Synopsis**: Overview with all available parameters.
- **Description**: A (long) description of the command, sometimes including the status of the command. For instance, the man-page of the `ifconfig` command explicitly states that this command is obsolete.
- **Options**: All the available parameters of a command, sometimes including examples.
- **Examples**: If the examples are not in the options section, there may be a separate section.
- **Files**: Files and directories that are important to this command.
- **See also**: Refers to other man-pages, info pages, and other sources of documentation. Some man-pages contains other sections such as notes, bugs, history, authors, and licenses.

Man-pages are divided into several sections; they are described in the description section in the man-page of `man`:

```
The table below shows the section numbers of the manual followed by the
types of pages they contain.

0   Header files (usually found in /usr/include)
1   Executable programs or shell commands
2   System calls (functions provided by the kernel)
3   Library calls (functions within program libraries)
4   Special files (usually found in /dev)
5   File formats and conventions eg /etc/passwd
6   Games
7   Miscellaneous (including macro packages and conventions), e.g.
    man(7), groff(7)
8   System administration commands (usually only for root)
9   Kernel routines [Non standard]
```

This sectioning is important to know about, especially if you want to search for documentation. To be able to search for documentation, you'll need to index the man-pages:

```
sudo mandb
```

> **TIP**
>
> Normally, after installing a package, the index is automatically updated. Sometimes the packager will have failed to add a post-install script to execute the `mandb` command. It's a good idea to execute the command manually if you can't find the information and you are pretty sure that there should be a man-page.

After that, you can use the `apropos` or `man -k` commands to find the information you'll need. It doesn't matter which one you choose, the syntax is the same. For example:

```
man -k -s 5 "time"
```

Search for the word time, limiting the search to the man-page section 5, configuration files:

```
localtime (5)          - Local timezone configuration file
ntp.conf (5)           - Network Time Protocol (NTP) daemon configuration file ...
systemd.timer (5)      - Timer unit configuration
time.conf (5)          - configuration file for the pam_time module
timesyncd.conf (5)     - Network Time Synchronization configuration files
timesyncd.conf.d (5)   - Network Time Synchronization configuration files
```

Using info documents

Info documents are another important source of information. The difference between man-pages and info pages is that info pages are more freely formatted, whereas man-pages are a sort of instruction manual for a certain command. Info documents are, most of the time, complete handbooks.

Info documents are, like man-pages, compressed and installed in the `/usr/share/info` directory. To read them, you can use `info` or the more modern `pinfo`. Both commands act as a text-based browser. If you are a big fan of the Emacs editor, you can use the InfoMode (`https://www.emacswiki.org/emacs/InfoMode`) to read the info documents.

One of the nice features is that you can directly jump to one of the hyperlinks in the document using `pinfo` or `info`:

```
pinfo '(pinfo) Keybindings'
```

The preceding example opens the man-page of `pinfo` and jumps directly to the section `Keybindings`.

The `pinfo` command has a search option, `-a`. If there is a match, it will automatically open the corresponding `info` document or man-page. If you don't want that behavior, use the `-p` parameter.

The `info` command has a search option as well: `-k`.

Other documentation

Another source of documentation is documentation provided by the Linux distribution vendor. The websites of Red Hat, SUSE, Canonical, and Debian host useful handbooks, Wikis, and so on. They can be very useful, especially for topics that are distribution-specific, such as software management.

There are two distributions that are not Microsoft-endorsed distributions, Gentoo and Arch Linux, with more excellent wikis on their websites. And of course, some of the information in these Wikis is specific to these distributions, but many articles are useful and will work on every distribution.

The Linux Foundation hosts another wiki at `https://wiki.linuxfoundation.org`, with documentation regarding specific topics such as networking, and standards such as the LSB, which will be covered later in this chapter. Other standards are covered by the freedesktop Organisation (`https://www.freedesktop.org`). They are also responsible for the Linux `init` system, SystemD, and the Linux firewall (FirewallD); both topics are discussed in `Chapter 5`, *Advanced Linux Administration*.

Last but not least, The Linux Documentation Project can be found at `http://www.tldp.org`. While many of the documents you can find there are very old, it's still a good starting point.

Working with text files

Part of the Unix philosophy is, *write programs to handle text streams, because that is a universal interface*. Communication between programs, configuration files, and many other things is implemented in plain text. This section is all about handling plain text.

Reading text

On the most fundamental level, reading the content of a file in plain text format means taking the content of this file and redirecting it to the standard output. The cat command is one utility that is able to do that—concatenate the content of one or more files (or another input channel) to the standard output:

```
[linvirt@CentOS-01 ~]$ cat /etc/shells
/bin/sh
/bin/bash
/sbin/nologin
/usr/bin/sh
/usr/bin/bash
/usr/sbin/nologin
/bin/tcsh
/bin/csh
```

Some nice parameters of this utility are:

- -A: Show all non-printable characters
- -b: Number lines, including empty lines
- -n: Number lines, except empty lines
- -s: Suppress repeated (!) empty blank lines

There is another utility similar to cat; the tac utilities concatenate the content in reverse order.

The problem with the cat command is that it just dumps the content to the standard output, without paginating the content and the scroll-back functionality for the terminals is not that good.

The utility more is a filter for paging. It displays the text one screen-full at a time (forward only) and provide a basic search engine that can be activated by using the forward slash. At the end of the file, more will exit, with or without the message Press space to continue.

The less utility is more advanced compared to the more utility. It has the following features:

- Ability to scroll forward, backward, and horizontally
- Advanced navigation

- Advanced search engine
- Multiple file handling
- Ability to display information about the file, such as filename and length
- Ability to invoke shell commands
- In more and less, the v command is available to switch to an editor, by default the VI editor.

> Both more and less are available on every distribution; however on some of the distributions, more is an alias for less. Use the type command to verify!

If you want to see only a specific number of lines at the top of a file, there is a utility called head. By default, it shows the first ten lines of a file. You can modify this behavior using the -n parameters for the number of lines and -c for a number of bytes/kilobytes.

The head utility is the opposite of tail; it shows the last 10 lines by default. It recognizes the same parameters as head to modify that behavior. But there is an extra parameter that makes this utility extremely useful for logging purposes. -f appends the output as the file grows; it's a way of following and monitoring the content of a file. A very well-known example is:

```
sudo tail -f /var/log/messages
```

Searching in text files

As stated, many things in Linux are managed by text streams and text files. Sooner or later you will want to search in this text. This can be done by using regular expressions. A regular expression is a pattern of special characters used to match strings in a search, typically made up of special characters called meta-characters. Regular expressions are used by many applications with a built-in processor, such as the Emacs and VI text editors, and utilities such as grep, awk, and sed. Many scripting and programming languages have support for regular expressions

In this book, I'll only cover the basics of this topic—just enough for use in daily system administration tasks.

Every regular expression is built around an atom. An atom specifies what text is to be matched and where it is to be found. It can be a known single-character item or a dot if you don't know the character, class, or range, such as:

`[a-z]`	From a to z
`[abc]`	From a, b, or c

Or a short-hand class. Examples of short-hand classes are:

`[[:alnum:]]`	Alphanumeric characters
`[[:alpha:]]`	Alpha characters
`[[:digit:]]`	Numbers
`[[:upper:]]`	Upper case characters
`[[:lower:]]`	Lower case characters
`[[:space:]]`	White space

Also important is where to find the next character:

`^`	Beginning of the line
`$`	End of the line
`\<`	Beginning of the word
`\>`	End of the word
`\A`	Start of a file
`\Z`	End of a file

Using a repetition operator, you can specify how many times a character should appear:

`{n}`	Exact *n* times
`{n,}`	Minimal *n* times
`{,n}`	Maximum *n* times
`{n,n}`	Minimal and maximal *n* times
`*`	Zero or more times
`+`	One or more times
`?`	Zero or one time

A reference for regular expressions can be found in:

```
man 7 regex
```

A few examples are as follows:

- If you search for the character b and the word boom is found, it will match the letter b. If you search for bo, it will match these characters in this order.
- If you search for bo{,2}m, the words bom and boom will match. But if the word booom exists, it will not match.
- If you search for ^bo{,2}m, there will be only a match if the word boom is at the beginning of a line.

One utility we've already mentioned is the grep utility to search in text files. There are multiple versions of this utility available; nowadays egrep is the most commonly used, because it has the most complete regular expression support including short hand ranges and the possibility to use the OR alternation operator |.

Common options are:

-i	Ignore case-sensitive
-v	Invert match
-A	Lines after match
-B	Lines before match
-n	Show line number
-o	Match only

A simple example of grep is:

```
[root@server1 student]# grep -B1 umask /etc/profile

# By default, we want umask to get set. This sets it for login shell
--
if [ $UID -gt 199 ] && [ "`/usr/bin/id -gn`" = "`/usr/bin/id -un`" ]; then
    umask 002
else
    umask 022
```

The awk is a utility that was created by the developers Weinberger and Kernighan. It is a scripting language used for manipulating data and generating reports. It scans a file, line by line, splits each input line into fields, compares input line/fields to a pattern, and performs action(s) on matched lines.

Let's look into an example:

```
awk -F: '/^root/ {print "Homedir of root:", $6}' /etc/passwd
```

It scans the file `/etc/passwd` and splits the content based on the field separator colon. It searches for the line starting with the string `root`, and prints some text and the sixth column.

Editing text files

Because text files are so important in Linux, a text editor is very important. Every distribution has one or more editors in their repositories, for both graphical and non-graphical environments. You can be sure that at least VIM, a modern VI implementation, and Emacs are available. There is an ongoing war between VI lovers and Emacs lovers—they have been insulting each other for decades and will do so for many decades to come.

The author of this book is not going to make the decision for you; instead, if you are already familiar with one of them, stick with it. If you don't know VI or Emacs, try them both for a while and decide for yourself.

There are also some lesser-known editors available:

- `nano`, a free clone of proprietary Pico, the text-editor component of the Pine email client
- `mcedit`, a part of the **Midnight Commander** (**MC**) file manager that can run stand-alone as well
- `joe`, which can emulate the keybindings of nano, Emacs, and a very old word processor called WordStar (Note: For CentOS, this editor is not available in the standard repository, but it is in a third-party repository).

> If you want to learn VI, execute the command `vimtutor`, a tutorial that comes with VIM. It's a good start for learning all the basics of navigation, the commands, and text editing in VI.
>
> Emacs comes with a very good help function that you can access in Emacs via *<Ctrl + h> + r*.

Another way to edit text streams and files is by using the non-interactive text editor `sed`. Instead of opening a file in a text editor-window, it processes a file or stream from the shell. It's a handy utility if you want to do the following:

- Automatically perform edits on file(s)
- Simplify the same edits on multiple files
- Write a conversion program—for example, to change between lowercase and uppercase or even more complex conversions

The syntax of the `sed` editor is very similar to the commands of the VI editor, and can be scripted.

The default behavior for `sed` is not to edit the file itself, but to dump the changes to the standard output. You can redirect this output to another file or use the `-i` parameter, which stands for **in place edit**, this mode will change the content of the file. The following command is by far the most well-known `sed` command:

```
sed -i 's/string/newstring/g' <filename>
```

It will search for a string, replace it, and continue searching and replacing to the end of the file.

Together with a little bit of scripting, in the same way you can edit multiple files:

```
for files in *conf; do sed -i 's /string/newstring/g' $files; done
```

You can limit the search to a single line:

```
sed -i '10 s/string/newstring' <filename>
```

The `info` page of `sed` is a great resource for all the available commands, and more importantly it has an example section if you want to know more.

Finding your way in the filesystem

The layout of the Linux filesystem is like all other members of the Unix family: very different from Windows. There is no concept of drive letters. Instead, there is a root filesystem (/), and everything else is available on the root filesystem, including other mounted filesystems.

In this section, you'll find out where you can find files, and why they are there.

File hierarchy system

In 2001, the Linux Foundation started the **Linux Standard Base Project** (**LSB**). Based on the POSIX specification, they created a project to develop and promote a set of open standards to increase compatibility among Linux distributions and enable software applications to run on any compliant system.

The **Filesystem Hierarchy Standard** (**FHS**) is a part of this project and defines the directory structure and directory contents. Of course, there are still some minor differences between distributions regarding the directory structure, but even on distributions that are not willing to fully support the LSB such as Debian, the directory structure follows the FHS standard.

The following screenshots are taken from a CentOS system, using the `tree` utility to show the directory structure.

In the root filesystem, the following directories are available:

```
[root@localhost ~]# tree -L 1 /
/
├── bin -> usr/bin
├── boot
├── dev
├── etc
├── home
├── lib -> usr/lib
├── lib64 -> usr/lib64
├── media
├── mnt
├── opt
├── proc
├── root
├── run
├── sbin -> usr/sbin
├── srv
├── sys
├── tmp
├── usr
└── var
```

The following directories are present in the screenshot:

- `/bin`: It contains programs that you need on a minimal system, to be executed by an unprivileged user such as a shell. On Red Hat-based systems, this directory is a symbolic link to `/usr/bin`.
- `/sbin`: It contains programs that you need on a minimal system, to be executed by a privileged user (`root`), such as filesystem repair utilities. On Red Hat Enterprise Linux-based systems, this directory is a symbolic link to `/usr/sbin`.
- `/dev`: Devices are mounted on a special filesystem called `devfs`. All peripheral devices are here, such as the serial port, disks, and CPUs—except the network interface.
- `/proc`: Processes are mounted on a special filesystem called `procfs`.
- `/sys`: Hardware information on the `sysfs` filesystem.
- `/etc`: It consists of editable text configuration files.
- `/lib`: Library for drivers and non-editable text configuration files.
- `/lib64`: Libraries for drivers, but no configuration files.
- `/boot`: Kernel and boot-loader.
- `/root`: User data for the user `root`.
- `/home`: User data for unprivileged users.
- `/media`: Removable media, such as CD-ROM and USB drives, are mounted here. At least read-only for every user.
- `/mnt`: Non-removable media, including remote storage. At least read-only for every user.
- `/run`: Files specific for a user or process, for instance, USB drivers that should be available for a specific user, or runtime information for a daemon.
- `/opt`: Optional software that is not a part of the distribution, such as third-party software.
- `/srv`: Static server data. It can be used for static websites, file servers, and orchestration software such as Salt or Puppet.
- `/var`: Dynamic data. Ranges from print spoolers and logging to dynamic websites.
- `/tmp`: Temporary files, not persistent during reboots. Nowadays, it's often a RAM filesystem (`tmpfs`) that is mounted on this directory. The directory itself is more or less deprecated and from an application perspective replaced with a directory in `/var` or `/run`.
- `/usr`: Software that is not critical in a way that you need it in a minimal software. It contains all extra software.

Using the `tree` command again to show the directory structure in `/usr`:

```
[root@localhost ~]# tree -L 1 /usr
/usr
├── bin
├── etc
├── games
├── include
├── lib
├── lib64
├── libexec
├── local
├── sbin
├── share
├── src
└── tmp -> ../var/tmp
```

The directory structure of `/usr` is very similar to the one in `/`. A few extra things are as follows:

- `/usr/etc`: If you recompile software that is already a part of the distribution, the configuration files should be in `/usr/etc`, so they can't conflict with files in `/etc`.
- `/usr/games`: Data for old games such as `fortune`, `figlet`, and `cowsay`.
- `/usr/include`: Development headers.
- `/usr/libexec`: Wrapper scripts. Let's say you need multiple versions of Java. They all need different libraries, environment variables, and so on. A wrapper script is there to call a specific version with the correct settings.
- `/usr/share`: Program data such as wallpaper, menu items, icons, and documentation.
- `/usr/src`: Linux kernel sources and sources from software that is included in the distribution.
- `/usr/local`: Software that you install and compile yourself.

The directory structure of /usr/local is the same as /usr:

```
[root@localhost ~]# tree -L 1 /usr/local
/usr/local
├── bin
├── etc
├── games
├── include
├── lib
├── lib64
├── libexec
├── sbin
├── share
└── src
```

This directory structure is there for software development. There is no need to have this directory in a production environment.

Optional software is placed in /opt. The main directory structure is /opt/<vendor>/<software>/, for example, /opt/google/chrome. A list of the possible vendor/provider names is maintained by the **Linux Assigned Names And Numbers Authority (LANANA)** on its website: http://www.lanana.org/lsbreg/providers/. For native Linux software, the same structure is used as with /usr and /usr/local, with one exception: you can choose between /conf and /etc in the software directory or in the /etc/opt directory. Non-native Linux software such as PowerShell can use its own structure within the software directory.

Mounting filesystems

It may be a good idea to define the root filesystem more precisely. A root filesystem is the filesystem where the root directory / is allocated. All other filesystems are mounted on directories created on this root filesystem. To find out what directories are local to the root filesystem and which ones are mount points, execute the findmnt command:

```
[student@server1 ~]$ findmnt
TARGET                              SOURCE         FSTYPE    OPTIONS
/                                   /dev/mapper/centos-root
                                                   xfs       rw,relatime,seclabel,a
├─/sys                              sysfs          sysfs     rw,nosuid,nodev,noexec
│ ├─/sys/kernel/security            securityfs     security  rw,nosuid,nodev,noexec
│ ├─/sys/fs/cgroup                  tmpfs          tmpfs     ro,nosuid,nodev,noexec
│ │ ├─/sys/fs/cgroup/systemd        cgroup         cgroup    rw,nosuid,nodev,noexec
│ │ ├─/sys/fs/cgroup/blkio          cgroup         cgroup    rw,nosuid,nodev,noexec
│ │ ├─/sys/fs/cgroup/hugetlb        cgroup         cgroup    rw,nosuid,nodev,noexec
```

Adding the -D parameter will show you the size of the filesystem and the amount of space that is available:

```
[student@server1 ~]$ findmnt -D
SOURCE                    FSTYPE      SIZE   USED   AVAIL  USE%  TARGET
devtmpfs                  devtmpfs    477M      0    477M    0%  /dev
tmpfs                     tmpfs     487.6M      0  487.6M    0%  /dev/shm
tmpfs                     tmpfs     487.6M   6.8M  480.9M    1%  /run
tmpfs                     tmpfs     487.6M      0  487.6M    0%  /sys/fs/cgroup
/dev/mapper/centos-root   xfs         12G    1.4G   10.6G   12%  /
```

The `findmnt` command is a great way to find out where a device is mounted, for instance:

```
findmnt /dev/sda1
```

It can also be the other way round:

```
findmnt /boot
```

If a directory is not a mount point, use the -T parameter:

```
findmnt -T /usr
```

In Chapter 4, *Advanced Linux Administration*, the different filesystems, and how to mount and automatically mount local and remote filesystems, are covered in detail.

Finding files on the filesystem

Searching for files on the filesystem can be done with the find command. Unfortunately, if you are not already familiar with this command, the man-page may be overwhelming and not very easy to read. However, if you understand the basics of this commands, the man-page will help you add parameters to search every property of a file and/or directory.

The first possible parameters of the find command are options. These affect the behavior of the find command should it follow symbolic links and debug and speed optimization options. Options are optional—most of the time you don't need them.

After the options, the next parameter tells the find command where to start the search process. It is not a very good idea to start at the root (/) directory; it takes too much time and can consume too much CPU activity on large filesystems. Remember the FHS—for instance, if you want to search configuration files, start searching in the /etc directory:

```
find /etc
```

The preceding command will show you all the files in /etc.

After the location, the next parameter is an expression, containing one or more tests. To list the most common tests, use the following:

- -type, f for file, d for directory, b for block device
- -name <pattern>
- -user and -group
- -perm
- -size

You can make combination of these tests, for instance: To search for files with filenames that end in conf use the following:

```
find /etc -type f -name '*conf'
```

For some of the tests, such as size and atime, it's possible to add a so-called comparison with a provided parameter:

- +n: Greater than n
- -n: Less than n
- n: Exactly n

The `find` commands search for files and directories and compare these to the value of *n*:

```
find / -type d -size +100M
```

This example will search for directories with content that exceeds 100 MB.

The last parameter is the action that should be executed on the files that were found. Examples include:

- `-ls`, output similar to the `ls` command
- `-print`, to print the filenames
- `-printf`, to format the output of print
- `-fprintf`, to write the formatted output to a file

The `-printf` parameter can be extremely useful. For instance, this command will search for files and list their size in bytes and the filename. After that, you can use the `sort` command to sort files by size:

```
find /etc -name '*conf' -printf '%s,%p\n' | sort -rn
```

There are some more dangerous actions as well, such as `-delete` to remove the files found, or `-exec` to execute an external command. Be very sure of the result of your search action before using these parameters. Most of the time, performance-wise, you are better off using the `xargs` utility anyway. This utility takes the results and converts them into arguments to a command. An example of such a command is the `grep` utility to search the content of the result:

```
find /etc/ -name '*' -type f| xargs grep "127.0.0.1"
```

Process management

Processes are used by the Linux kernel, started by a user, or created by other processes. All processes are child processes of process number one, which will be covered in the next chapter. In this section, we learn to identify processes and how to send a signal to a process.

View processes

If you start a program, a **process ID** (**PID**) is assigned to the process and a corresponding directory is created in `/proc`.

In Bash, you can find the PID of the current shell with the command:

```
echo $$
```

You can also find the PID of the parent shell:

```
echo $PPID
```

To find the PID of a program on your filesystem, the utility `pidof` is available, for instance:

```
pidof ssh
```

If you want to use `pidof` to find running scripts, including the PID of the shell that is used by a script, you have to add the `-s` parameter.

Let's have a look into the `proc` directory of the current shell:

```
[root@localhost ~]# cd /proc/$$
[root@localhost 1226]# ls
attr             cpuset    limits      net             projid_map   stat
autogroup        cwd       loginuid    ns              root         statm
auxv             environ   map_files   numa_maps       sched        status
cgroup           exe       maps        oom_adj         schedstat    syscall
clear_refs       fd        mem         oom_score       sessionid    task
cmdline          fdinfo    mountinfo   oom_score_adj   setgroups    timers
comm             gid_map   mounts      pagemap         smaps        uid_map
coredump_filter  io        mountstats  personality     stack        wchan
```

You can see all the properties of this process. To name a few:

- `cmdline`: The command that is executed to create this process
- `environ`: The environment variables that are available to this process
- `status`: The status of the file, the UID, and the GID of the user/group that owns the process

If you execute `cat environ`, the output is difficult to read, because the end-of-line character is `\0` instead of `\n`. You can fix this using the `tr` command to translate the `\0` into `\n`:

```
cat /proc/$$/environmen | tr "\0" "\n"
```

The `proc` directory is very interesting for troubleshooting, but there are also many tools that use this information to produce a more human-friendly output. One of these utilities is the `ps` command. There is something strange with this command; it supports three different types of parameter:

- **Unix style**: Preceded by a dash. Commands can be grouped. `ps -ef` is the same as `ps -e -f`.
- **BSD style**: Not preceded by a dash. Commands can be grouped. `ps ax` is the same as `ps a x`.
- **GNU style**: Preceded by a double dash and a long-named option. Commands cannot be grouped.

Output formatting for the three styles are not the same, but you can modify the behavior with options. A comparison is as follows:

```
[root@localhost ~]# ps -ef | head -5
UID          PID    PPID  C STIME TTY          TIME CMD
root           1       0  0 02:15 ?        00:00:01 /usr/lib/systemd/systemd --swi
tched-root --system --deserialize 21
root           2       0  0 02:15 ?        00:00:00 [kthreadd]
root           3       2  0 02:15 ?        00:00:00 [ksoftirqd/0]
root           5       2  0 02:15 ?        00:00:00 [kworker/0:0H]
[root@localhost ~]# ps aux | head -5
USER        PID %CPU %MEM    VSZ   RSS TTY      STAT START   TIME COMMAND
root          1  0.0  0.6 128168  6836 ?        Ss   02:15   0:01 /usr/lib/syste
md/systemd --switched-root --system --deserialize 21
root          2  0.0  0.0      0     0 ?        S    02:15   0:00 [kthreadd]
root          3  0.0  0.0      0     0 ?        S    02:15   0:00 [ksoftirqd/0]
root          5  0.0  0.0      0     0 ?        S<   02:15   0:00 [kworker/0:0H]
```

The processes between square brackets are kernel processes.

You can query for specific values, for instance:

```
ps -q $$ -o comm
```

This is the same as:

```
cat /proc/$$/cmdline
```

Another utility that can help you search for a process is `pgrep`. It greps on values such as the name and user and shows the PID by default. The output can be formatted using parameters such as `-l` to list the process name, or `-o` to add the full command to the output.

An interactive way to monitor processes uses the `top` command:

```
top - 03:12:45 up 57 min,  5 users,  load average: 0.00, 0.01, 0.05
Tasks: 104 total,   1 running, 103 sleeping,   0 stopped,   0 zombie
%Cpu(s):  0.0 us,  0.3 sy,  0.0 ni, 99.7 id,  0.0 wa,  0.0 hi,  0.0 si,  0.0 st
KiB Mem :   998636 total,   668612 free,   165676 used,   164348 buff/cache
KiB Swap:  2097148 total,  2097148 free,        0 used.   657180 avail Mem

  PID USER      PR  NI    VIRT    RES    SHR S %CPU %MEM     TIME+ COMMAND
 2042 root      20   0  157584   2132   1500 R  0.3  0.2   0:00.03 top
    1 root      20   0  128168   6836   4068 S  0.0  0.7   0:01.95 systemd
    2 root      20   0       0      0      0 S  0.0  0.0   0:00.00 kthreadd
    3 root      20   0       0      0      0 S  0.0  0.0   0:00.06 ksoftirqd/0
```

The values in the columns for a process visible in `top` are the same as in `ps`. In the man-page of `top` you can find a good explanation of what they mean. Some of them will be covered in later chapters.

The `top` command or the more fancier `htop` command can help you to quickly identify processes taking too much memory or CPU and send a signal to the process. If you want detailed and advanced process monitoring and troubleshooting it's better to use the tooling available in Azure. This is covered in `Chapter 12`, *Monitoring Your Workload in Azure*.

Sending signals to a process

In man-page section 7, you can find a man-page about signals. A signal is a message to a process, for instance, to change the priority or to kill a process. There are many different signals described in this manual, but only a few are really important:

- Signal 1: It hangs the process; it will reload everything that is attached to a process. Commonly used to reread a changed configuration file.
- Signal 2: It is same as *Ctrl + C* or *<Ctrl + Break*.
- Signal 3: Normal quitting of a process; the same as *Ctrl + D*.
- Signal 15: Default signal, used to terminate a command, giving the terminal time to clean up everything nicely.

- Signal 9: Kill a command without cleanup. This is dangerous and can make your system unstable and sometimes even vulnerable.

To send a signal to a process, you can use the `top` (shortcut k) or `kill` command. For instance:

```
kill -HUP <PID>
```

There is a nice utility you can use to grep on a process or group of processes; it sends a signal at once: `pkill`. It's similar to `pgrep`. Selection is possible on values such as `name` and `uid`.

Discretionary Access Control

Discretionary Access Control (**DAC**) is a security implementation to restrict access to objects, such as files and directories. A user or a group of users gets access based on ownership and the permissions on the objects.

In cloud environments, user and group management is maybe not a part of your daily job. It's often delegated to Identity Management Systems such as an **Active Directory** (**AD**), and you don't need that many user accounts; authentication and authorization at an application level are more important nowadays. But it's still a good idea to be able to verify users and know how the underlying system works.

User management

If you deploy a virtual machine in Azure, in the wizard you'll specify a user, which will be created by the Azure Agent in the virtual machine—for instance, if you deploy a virtual machine with PowerShell:

```
PS /Users/frederik> New-AzureRmVM -Name "CentOS-01" -Location westus `
>> -ResourceGroupName MyResource1 -ImageName CentOS `
>> -Size Standard_B1S

cmdlet New-AzureRmVM at command pipeline position 1
Supply values for the following parameters:
Credential
User: linvirt
Password for user linvirt: **********
```

You can use this account to log in. It's a normal user, also called an unprivileged user, which doesn't have administrative privileges. To gain administrative privileges you need the `sudo` command; `sudo` means: do as su, referring to the `su` command. Without parameters, the `su` command switches your current user to another user, root—the administrator account in Linux.

> If you want root privileges, in some of the Linux images in Azure you can't use the `su` command. It's disabled by default. To get a root shell, you can use `sudo -s`. By default, the `sudo` command will ask you for *your* password.

To get more information about this user account, use the `getent` command to get an entity from the `passwd` database where the user information is stored. This `passwd` database can be local (`/etc/passwd`) or remote:

```
sudo getent passwd <username>
```

```
[linvirt@CentOS-01 ~]$ sudo getent passwd linvirt
[sudo] password for linvirt:
linvirt:x:1000:1000::/home/linvirt:/bin/bash
```

The output of this command is a colon-separated list:

- User account name
- Password is not configured here
- User ID
- Primary group ID
- **General Electric Comprehensive Operating System (GECOS)** field for extra account information
- Home directory for this user
- Default shell

In the early days of the Unix Operating System family, the password was stored in the `/etc/passwd` file, but for security reasons the hashed password was moved to `/etc/shadow`. The password can be changed with:

```
sudo passwd <username>
```

If you want to change the password of the current user, you don't need to use `sudo`, and don't need to specify the username. You can view the entry in the `/etc/shadow` file with `getent`:

```
[linvirt@CentOS-01 ~]$ sudo getent shadow linvirt
linvirt:$
                                    1:17645:0:99999:7:::
```

The columns after the hashed password contain ageing information that can be viewed (and changed) with the `chage` command. The notation in the shadow database is notated in number of days since EPOCH (the virtual birthday of Unix: January 1 1970). The `chage` commands translates it into a more human readable form:

```
[linvirt@CentOS-01 ~]$ chage -l linvirt
Last password change                                    : Apr 24, 2018
Password expires                                        : never
Password inactive                                       : never
Account expires                                         : never
Minimum number of days between password change          : 0
Maximum number of days between password change          : 99999
Number of days of warning before password expires       : 7
```

Let's go back to the `passwd` database. The numbering of the user ID is defined in the file `/etc/login.defs`. ID 0 is reserved for the root account. IDs 1 to 200 are reserved for `admin` accounts that are not in use any longer in modern Linux systems. In Red Hat-based distributions the range 201–999 is reserved for system accounts and daemons run under these accounts. The range for the unprivileged accounts is between 1,000 and 60,000 for local users and >60,000 for remote users (for example, AD or LDAP users). There can be small differences between Linux distributions!

Many distributions are configured with the so-called **User Private Group** (**UPG**) scheme, thanks to the directive in the file `/etc/login.defs`:

USERGROUPS_ENAB yes

This means that if you create a user, automatically a primary group is created with the same name as the login. If you disable this functionality, a newly created user becomes a member of another group automatically, defined in `/etc/default/useradd`:

```
GROUP=100
```

The GECOS field can be changed with the `chfn` command:

```
[linvirt@CentOS-01 ~]$ sudo chfn linvirt
[sudo] password for linvirt:
Changing finger information for linvirt.
Name []: Jane Roe
Office []: 112
Office Phone []: 00-01
Home Phone []: 00-02
```

> The `chfn`, change finger, command refers to an old utility, `finger`, which is not installed by default but it is still available in repositories. A finger daemon that makes the GECOS information available via the network is available as well, but it's considered a security risk.

The default shell while creating a user is defined in `/etc/default/useradd`. You can change the default shell to another using the `chsh` command. The shell must be listed in the file `/etc/shells`:

```
chsh -s /bin/tcsh linvirt
```

For the purpose of this book, keep Bash as the default.

In this section, you learned how to verify and change the properties of an existing local user. Of course, you can add additional users as well:

```
sudo useradd <username>
```

Group management

A user is always a member of one group, the primary group, that is—as discussed in a previous paragraph—defined in the `passwd` database.

Besides being a member of a primary group, additional group memberships can be added. This can be necessary to get access to a group directory/share or to delegate privileges in the `sudo` configuration. You can add existing additional groups with the `--groups` parameter of the `useradd` command during the creation of a user or afterwards with `usermod` or `groupmems`.

Let's create a new user and a new group and verify the results:

```
sudo useradd student

sudo passwd student

sudo getent passwd student

sudo groupadd staff

sudo getent group staff
```

Make the user `student` a member of the group `staff`:

```
sudo groupmems -g staff -a student

sudo groupmems -g staff -l

sudo getent group staff
```

You can change your primary group temporarily with **switch group** (`sg`):

```
su student

id -g

sg staff
```

> **TIP**
>
> It's not very common, but you can add a password to a group account using the `gpasswd` command. This way, a user that is not a member of this group can still use `sg` and enter the `passwd` for the group.

A very special, already existing, group is the wheel group. In the `sudo` configuration, a user that is a member of this group is able to execute commands that need administrative privileges. In Ubuntu, this group is not available; instead there is a group called sudo available for the same purpose.

Login management

Login into a Linux system is registered, tracked, and managed by a service called `systemd-logind` and a corresponding command: `loginctl`.

The parameters of this command are divided into sections for users, sessions, and seats. To do some exercises with these parameters, open a second `ssh` session to your virtual machine using the credentials of the student account. Execute the commands in the first `ssh` session.

First list the sessions:

```
loginctl list-sessions
```

Then view the properties of the session using the session ID:

```
loginctl show-session <session number>
```

```
[linvirt@CentOS-01 ~]$ loginctl list-sessions
   SESSION        UID USER              SEAT
        43       1001 student
        42       1000 linvirt

2 sessions listed.
[linvirt@CentOS-01 ~]$ loginctl show-session 43
Id=43
User=1001
Name=student
Timestamp=Tue 2018-04-24 12:16:08 UTC
TimestampMonotonic=19702968317
VTNr=0
Remote=yes
RemoteHost=77.95.96.78
Service=sshd
```

View the user properties:

```
loginctl show-user <username>
```

Switch to the second SSH session and execute man man.

Now switch back to the first SSH session and view the status of the student using the `user-status` parameter:

```
student (1001)
           Since: Tue 2018-04-24 12:16:08 UTC; 14min ago
           State: active
        Sessions: *43
            Unit: user-1001.slice
                 └─session-43.scope
                   ├─37090 sshd: student [priv]
                   ├─37097 sshd: student@pts/1
                   ├─37098 -bash
                   ├─37475 man man
                   └─37487 less -s
```

Finally, terminate the session:

```
sudo loginctl terminate-session <session id>
```

There is also a `terminate-user` parameter that can become handy if there are multiple users in one session.

Summary

This chapter was a sort of crash course on how to survive in Linux if you are more or less unfamiliar with this operating system. This chapter was not about how to become a senior Linux administrator.

In daily life as an administrator in Azure, you may not execute everything in this chapter. For instance, you don't create users in a virtual machine. But you should be able to verify users configured in an identity management system such as AD and that they are able to log in.

This chapter was all about using shells, the structure of the filesystem, and finding files. We looked at the role of text files in Linux, and how to process and edit them. We worked with processes, and how to view them and kill them. And last but not least, we looked at user and group management.

In Chapter 5, *Advanced Linux Administration*, we're going more in depth with Linux and looking at topics such as software management, storage, networking, and SystemD.

Questions

In this chapter, instead of answering some questions, I want you to do an exercise:

1. Create the users Lisa, John, Karel, and Carola.
2. Set the password for these users to welc0meITG.
3. Verify the existence of these users.
4. Create the finance and staff groups.
5. Make the users Lisa and Carola members of finance, and Karel and John members of staff.
6. Create the directory `/home/staff` and `/home/finance` and set the group ownership of this directory to staff and home, respect
7. Give the group staff read-access into the finance directory
8. Make sure that newly created files gets the correct group ownership and permissions

Further reading

There are many books that are published for users that are new to the Linux Operating System. Here I name a few of my personal favorites.

The book by Sander van Vugt, *Beginning the Linux Command Line* (ISBN 978-143021889), is one of the best introductions to Linux, with a great eye for detail, and covers all relevant commands.

I also enjoyed reading the book by Petru Işfan and Bogdan Vaida, *Working with Linux - Quick Hacks for the Command Line* (ISBN 978-1787129184). It's a strange collection of nice tips and tricks, and sometimes that is all you need.

If you are able to read German, all the books by Michael Kofler (`https://kofler.info`) should be on your bookshelf, even if you are an experienced Linux user!

If you want to learn VI, I strongly suggest you read the book by Drew Neil, *Practical VIM: Edit Text at the speed of Thought* (ISBN 978-1680501278). Even if you are already familiar with this editor, I do think that you will learn many new things. To learn Emacs, read the book by Mickey Peterson: *Mastering Emacs* (`https://www.masteringemacs.org`).

The Microsoft website hosts very good documentation on regular expressions: `https://docs.microsoft.com/en-us/dotnet/standard/base-types/regular-expressions`. And I do like the website `http://regexone.com` if you want to practice using regular expressions.

The `awk` utility comes with a big manual itself (`https://www.gnu.org/software/gawk/manual/gawk.html`), but it's maybe not the best place to start. Shiwang Kalkhanda did a very good job in *Learning AWK Programming* (ISBN 978-1788391030), producing a very readable book. Don't be afraid of the word *Programming* in this title, especially if you are not a developer; you should read this book.

4
Managing Azure

In Chapter 2, *Getting Started with the Azure Cloud*, we took our first steps on a journey into the world of Azure. We discovered that there are many ways to manage an Azure environment and that these include Azure portal and command-line interfaces. You can use the command-line interfaces within the the Azure portal to run them on your workstation. Later on in the book, we'll see that there are other great possibilities, using automation and orchestration solutions. At the end of chapter, we created a Linux virtual machine and explored the basics of the Linux environment in Chapter 3, Basic Linux Administration.

Before we continue our journey, covering more advanced topics, this chapter covers components of the Azure infrastructure that are needed for our workloads, virtual machines, and containers. We're talking about components that we already used in the previous chapters, sometimes even without knowing that we did.

Basically, this chapter is about Azure resources. And, remember, they are all part of a resource group, a logical container into which resources are deployed and managed.

> In this book, the author tries to be as agnostic as possible, regarding the available interfaces. Because this chapter is more about the theory than the interfaces, I'll only use the PowerShell as an example.

Technical requirements

For this chapter, basic knowledge of storage and networking is required. In the *Further reading* section, you can find some suggestions to prepare yourself.

It's not necessary, but it's a good idea to have at least one virtual machine up and running. This way, you can not only create new resources in this chapter, but also look at the properties of an existing virtual machine. In this section, I created an Ubuntu virtual machine named `ubuntu01` in the resource group `chapter4` for the examples.

Set variables for the resource group and the location:

```
$myRG = "chapter4"
$myLocation = "westus"
$myTestVM = "ubuntu01"
```

Create the resource group:

```
New-AzureRMResourceGroup -Name $myRG -Location $myLocation
```

Create the virtual machine:

```
New-AzureRmVm `
  -ResourceGroupName $myRG `
  -Name $myTestVM `
  -ImageName UbuntuLTS `
  -Location $myLocation `
  -VirtualNetworkName "$myTestVM-Vnet" `
  -SubnetName $myTestVM-Subnet `
  -SecurityGroupName "$myTestVM-NSG" `
  -PublicIpAddressName $myTestVM-pip
```

For now, the parameters used in this example are not important; at the end of this chapter, you'll be able to understand them all.

Not a real requirement, but nice to have, is the Azure Storage Explorer utility, which is available for free at `https://azure.microsoft.com/en-us/features/storage-explorer`. This is a stand-alone utility to install on your workstation. The Storage Explorer is also available as an option in the Azure Portal.

Storage services

In Azure, we have different types of data or storage services:

- **Blob storage**: An optimized storage object, to store massive amounts of unstructured data, such as text or binary data. It's often used to make the data available for other resources, for instance, to store VHD files that can be used to create virtual disks. Another use case is to use it as storage for audio and video files. Making the blob publicly accessible, it's even possible to stream the data.

- **Azure Files**: CIFS shares hosted files in Azure.
- **Azure Queue storage**: Passing messages from one resource to another, especially for serverless services such as Azure Web App and Functions. It can also be used to create a backlog of work to process asynchronously.
- **Table storage**: This is for the Azure CosmoDB service.
- **Disk storage**: This is for managed and unmanaged disks.

In this chapter, I will only cover Blob storage, Azure Files, and disk storage, because Queues and Table storage are there for a very specific solution that are important for application developers only.

> If you have an enormous amount of data you want to store in the cloud, uploading can take too much time. Microsoft has a service called **Azure Data Box Disks**. They send encrypted SSDs to your data center. Copy the data and send it back. For more information visit: `https://docs.microsoft.com/en-gb/azure/databox/data-box-disk-overview`.

Storage accounts

A key component in the storage services is the storage account. It's needed to access the storage. It also defines the type of storage that is behind the service.

There are three different kinds of storage accounts:

- **Storage**: The old type of deprecated storage account doesn't support all features (for instance, there is no archive option). It's often more expensive than the newer Version 2.
- **StorageV2**: This is a newer storage account. It supports all types of storage and the latest features for blobs, files, queues, and tables.
- **Blob storage**: This has not been deprecated yet, but there is no reason to use it any longer. The biggest problem with this account type is that you can't store files such as VHDs.

> You don't need to create a storage account for managed disks. However, if you want to store virtual machine boot diagnostic data, you'll need one.

Another property is the SKU, as already covered in `Chapter 2`, *Getting Started with the Azure Cloud*. It specifies what type of replication applies to the storage account. Here are the available types:

- **Standard_LRS**: Locally-redundant storage
- **Premium_LRS**: Same as LRS, but supports blobs
- **Standard_GRS**: Geo-redundant storage
- **Standard_RAGRS**: Read-access geo-redundant storage
- **Standard_ZRS**: Zone-redundant storage

The last important property is the access tier; it specifies the optimization of the storage. There are three types available:

- **Hot storage tier**: Optimized for storing data that is accessed frequently.
- **Cool storage tier**: Optimized for storing data that is infrequently accessed and stored for at least 30 days.
- **Archive storage tier**: Optimized for storing data that is rarely accessed and stored for at least 180 days with flexible latency requirements. It's only available for Blob storage.

The choice made for the access tier also affects the costs, for instance, the archive storage offers the lowest storage costs but also the highest access costs.

> This property is not available for the older storage accounts.

The storage account name must be between three and 24 characters in length and use numbers and lowercase letters only. They must be unique in Azure. It is suggested by Microsoft to use a globally unique name and a random number:

```
New-AzureRMStorageAccount `
  -ResourceGroupName <resource group> `
  -SkuName <sku> `
  -Location <location> `
  -Kind StorageV2 `
  -AccessTier <access tier> `
  -name <storage account>
```

Here is an example:

```
$mySA = New-AzureRMStorageAccount `
    -ResourceGroupName $myRG `
    -SkuName Standard_LRS `
    -Location $myLocation `
    -Kind StorageV2 `
    -AccessTier Hot `
    -name chapter4$(Get-Random -Minimum 1001 -Maximum 9999)
```

Check the available accounts in your subscription:

```
Get-AzureRMStorageAccount | Select StorageAccountName, Location
```

```
PS /Users/frederik> Get-AzureRMStorageAccount | Select StorageAccountName, Location

StorageAccountName Location
------------------ --------
chapter42585       westus
```

Ask for more details using the following:

```
Get-AzureRMStorageAccount `
    -ResourceGroupName <resource group> `
    -Name <storage account>
```

Storage accounts are protected by keys. You'll need this key if you want access to the storage account. A set of two keys are automatically created during the creation of the account. If you are still in the same session when you created the account, you can receive it:

```
$mySA | Get-AzureRmStorageAccountKey | Format-Table -Wrap
```

Otherwise, you can use the following:

```
Get-AzureRMStorageAccountKey `
    -ResourceGroupName <resource group>`
    -Name <storage account name>
```

```
PS /Users/frederik> Get-AzureRMStorageAccountKey -ResourceGroupName $myRG -Name chapter42585 | Selec
t KeyName,Value

KeyName Value
------- -----
key1    A5Jd46nZattrWNUYky
key2    u2vr1BmF7Y4DEzv/JM
```

Managed disks

If you create a virtual machine, this machine will have at least two disks that are stored in an (not in the one you created) Azure Storage account: an operating system disk, created based on an image, and a temporary disk. All the disks are in VHD format.

You can also add extra data disks. First, create the disk configuration:

```
New-AzureRmDiskConfig -Location <location>`
  -DiskSizeGB <size> -OsType Linux -SkuName <sku>   `
  -CreateOption empty
```

Here is an example:

```
$diskconfig = New-AzureRmDiskConfig -Location $myLocation `
  -DiskSizeGB 5 -OsType Linux -SkuName Standard_LRS `
  -CreateOption empty
```

```
PS /Users/frederik> $diskconfig


ResourceGroupName   :
ManagedBy           :
Sku                 : Microsoft.Azure.Management.Compute.Models.DiskSku
Zones               :
TimeCreated         :
OsType              : Linux
CreationData        : Microsoft.Azure.Management.Compute.Models.CreationData
DiskSizeGB          : 5
EncryptionSettings  :
ProvisioningState   :
Id                  :
Name                :
Type                :
Location            : westus
Tags                :
```

Now, you can create the actual disk:

```
New-AzureRmDisk -ResourceGroupName <resource group name> `
  -DiskName <disk name> -Disk <disk configuration>
```

For example:

```
$Disk01 = New-AzureRmDisk -ResourceGroupName $myRG `
  -DiskName 'Disk01' -Disk $diskconfig
```

```
PS /Users/frederik> $Disk01


ResourceGroupName  : chapter4
ManagedBy          :
Sku                : Microsoft.Azure.Management.Compute.Models.DiskSku
Zones              :
TimeCreated        : 08/09/2018 08:27:06
OsType             : Linux
CreationData       : Microsoft.Azure.Management.Compute.Models.CreationData
DiskSizeGB         : 5
EncryptionSettings :
ProvisioningState  : Succeeded
Id                 : /subscriptions/88                        69/resourceG
                     oviders/Microsoft.Compute/disks/Disk01
Name               : Disk01
Type               : Microsoft.Compute/disks
Location           : westus
Tags               : {}
```

You can now add the data disk to the virtual machine. Start with a variable that contains the virtual machine properties:

```
$myVM = Get-AzureRmVM -ResourceGroupName <resource group>`
  -Name <virtual machine name>
```

The next step is to add the data disk, providing the same disk name, to the virtual machine. To do so, you'll need the disk ID:

```
Get-AzureRMDisk -DiskName <disk name> | select Id
```

Add the data disk:

```
Add-AzureRmVMDataDisk -VM $myVM -Name <disk name> `
  -ManagedDiskId <disk id> -Lun <lun number> -CreateOption Attach
```

A **Logical Unit Number** (**LUN**) is a number used to identify the storage in the virtual machine. You can start numbering with zero. Finally, update the virtual machine settings:

```
Update-AzureRmVM `
  -ResourceGroupName <resource group> `
  -VM <virtual machine>
```

The complete example is as follows:

```
$myVM = Get-AzureRmVM -ResourceGroupName $myRG -Name $myTestVM

Add-AzureRmVMDataDisk -VM $myVM -Name Disk01 `
  -ManagedDiskId $Disk01.Id -Lun 1 -CreateOption Attach
```

```
PS /Users/frederik> Add-AzureRmVMDataDisk -VM $myVM -Name Disk01 `
>>    -ManagedDiskId $Disk01.Id -lun 1 -CreateOption Attach


ResourceGroupName : chapter4
Id                : /subscriptions/8                              69/resourceGr
viders/Microsoft.Compute/virtualMachines/ubuntu01
VmId              : be7dd051-1adc-4b3b-9484-f0b86b895ea4
Name              : ubuntu01
Type              : Microsoft.Compute/virtualMachines
Location          : westus
Tags              : {}
HardwareProfile   : {VmSize}
NetworkProfile    : {NetworkInterfaces}
OSProfile         : {ComputerName, AdminUsername, LinuxConfiguration, Secrets}
ProvisioningState : Succeeded
StorageProfile    : {ImageReference, OsDisk, DataDisks}
```

```
Update-AzureRmVM -ResourceGroupName $myRG -VM $myVM
```

```
PS /Users/frederik> Update-AzureRmVM -ResourceGroupName $myRG -VM $myVM

RequestId IsSuccessStatusCode StatusCode ReasonPhrase
--------- ------------------- ---------- ------------
                         True         OK OK
```

Verify the result:

```
$myVM.StorageProfile.DataDisks
```

Or even better:

```
$(Get-AzureRmVM -Name $myTestVM `
  -ResourceGroupName $myRG).StorageProfile.DataDisks
```

```
PS /Users/frederik> $(Get-AzureRmVM -Name $myTestVM -ResourceGroupName $myRG).StorageProfile.DataDisks


Name            : Disk01
DiskSizeGB      : 5
Lun             : 1
Caching         : None
CreateOption    : Attach
SourceImage     :
VirtualHardDisk :
```

Azure Files

Instead of adding data disks to a virtual machine, you can use **Azure Files**. This service offers a CIFS share (SMB 2.1 and 3.0 protocol) to virtual machines (or even the outside world).

Azure Files needs a storage account and supports only Standard_LRS, Standard_ZRS and Standard_GRS SKU types. There are no premium storage or other access tiers than the standard (hot) available. (At the time of writing, sources at Microsoft state that there is no timeline available for the introduction of these features.)

Please note that you really want the SMB 3.0 protocol for performance reasons. This means that you need a recent Linux distribution:

- RHEL-based distributions 7.5 or higher
- Ubuntu 16.04 or higher
- Debian 9
- SUSE SLE 12 SP3 / OpenSUSE LEAP 42.3 or higher

And, you need to force Version 3 with the mount option: **vers=3.0**.

The first step involves creating the Azure Files share:

```
New-AzureStorageShare `
  -Name <share name> -Context <storage account context>
```

For the storage account context, you can use the variable that was used to create the storage account or create the variable again:

```
$mySA = Get-AzureRmVM -Name $myTestVM -ResourceGroupName $myRG
```

For example:

```
$myShare01 = New-AzureStorageShare `
  -Name "myshare01-staff" -Context $mySA.Context
```

```
PS /Users/frederik> $myShare01


   File End Point: https://chapter42585.file.core.windows.net/

Name                                                          LastModified
----                                                          ------------
myshare01-staff                                               08/09/2018...
```

To review the properties of the created share, execute the following command:

```
(Get-AzureStorageShare -Context $mySA.Context).Uri
```

```
PS /Users/frederik> (Get-AzureStorageShare -Context $mySA.Context).Uri

AbsolutePath    : /myshare01-staff
AbsoluteUri     : https://chapter42585.file.core.windows.net/myshare01-staff
LocalPath       : /myshare01-staff
Authority       : chapter42585.file.core.windows.net
HostNameType    : Dns
IsDefaultPort   : True
IsFile          : False
IsLoopback      : False
PathAndQuery    : /myshare01-staff
Segments        : {/, myshare01-staff}
IsUnc           : False
Host            : chapter42585.file.core.windows.net
Port            : 443
Query           :
Fragment        :
Scheme          : https
OriginalString  : https://chapter42585.file.core.windows.net:443/myshare01-staff
DnsSafeHost     : chapter42585.file.core.windows.net
IdnHost         : chapter42585.file.core.windows.net
IsAbsoluteUri   : True
UserEscaped     : False
UserInfo        :
```

In Linux, you can mount it manually with the following code:

```
mount -t cifs \
  -o vers=3.0,username=<storage account>,password=<storage key>\
  //<storage account name>.file.core.windows.net/<share> \
  /<mount point>
```

For example:

```
mkdir /mnt/staff
mount -t cifs -o vers=3.0,username=chapter42585,password=.... \
  //chapter42585.file.core.windows.net/myshare-01.staff /mnt/staff
```

More information about mounting shares is available in Chapter 5, *Advanced Linux Administration,* under the section *Mounting remote filesystems.* The following is an example of a mount unit for Azure Files:

```
[Unit]
Description = Staff Share

[Mount]
```

```
What = //chapter42585.file.core.windows.net/myshare-01.staff
Where = /mnt/staff
Type = cifs
Options = vers=3.0,credentials=/root/.staff
```

Where the `file` `/root/.staffs` contains the entries:

```
username=<storage account>
password=<key>
```

Another great way to verify the share and manage the content is with the Azure Storage Explorer. Start the Azure Storage Explorer on your workstation, connect to Azure using your storage account and the corresponding key, to verify that the share exists:

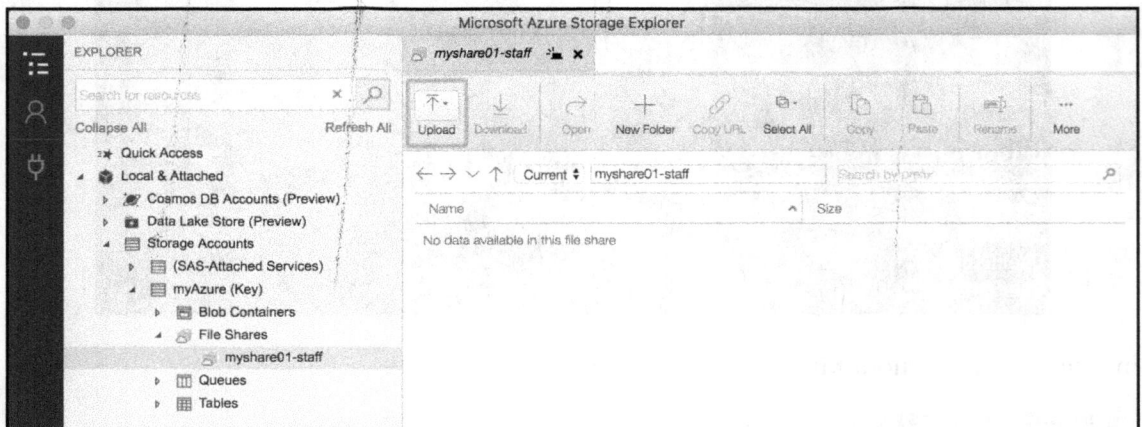

Blob storage

Azure Blob Storage is a storage service that stores unstructured data in the cloud as objects. Blob is object-based storage that can store any type of data.

Azure File Shares are a great way to keep your data out of the virtual machine. But, it's file-based, and that's not the fastest choice for every data type. For instance, streaming from Azure Files, while possible, does not perform very well; uploading very big files can also be very challenging. Blob storage is a solution for that and it scales much better: 5 TB for a Azure File Share, 500 TB for a single Blob container.

In shares, you have directories; in Blob storage, there is something similar called a **container object**; normally, these are files; in Blob storage, it's a blob object.

To be able to upload a blob, you have to create a container first:

```
New-AzureStorageContainer -Name <container name> `
  -Context <context of storage account> -Permission blob
```

For example:

```
$myContainer = New-AzureStorageContainer `
  -Name container01 `
  -Context $mySA.context -Permission blob
```

```
PS /Users/frederik> $myContainer


   Blob End Point: https://chapter42585.blob.core.windows.net/

Name                 PublicAccess         LastModified
----                 ------------         ------------
container01          Blob                 2018-08-09 08:54:35Z
```

There are three types of permissions available:

- **Container**: Provides full read access to a container and its blobs. Clients can enumerate blobs in the container through anonymous request; other containers are not visible.
- **Blob**: Provides read access to blob data throughout a container through anonymous request, but does not provide access to container data. Other blobs are not visible.
- **Off**: Restricts access to just the storage account owner.

You can use the Azure Storage Explorer again to view the container:

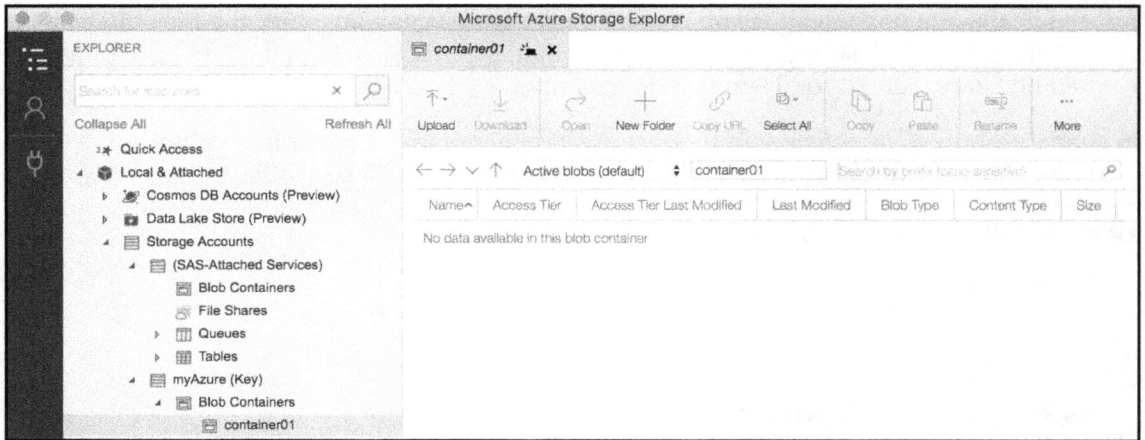

Using PowerShell, you can create a blob:

```
Set-AzureStorageBlobContent -File <filename> `
  -Container <container> -Blob <blobname> `
  -Context $mySA.context
```

You can verify the result using the following command:

```
Get-AzureStorageBlob -Container <container name> `
  -Context $mySA.context | select Name
```

Now you can upload a file to the container, making it into a blob, for instance:

```
Set-AzureStorageBlobContent -File "/Pictures/image.jpg" `
  -Container $containerName ` -Blob "Image1.jpg" `
  -Context $mySA.context
```

You can also list the result:

```
Get-AzureStorageBlob -Container <container> `
  -Context $mySA.context | select Name
```

You can mount the blob from Linux using **Blobfuse;** for more information see: https://github.com/Azure/azure-storage-fuse and https://docs.microsoft.com/en-us/azure/storage/blobs/storage-how-to-mount-container-linux.

An alternative solution to copy data into a Blob is **AzCopy** (more information is available at https://docs.microsoft.com/en-us/azure/storage/common/storage-use-azcopy-linux).

But, honestly, most of the time, this is not the way you are going to use Blob storage. Blob storage is not something you want access to on an operating system level, but rather on an application level to store objects such as images and to make them publicly available. Microsoft provides great examples for getting started at https://github.com/Azure-Samples?utf8=%E2%9C%93&q=storage-blobs.

In Chapter 7, *Deploying Your Virtual Machine*, there is a good example of an exception: uploading a VHD file to create a custom image using this VHD.

Networking

Virtual networks is the service in Azure that provides you with the following:

- Connectivity to your workload
- Connectivity from your workload to the outside world
- Connectivity between virtual machines
- Other connectivity options, such as VPN tunnels
- Traffic filtering
- Advanced routing options including BGP routes through an VPN tunnel

Virtual network

The most important component of the virtual networks service is the **virtual network**, or **VNet** for short.

Let's start with the simplest version of creating a VNet. To be honest, it's often the best way to do it; you'll probably need more commands to configure everything, but it makes it very clear what the purpose of your commands is:

```
New-AzureRmVirtualNetwork -Name <vnet name> `
  -ResourceGroupName <resource group> -Location <location>`
  -AddressPrefix <network>
```

For example:

```
$myVnet = New-AzureRmVirtualNetwork -Name MyVirtualNetwork `
  -ResourceGroupName $myRG -Location $myLocation `
  -AddressPrefix "10.0.0.0/16"
```

```
PS /Users/frederik> $myVnet


Name                    : MyVirtualNetwork
ResourceGroupName       : chapter4
Location                : westus
Id                      : /subscriptions/88                          9/resour
                          oviders/Microsoft.Network/virtualNetworks/MyVirtualNetwork
Etag                    : W/"a9e                      -15a75d7aec18"
ResourceGuid            : 9ccc6b48-95ce-47f2-bea1-90a0dbb8e5ad
ProvisioningState       : Succeeded
Tags                    :
AddressSpace            : {
                              "AddressPrefixes": [
                                "10.0.0.0/16"
                              ]
                          }
DhcpOptions             : {}
Subnets                 : []
VirtualNetworkPeerings  : []
EnableDdosProtection    : false
DdosProtectionPlan      : null
EnableVmProtection      : false
```

The address space or address prefix is the network that can be used by one or more subnets. It's possible to add additional address spaces.

Subnets

As stated, the subnet is created within a VNet. All traffic between different subnets in the same network is routed in Azure, so they are able to reach one another. Of course, you can modify that behavior, for instance, if you want to use a load balancer.

Again, I take the simplest command possible, for the same reason as for VNets:

```
Add-AzureRmVirtualNetworkSubnetConfig `
  -AddressPrefix <subnet> -Name <subnet> `
  -VirtualNetwork <vnet>
```

For example:

```
$mySubnet = Add-AzureRmVirtualNetworkSubnetConfig `
  -AddressPrefix 10.0.1.0/24 -Name MySubnet `
  -VirtualNetwork $myVnet
```

```
PS /Users/frederik> $myVnet


Name                    : MyVirtualNetwork
ResourceGroupName       : chapter4
Location                : westus
Id                      : /subscriptions/88525bff-081c-45ad-
                          oviders/Microsoft.Network/virtualN
Etag                    : W/"a9efc831-f2d0-4ae5-bb87-15a75d7
ResourceGuid            : 9ccc6b48-95ce-47f2-bea1-90a0dbb8e5
ProvisioningState       : Succeeded
Tags                    :
AddressSpace            : {
                                "AddressPrefixes": [
                                  "10.0.0.0/16"
                                ]
                          }
DhcpOptions             : {}
Subnets                 : [
                            {
                                "Name": "MySubnet",
                                "AddressPrefix": "10.0.1.0/24"
                            }
                          ]
VirtualNetworkPeerings  : []
EnableDdosProtection    : false
DdosProtectionPlan      : null
EnableVmProtection      : false
```

As you can see in this example, I didn't use the full network, only a part of it.

Alternatively, verification can be done using the following command:

```
Get-AzureRmVirtualNetworkSubnetConfig `
  -VirtualNetwork $myVnet
```

```
PS /Users/frederik> Get-AzureRmVirtualNetworkSubnetConfig -VirtualNetwork $myVnet


Name                     : MySubnet
Id                       :
Etag                     :
ProvisioningState        :
AddressPrefix            : 10.0.1.0/24
IpConfigurations         : null
ResourceNavigationLinks  : null
NetworkSecurityGroup     : null
RouteTable               : null
ServiceEndpoints         : null
```

The first IP address of the subnet is the gateway for network traffic coming from the virtual machine; it provides the following:

- A default gateway, with **Source Network Address Translation** (**SNAT**) to gain internet access. To be able to do so, a public IP address must be configured.
- It provides the DNS server, if not configured otherwise.
- It provides the DHCP server.

The last part of the VNet configuration involves attaching the newly created subnet:

```
$mySubnet | Set-AzureRmVirtualNetworkSubnetConfig `
  -VirtualNetwork $myVnet -Name $mySubnet.name `
  -AddressPrefix 10.0.1.0/24 | set-AzureRmVirtualNetwork
```

Network Security Group

Network Security Group (**NSG**) is the next component we need to take care of. It is essentially access control lists that are associated with a subnet. It also provides port forwarding to the virtual machines or containers. The rules are applied to all interfaces that are attached to the subnet.

The first step is to create an NSG:

```
New-AzureRMNetworkSecurityGroup `
  -ResourceGroupName <resource group>`
  -Location <location> -Name <nsg name>
```

For example:

```
$myNSG = New-AzureRMNetworkSecurityGroup `
  -ResourceGroupName $myRG -Location $myLocation -Name myNSG1
```

In the enormous output, you can find several sections; one of the sections is named `Default Security Rules`. This section contains a set of rules, given in order of priority:

- Allow inbound traffic from all VMs in VNet (`AllowVnetInBound`)
- Allow inbound traffic from Azure load balancer (`AllowAzureLoadBalancerInBound`)
- Deny all inbound traffic (`DenyAllInBound`)
- Allow outbound traffic from all VMs to all VMs in VNET (`AllowVnetOutBound`)
- Allow outbound traffic from all VMs to internet (`AllowInternetOutBound`)
- Deny all outbound traffic (`DenyAllOutBound`)

Before going into the rules, let's associate the subnet with the NSG:

```
Set-AzureRmVirtualNetworkSubnetConfig -Name <subnet> `
  -VirtualNetwork <vnet> -NetworkSecurityGroupID <nsg id> `
  -AddressPrefix 10.0.1.0/24
```

For example:

```
$NSGSubnet = Set-AzureRmVirtualNetworkSubnetConfig `
  -Name $myVnet.Subnets.Name `
  -VirtualNetwork $myVnet `
  -NetworkSecurityGroupID $myNSG.Id `
  -AddressPrefix 10.0.1.0/24

$NSGSubnet|Set-AzureRmVirtualNetwork
```

```
Name                      : MyVirtualNetwork
ResourceGroupName         : chapter4
Location                  : westus
Id                        : /subscriptions/88525bff-081c-45ad-ba31-4e79cd539e69/resourceGr
                            oviders/Microsoft.Network/virtualNetworks/MyVirtualNetwork
Etag                      : W/"e3ae26e5-a72f-4d23-8cc7-abf75c4df92f"
ResourceGuid              : 9ccc6b48-95ce-47f2-bea1-90a0dbb8e5ad
ProvisioningState         : Succeeded
Tags                      :
AddressSpace              : {
                              "AddressPrefixes": [
                                "10.0.0.0/16"
                              ]
                            }
DhcpOptions               : {
                              "DnsServers": []
                            }
Subnets                   : [
                              {
                                "Name": "MySubnet",
                                "Etag": "W/\"e3ae26e5-a72f-4d23-8cc7-abf75c4df92f\"",
                                "Id": "/subscriptions/8852                                9
                            chapter4/providers/Microsoft.Network/virtualNetworks/MyVirtual
                            MySubnet",
                                "AddressPrefix": "10.0.1.0/24",
                                "IpConfigurations": [],
                                "ResourceNavigationLinks": [],
                                "NetworkSecurityGroup": {
                                  "Id": "/subscriptions/88525bff-081c-45ad-ba31-4e79cd539e
                            s/chapter4/providers/Microsoft.Network/networkSecurityGroups/m
                                },
                                "ServiceEndpoints": [],
                                "ProvisioningState": "Succeeded"
                              }
                            ]
VirtualNetworkPeerings    : []
EnableDdosProtection      : false
DdosProtectionPlan        : null
EnableVmProtection        : false
```

If we want access to our virtual machines using SSH, then we need to add a security rule:

```
$myNSG | Add-AzureRmNetworkSecurityRuleConfig -Name SSH `
  -Description "Allow SSH" `
  -Access Allow -Protocol Tcp -Direction Inbound `
  -Priority 100 `
  -SourceAddressPrefix Internet -SourcePortRange * `
```

```
-DestinationAddressPrefix * `
-DestinationPortRange 22 | Set-AzureRmNetworkSecurityGroup
```

The `-SourceAddressPrefix` parameter is a sort of a shorthand for everything that is outside the VNet and reachable by public internet. Other values are as follows:

- `VirtualNetwork`: Everything within this VNet and other connected networks
- `AzureLoadBalancer`: If you are using the Azure Load Balancer that provides access to your virtual machines
- `*`: Everything

`Priority` ranges from `100` to `4096`. Higher numbers are created by Azure and can be overruled. The lower is the priority number, the higher is the priority of the rule.

To verify, execute the following commands:

```
$myNSG | select SecurityRules
```

```
$myNSG.SecurityRules
```

```
PS /Users/frederik> $myNSG | select SecurityRules

SecurityRules
-------------
{SSH}


PS /Users/frederik> $myNSG.SecurityRules


Name                                    : SSH
Id                                      :
Etag                                    :
ProvisioningState                       :
Description                             : Allow SSH
Protocol                                : Tcp
SourcePortRange                         : {*}
DestinationPortRange                    : {22}
SourceAddressPrefix                     : {Internet}
DestinationAddressPrefix                : {*}
SourceApplicationSecurityGroups         : null
DestinationApplicationSecurityGroups    : null
Access                                  : Allow
Priority                                : 100
Direction                               : Inbound
```

Alternatively, use the following command:

```
$myNSG | Get-AzureRmNetworkSecurityRuleConfig
```

Public IP address and network interface

To be able to access the virtual machine from the internet, a public IP address is needed and a DNS label.

An IP address can be static or dynamic. The DNS name must be unique in Azure. I prefer to generate it with a more or less random fixed prefix, especially for dynamically allocated IP addresses. But, even if it's static, it's easier to add aliases in DNS zones than modifying scripts over and over again, or using dynamic DNS:

```
$pip = New-AzureRmPublicIpAddress `
  -ResourceGroupName $myRG `
  -Location $myLocation -AllocationMethod Dynamic `
  -Name "<prefix>$(Get-Random)"
```

```
PS /Users/frederik> $pip


Name                      : loa979720432
ResourceGroupName         : chapter4
Location                  : westus
Id                        : /subscriptions/88525bff-081c-45ad-ba31-4e79
                            providers/Microsoft.Network/publicIPAddress
Etag                      : W/"28b8d5ad-6c90-4b8e-b113-3f9404e61afa"
ResourceGuid              : 664c331f-5feb-40d0-85e8-d5df32495b26
ProvisioningState         : Succeeded
Tags                      :
PublicIpAllocationMethod  : Dynamic
IpAddress                 : Not Assigned
PublicIpAddressVersion    : IPv4
IdleTimeoutInMinutes      : 4
IpConfiguration           : null
DnsSettings               : null
Zones                     : {}
Sku                       : {
                                "Name": "Basic"
                            }
IpTags                    : []
```

If the allocation method is `Dynamic`, the IP address is not allocated until the IP address is assigned to a network interface.

To create the network interface, use the following command:

```
$nic = New-AzureRmNetworkInterface -Name myNic `
  -ResourceGroupName $myRG -Location $myLocation `
  -SubnetId $myVnet.Subnets[0].Id -PublicIpAddressId $pip.Id `
  -NetworkSecurityGroupId $myNSG.Id
```

> **TIP**
>
> If you get an error on the `SubnetId`, try to set the `myVnet` variable again
> and run the `$myVnet = Get-AzureRmVirtualNetwork -Name`
> `$myVnet.Name `
>   `-ResourceGroupName $myRG` command.

To verify the result, execute the following command:

```
$nic.ipConfigurations
```

```
PS /Users/frederik> $nic.IpConfigurations


Name                                        : ipconfig1
Id                                          : /subscriptions/88525bff-081c-45ad-ba31-4
                                              ups/chapter4/providers/Microsoft.Network
                                              c/ipConfigurations/ipconfig1
Etag                                        : W/"45b8a6f2-59a6-447e-973a-5133018eecc4"
Primary                                     : True
ProvisioningState                           : Succeeded
PrivateIpAddress                            : 10.0.1.4
PrivateIpAddressVersion                     : IPv4
PrivateIpAllocationMethod                   : Dynamic
Subnet                                      : {
                                                  "Id": "/subscriptions/88525bff-081c-45
                                              sourceGroups/chapter4/providers/Microsof
                                              ks/MyVirtualNetwork/subnets/MySubnet",
                                                  "ResourceNavigationLinks": [],
                                                  "ServiceEndpoints": []
                                              }
PublicIpAddress                             : {
                                                  "IpTags": [],
                                                  "Zones": [],
                                                  "Id": "/subscriptions/88525bff-081c-45
                                              sourceGroups/chapter4/providers/Microsof
                                              sses/loa1539965299"
                                              }
LoadBalancerBackendAddressPools             : []
ApplicationGatewayBackendAddressPools       : []
LoadBalancerInboundNatRules                 : []
ApplicationSecurityGroups                   : []
```

Components for your virtual machine

Let's sum up the components covered in this chapter, which you need, as a requirement, before we can deploy a virtual machine. Yes, in the case of the storage account, it's not a real requirement, but do you want to work without being able to receive boot diagnostics in times of trouble?

> Every resource mentioned here is also in use by the Azure container service and the Azure Kubernetes service.

In this section, tables are provided with the needed components and the corresponding commands in PowerShell and Bash. It can be used together with the help available in PowerShell (`help <cmdlet>`, Azure CLI (add `--help` parameter to the command) or the Azure online documentation.

Azure profile

The Azure profile compromises the settings needed to describe your Azure environment:

Requirement	PowerShell	Azure CLI
Subscription ID	Get-AzureRmSubscription	az account list
Tenant ID	Get-AzureRmSubscription	az account list

Resource group

The resource group is needed to contain and manage resources:

Requirement	PowerShell	Azure CLI
Create resource group	New-AzureRmResourceGroup	az group create
View resource group	Get- AzureRmResourceGroup	az group list	show

Storage account

The storage account is needed if you want to store data outside your virtual machine/container:

Requirement	PowerShell	Azure CLI
Create storage account	New-AzureRMStorageAccount	az storage account create
View storage account	Get-AzureRMStorageAccount	az storage account show | list
View storage account keys	Get-AzureRMStorageAccountKey	az storage account keys list

Virtual network

Virtual networking is needed for communication between virtual machines/containers and communication to/from the outside world:

Requirement	PowerShell	Azure CLI
Create virtual network	New-AzureRmVirtualNetwork	az network vnet create
Create subnet	Add-AzureRmVirtualNetworkSubnetConfig Set-AzureRmVirtualNetworkSubnetConfig	az network vnet subnet create
View virtual network	Get-AzureRmVirtualNetwork	az network vnet list | show
View subnet	Get-AzureRmVirtualNetworkSubnetConfig	az network vnet subnet list | show

NSG

The NSG consists of ACLs to protect your workloads and allow access where needed. It is, together with the public IP address, also needed for the port forwarding to the virtual machine/container:

Requirement	PowerShell	Azure CLI
Create NSG	New-AzureRMNetworkSecurityGroup	az network nsg create
Associate subnet with NSG	Set-AzureRmVirtualNetworkSubnetConfig	az network vnet subnet update
Add NSG rule	Add-AzureRmNetworkSecurityRuleConfig Set-AzureRmNetworkSecurityGroup	az network nsg rule create
View NSG	Get-AzureRmNetworkSecurityGroup	az network nsg show | list
View NSG rules	Get-AzureRmNetworkSecurityRuleConfig	az network nsg rule show | list

Public IP address and network interface

The public IP address provides access from the outside world into the virtual machine/container. It's necessary for **Port Address Translation** (**PAT**) and SNAT:

Requirement	PowerShell	Azure CLI
Create public IP address	`New-AzureRmPublicIpAddress`	`az network public-ip create`
Create NIC	`New-AzureRmNetworkInterface`	`az network nic create`
List public IP address	`Get-AzureRmPublicIpAddress`	`az network public-ip show	list`

Summary

With the information in this chapter, you should be able to have a better understanding of the things you already encountered in `Chapter 2`, *Getting Started with the Azure Cloud*.

In this chapter, we explored all the Azure components that are needed before you can create your workload in Azure:

- You'll need a storage account for the virtual machine boot diagnostic extension.
- You'll want a storage account to store data outside your virtual machine.
- Networking components are needed to be able to communicate with your virtual machine, enable communication between your machines, and the virtual machine able to reach the internet.

The information that is provided is useful for receiving the information you'll probably need to identify components, for instance, whether you'll need to troubleshoot your workload, or getting a better understanding of your Azure infrastructure.

In the next chapter, we can use the information and commands provided in this chapter to identify and configure it in the Linux operating system. Besides network and storage topics, we'll explore other system administration tasks, such as software and service management.

Questions

1. Which resources are required before you can create your virtual machine?
2. Which resources are recommended for a virtual machine?
3. In the examples, a random number generator was used several times—why?
4. What is the purpose of the `AddressPrefix` on a network?
5. What is the purpose of the `AddressPrefix` on a subnet?
6. What is the purpose of the NSG?
7. Why is the public IP address needed for communication with the outside world?
8. What is the difference between a static and a dynamically allocated public IP address?

Further reading

The book, *Implementing Microsoft Azure Infrastructure Solutions* from Microsoft Press, is intended as a reference guide for studying the 70-533 exam. It explains every part of the Azure infrastructure in great detail, using the Azure portal and the command-line interfaces.

If you are newly into networking, another book, which is also written as a study guide for an exam, is the *Network+ Certification Guide* by Anthony Sequeira. The first five chapters are an excellent read as an introduction to networking. Much older and more difficult to read is the freely available TCP/IP Redbook from IBM (`https://www.redbooks.ibm.com/redbooks/pdfs/gg243376.pdf`); it covers much more than you need to know, but if you are interested in the topic, it's a must-read. Even if you are not interested in taking the Cisco ICND1 exam, Neil Anderson recorded a video at PacktPub, which gives you, besides the Cisco part, a very good introduction to networking.

On the website, `https://www.petri.com`, you can find some nice background articles about Azure Storage and Azure Files.

> **TIP**
> Please be aware that the Azure environment is continuously changing, especially regarding storage and networking; it is important to validate sources against the documentation available on the Microsoft website(s). The date of publishing is maybe the first thing you will want to check.

Advanced Linux Administration

5

In Chapter 3, *Basic Linux Administration*, some basic Linux commands were covered and you learned how to find your way in the Linux environment. After that, in Chapter 4, *Managing Azure*, we took a deep dive into the Azure architecture.

With the knowledge from these two chapters, we're ready to continue our journey in Linux and explore the following topics:

- Software management
- Storage management
- Network management
- System management

Technical requirements

For the purpose of this chapter, you'll need to deploy a Linux virtual machine in Azure, with the distribution of your choice.

In terms of sizing, you'll need at least 2 GB of temporary storage, and the ability to add a minimum of three extra disks. For instance, the B2S virtual machine size is a good starting point.

Software management

In the old days, installing software was a matter of extracting an archive to a filesystem. There are several problems with this approach:

- It's difficult to remove the software if the files are copied into directories that are also used by other software

- It's difficult to upgrade software; maybe the files are still in use, or they are renamed for whatever reason
- It's difficult to handle shared libraries

That's why Linux distributions invented software managers.

The RPM software manager

In 1997, Red Hat released the first version of their package manager, RPM. Other distributions such as SUSE adopted this package manager. RPM is the name of the utility rpm, as well as the name of the format and the filename extension.

The RPM package contains the following:

- A CPIO archive
- Metadata with information about the software, such as a description and dependencies
- Scriptlets for pre- and post-installation scripts

In the past, Linux administrators used the rpm utility to install/update and remove software on a Linux system. If there was a dependency, the rpm command is able to tell exactly which other packages you'll need to install. The rpm utility is not able to fix the dependencies or possible conflicts between packages.

Nowadays, we don't use the rpm utility any longer to install or remove software; instead, we use more advanced software installers. After the installation of software with yum (Red Hat/CentOS) or zypper (SUSE), all the metadata goes into a database. Querying this rpm database with the rpm command can be very handy.

A list of the most common rpm query parameters are as follows:

Parameter	Description
-qa	List all installed packages.
-qi <software>	List information.
-qc <software>	List installed configuration files.

`-qd` `<software>`	List installed documentation and examples.
`-ql` `<software>`	List all installed files.
`-qf` `<filename>`	Shows the package that installed this file
`-V <software>`	Verify the integrity/changes after the installation of a package; use `-va` to do it for all installed software.
`-qp`	Use this parameter together with other parameters if the package is not already installed. It's especially useful if you combine this parameter with `--script` to investigate the pre- and post-installation scripts in the package.

The following screenshot is an example of getting information about the installed SSH server package:

```
[linvirt@centos ~]$ rpm -qa | grep openssh
openssh-server-7.4p1-13.el7_4.x86_64
openssh-7.4p1-13.el7_4.x86_64
openssh-clients-7.4p1-13.el7_4.x86_64
[linvirt@centos ~]$ rpm -qc openssh-server
/etc/pam.d/sshd
/etc/ssh/sshd_config
/etc/sysconfig/sshd
[linvirt@centos ~]$ rpm -qd openssh-server
/usr/share/man/man5/moduli.5.gz
/usr/share/man/man5/sshd_config.5.gz
/usr/share/man/man8/sftp-server.8.gz
/usr/share/man/man8/sshd.8.gz
[linvirt@centos ~]$ rpm -qf /etc/ssh/sshd_config
openssh-server-7.4p1-13.el7_4.x86_64
[linvirt@centos ~]$ rpm -V openssh-server
..?....T.  c /etc/ssh/sshd_config
..?......  c /etc/sysconfig/sshd
```

The output of the −V parameter is telling us that the modification time has changed since the installation. Let's make another change in the sshd_config file:

```
sudo cp /etc/ssh/sshd_config /tmp

sudo sed -i 's/#Port 22/Port 22/' /etc/ssh/sshd_config
```

If you verify the installed package again, there is an S added to the output, indicating that the file size is different, and a T, indicating the modification time has changed:

```
linvirt@debian:~$ dpkg -l xxd
Desired=Unknown/Install/Remove/Purge/Hold
| Status=Not/Inst/Conf-files/Unpacked/halF-conf/Half-inst/trig-aWait/Trig-pend
|/ Err?=(none)/Reinst-required (Status,Err: uppercase=bad)
||/ Name           Version        Architecture Description
+++-==============-==============-============-=======================================
ii  xxd            2:8.0.0197-4   amd64        tool to make (or reverse) a hex d
```

Other possible characters in the output are as follows:

S	File size
M	Mode (permissions)
5	Checksum
D	Major/minor on devices
L	Readlink mismatch
U	User ownership
G	Group ownership
T	Modification time
P	Capabilities

For text files, the diff command can help to show the differences between the backup in the /tmp directory and the configuration in /etc/ssh:

```
sudo diff /etc/ssh/sshd_config /tmp/sshd_config
```

Restore the original file as follows:

```
sudo cp /tmp/sshd_config /etc/ssh/sshd_config
```

The DPKG software manager

The Debian distribution doesn't use the RPM format; instead it uses the DEB format, invented in 1995. The format is in use on all Debian and Ubuntu-based distributions.

A DEB package contains:

- A file, `debian-binary`, with the version of the package
- An archive file, `control.tar`, with metadata (package name, version, dependencies, and maintainer)
- An archive file, `data.tar`, containing the actual software

Management of DEB packages can be done with the `dpkg` utility. Like `rpm`, the utility is not in use any longer to install software. Instead, the more advanced `apt` command is used.

All the metadata goes into a database that can be queried with `dpkg` or `dpkg-query`.

The important parameters of `dpkg-query` are as follows:

`-l`	List all packages without parameters, but you can use wildcards, for example, `dpkg -l *ssh*`
`-L <package>`	List files in an installed package
`-p <package>`	Show information about the package
`-s <package>`	Show the state of a package

The first column from the output of `dpkg -l` also shows a status:

```
linvirt@debian:~$ dpkg -l xxd
Desired=Unknown/Install/Remove/Purge/Hold
| Status=Not/Inst/Conf-files/Unpacked/halF-conf/Half-inst/trig-aWait/Trig-pend
|/ Err?=(none)/Reinst-required (Status,Err: uppercase=bad)
||/ Name            Version         Architecture Description
+++-===============-===============-============-===================================
ii  xxd             2:8.0.0197-4    amd64        tool to make (or reverse) a hex d
```

The first character in the first column is the desired action, the second is the actual state of the package, and a possible third character indicates an error flag (R). `ii` means that the package is installed.

Possible desired states are as follows:

- (u) unknown
- (h) hold
- (r) remove
- (p) urge

Important package states are as follows:

- n(ot) installed
- H(a)lf installed
- Hal(F) configured

Software management with YUM

Your Update Manager or **Yellowdog Updater Modified** (**YUM**) is a modern software management tool that was introduced by Red Hat in Enterprise Linux version 5, replacing the up2date utility. It is currently in use in all Red Hat-based distributions, but will be replaced with dnf, which is used by Fedora. The good news is that dnf is syntax-compatible with yum.

Yum is responsible for the following:

- Installing software, including dependencies
- Updating software
- Removing software
- Listing and searching for software

Important basic parameters are as follows:

Command	Description
yum search	Search for software based on package name/summary
yum provides	Search for software based on a filename in a package
yum install	Install software
yum info	Information and status
yum update	Updates all software
yum remove	Remove software

You can also install patterns of software, for instance the pattern or group *File and Print Server* is a very convenient way to install the NFS and Samba file servers together with the Cups print server:

Command	Description
yum groups list	List the available groups.
yum groups install	Install a group.
yum groups info	Information about a group, including the group names that are in use by the Anaconda installer. This information is important for unattended installations.
yum groups update	Update software within a group.
yum groups remove	Remove the installed group.

Another nice feature of yum is working with history:

Command	Description
yum history list	List the tasks executed by yum
yum history info <number>	List the content of a specific task
yum history undo <number>	Undo the task; a redo is also available

The yum command is using repositories to be able to do all the software management. To list the currently configured repositories, use:

```
yum repolist
```

To add another repository, you'll need the tool yum-config-manager that creates and modifies the configuration files in /etc/yum.repos.d. For instance, if you want to add a repository to install Microsoft SQL Server, use the following:

```
yum-config-manager --add-repo \
  https://packages.microsoft.com/config/rhel/7/\
  mssql-server-2017.repo
```

The yum functionality can be extended with plugins, for instance to select the fastest mirror, enabling the filesystem / LVM snapshots and running yum as a scheduled task (cron).

Software management with Zypp

SUSE, like Red Hat, using RPM for package management. But instead of using yum, they use another tool set with Zypp (also known as libZypp) as backend. Software management can be done with the graphical configuration software YaST or the command-line interface tool Zypper.

> Yum and DNF are also available in the SUSE software repositories. You can use them to manage (limited to install and remove) software on your local system, but that's not why they are available. The reason is Kiwi: an application to build OS images and installers.

Important basic parameters are:

Command	Description
zypper search	Search for software
zypper install	Install software
zypper remove	Remove software
zypper update	Update software
zypper dist-upgrade	Perform a distribution upgrade
zypper info	Show information

There is a search option to search for a command, what-provides, but it's very limited. If you don't know the package name, there is a utility called cnf instead. Before you can use cnf, you'll need to install scout; this way, the package properties can be searched:

```
sudo zypper install scout
```

After that, you can use `cnf`:

```
linvirt@suse01:~> sudo cnf finger

The program 'finger' can be found in the following package:
 * finger [ path: /usr/bin/finger, repository: zypp (openSUSE-Leap-42.3-Oss) ]

Try installing with:
    zypper install finger

linvirt@suse01:~> sudo zypper install finger
Loading repository data...
Reading installed packages...
Resolving package dependencies...

The following NEW package is going to be installed:
  finger

1 new package to install.
Overall download size: 18.9 KiB. Already cached: 0 B. After the operation,
additional 31.6 KiB will be used.
Continue? [y/n/...? shows all options] (y):
```

If you want to update your system to a new distribution version, you have to modify the repositories first. For instance, if you want to update from SUSE LEAP 42.3 to version 15.0, execute the following procedure:

1. First, install the available updates for your current version:

   ```
   sudo zypper update
   ```

2. Update to the latest version in the 42.3.x releases:

   ```
   sudo zypper dist-upgrade
   ```

3. Modify the repository configuration:

   ```
   sudo sed -i 's/42.3/15.0/g' /etc/zypp/repos.d/repo*.repo
   ```

4. Initialize the new repositories:

```
sudo zypper refresh
```

5. Install the new distribution:

```
sudo zypper dist-upgrade
```

6. Of course, you have to reboot after the distribution upgrade.

Besides installing packages, you can install the following:

- `patterns`: Groups of packages, for instance to install a complete web server including PHP and MySQL (also known as lamp)
- `patches`: Incremental updates for a package
- `products`: Installation of an additional product

To list the available patterns, use:

```
zypper patterns
```

To install them, use:

```
sudo zypper install --type pattern <pattern>
```

The same procedure applies to patches and products.

Zypper uses online repositories to view the currently configured repositories:

```
sudo zypper repos
```

You can add repositories with the `addrepo` parameter, for instance: To add a community repository for the latest PowerShell version on LEAP 15.0:

```
sudo zypper addrepo \
  https://download.opensuse.org/repositories\
  /home:/aaptel:/powershell-stuff/openSUSE_Leap_15.0/\
  home:aaptel:powershell-stuff.repo
```

If you add a repository, you always need to refresh the repositories:

```
sudo zypper refresh
```

> SUSE has the concept of repositories that can or cannot be trusted. If a vendor is not trusted, you need to add the `--from` parameter to the install command. Alternatively, you can add a configuration file to `/etc/vendors.d`. For example:
> ```
> [main]
> vendors = suse,opensuse,obs://build.suse.de
> ```

The vendor of a package can be found with `zypper info`.

Software management with apt

In Debian/Ubuntu-based distributions, software management is done via the `apt` utility, which is a recent replacement for the utilities `apt-get` and `apt-cache`.

The most-used commands include:

Command	Description
apt list	List packages
apt search	Search in descriptions
apt install	Install a package
apt show	Show package details
apt remove	Remove a package
apt update	Update catalog of available packages
apt upgrade	Upgrade the installed software
apt edit-sources	Edit the repository configuration

Repositories are configured in `/etc/apt/sources.list` and files in the `/etc/apt/sources.list.d/` directory. Alternatively, there is a command, `apt-add-repository`, available:

```
apt-add-repository \
  'deb http://myserver/path/to/repo stable'
```

The `apt` repositories have the concept of release classes:

- Old stable, tested in the previous version of a distribution
- Stable
- Testing
- Unstable

They also have the concept of components:

- **Main**: Tested and provided with support and updates
- **Contrib**: Tested and provided with support and updates, but there are dependencies that are not in main, but for instance, in non-free
- **Non-free**: Software that isn't compliant with the Debian Social Contract Guidelines (`https://www.debian.org/social_contract#guidelines`)

Ubuntu adds some extra components:

- **Universe**: Community provided, no support, updates possible
- **Restricted**: Proprietary device drivers
- **Multiverse**: Software restricted by copyright or legal issues

Networking

In Azure, the network settings, such as your IP address and DNS settings, are provided via DHCP. The configuration is very similar to the configuration of physical machines or virtual machines running on another platform. The difference is that the configuration is provided by Azure and normally shouldn't be changed.

In this section, you'll learn to identify the network configuration in Linux and how to match that information with the settings in Azure that were covered in the previous chapter.

Identifying the network interfaces

During the boot process and afterwards, the Linux kernel is responsible for hardware identification. When the kernel identifies the hardware, it hands the collected information over to a process, a running daemon, called `systemd-udevd`. This daemon does the following:

- Loads the network driver if necessary

- Can be responsible for device naming
- Updates /sys with all the available information

The udevadm utility can help you to show the identified hardware:

```
[linvirt@CentOS-01 ~]$ sudo udevadm info -p /sys/class/net/eth*
P: /devices/LNXSYSTM:00/device:00/PNP0A03:00/device:08/VMBUS:01/vmbus_15/net/eth0
E: DEVPATH=/devices/LNXSYSTM:00/device:00/PNP0A03:00/device:08/VMBUS:01/vmbus_15/net/eth0
E: ID_NET_DRIVER=hv_netvsc
E: ID_NET_NAME_MAC=enx000d3a3ae27f
E: ID_OUI_FROM_DATABASE=Microsoft Corp.
E: ID_PATH=acpi-VMBUS:01
E: ID_PATH_TAG=acpi-VMBUS_01
E: IFINDEX=2
E: INTERFACE=eth0
E: SUBSYSTEM=net
E: SYSTEMD_ALIAS=/sys/subsystem/net/devices/eth0
E: TAGS=:systemd:
E: USEC_INITIALIZED=135398
E: net.ifnames=0
```

You can also reach the /sys/class/net directory and view the cat command with the available files, but that's not a very user-friendly method and normally there is no need to do it this way, because there are utilities that parse all the available information.

The most important utility is the ip command. Let's start with listing the available network interfaces:

```
ip link show
```

Once listed, you can be more specific:

```
ip link show dev eth0
```

```
[linvirt@CentOS-01 ~]$ ip link show
1: lo: <LOOPBACK,UP,LOWER_UP> mtu 65536 qdisc noqueue state UNKNOWN mode DEFAULT
  qlen 1
     link/loopback 00:00:00:00:00:00 brd 00:00:00:00:00:00
2: eth0: <BROADCAST,MULTICAST,UP,LOWER_UP> mtu 1500 qdisc pfifo_fast state UP mo
de DEFAULT qlen 1000
     link/ether 00:0d:3a:3a:e2:7f brd ff:ff:ff:ff:ff:ff
[linvirt@CentOS-01 ~]$ ip link show dev eth0
2: eth0: <BROADCAST,MULTICAST,UP,LOWER_UP> mtu 1500 qdisc pfifo_fast state UP mo
de DEFAULT qlen 1000
     link/ether 00:0d:3a:3a:e2:7f brd ff:ff:ff:ff:ff:ff
```

The meaning of all the status flags, such as LOWER_UP, can be found in man 7 netdevice.

Identifying the IP address

After learning the naming of the network interface, the `ip` utility can be used to show the IP address configured on the network interface, as shown in the following screenshot:

```
[linvirt@CentOS-01 ~]$ ip addr show
1: lo: <LOOPBACK,UP,LOWER_UP> mtu 65536 qdisc noqueue state UNKNOWN qlen 1
    link/loopback 00:00:00:00:00:00 brd 00:00:00:00:00:00
    inet 127.0.0.1/8 scope host lo
       valid_lft forever preferred_lft forever
    inet6 ::1/128 scope host
       valid_lft forever preferred_lft forever
2: eth0: <BROADCAST,MULTICAST,UP,LOWER_UP> mtu 1500 qdisc pfifo_fast state UP ql
en 1000
    link/ether 00:0d:3a:3a:e2:7f brd ff:ff:ff:ff:ff:ff
    inet 192.168.1.4/24 brd 192.168.1.255 scope global eth0
       valid_lft forever preferred_lft forever
    inet6 fe80::20d:3aff:fe3a:e27f/64 scope link
       valid_lft forever preferred_lft forever
[linvirt@CentOS-01 ~]$ ip addr show eth0
2: eth0: <BROADCAST,MULTICAST,UP,LOWER_UP> mtu 1500 qdisc pfifo_fast state UP ql
en 1000
    link/ether 00:0d:3a:3a:e2:7f brd ff:ff:ff:ff:ff:ff
    inet 192.168.1.4/24 brd 192.168.1.255 scope global eth0
       valid_lft forever preferred_lft forever
    inet6 fe80::20d:3aff:fe3a:e27f/64 scope link
       valid_lft forever preferred_lft forever
```

Showing the route table

The route table can be shown per device or per subnet:

```
[linvirt@CentOS-01 ~]$ ip route show dev eth0
default via 192.168.1.1
168.63.129.16 via 192.168.1.1  proto static
169.254.0.0/16  scope link  metric 1002
169.254.169.254 via 192.168.1.1  proto static
192.168.1.0/24  proto kernel  scope link  src 192.168.1.4
[linvirt@CentOS-01 ~]$ ip route show 0.0.0.0/0
default via 192.168.1.1 dev eth0
```

Another nice feature is that you can query which device and gateway is used to reach a specific IP:

```
[linvirt@CentOS-01 ~]$  ip route get 9.9.9.9
9.9.9.9 via 192.168.1.1 dev eth0  src 192.168.1.4
        cache
```

Network configuration

The `ip` command is mainly used to verify settings. The persistent configuration is normally managed by another daemon. Red Hat Enterprise Linux distributions uses `NetworkManager` in SLE and OpenSUSE LEAP. `wicked` is used in Ubuntu 17.10 and later. `systemd-networkd` and `systemd-resolved`, earlier versions of Ubuntu, completely rely on the DHCP client configured in `/etc/network/interfaces.d/*cfg` files.

In Ubuntu, the Azure Linux Guest Agent creates two files in the directory `/run/systemd/` network. One is a link file named `10-netplan-eth0.link` to preserve the device name, based on the MAC address:

```
[Match]
MACAddress=00:....

[Link]
Name=eth0
WakeOnLan=off
```

The other is `10-netplan-eth0.network` for the actual network configuration:

```
[Match]
MACAddress=00:...
Name=eth0

[Network]
DHCP=ipv4

[DHCP]
UseMTU=true
RouteMetric=100
```

If you have more than one network interface, multiple sets of files are created.

In SUSE, the Azure Linux Guest Agent creates a file, `/etc/sysconfig/network/ifcfg-eth0`, with the following content:

```
BOOTPROTO='dhcp'
DHCLIENT6_MODE='managed'
MTU=''
REMOTE_IPADDR=''
STARTMODE='onboot'
CLOUD_NETCONFIG_MANAGE='yes'
```

The `wicked` daemon reads this file and uses it for the network configuration. Like Ubuntu, multiple files are created if you have more than one network interface. The status of the configuration can be viewed with the `wicked` command:

```
linvirt@suse:/etc/sysconfig/network> sudo wicked show eth0
eth0            up
        link:   #2, state up, mtu 1500
        type:   ethernet, hwaddr 00:0d:3a:2a:89:29
        config: compat:suse:/etc/sysconfig/network/ifcfg-eth0
        leases: ipv4 dhcp granted
        leases: ipv6 dhcp requesting
        addr:   ipv4 10.1.0.4/24 [dhcp]
        route:  ipv4 default via 10.1.0.1 proto dhcp
        route:  ipv4 168.63.129.16/32 via 10.1.0.1 proto dhcp
        route:  ipv4 169.254.169.254/32 via 10.1.0.1 proto dhcp
```

In RHEL and CentOS, the `ifcfg-` files are created in the directory `/etc/sysconfig/network-scripts`:

```
DEVICE=eth0
ONBOOT=yes
BOOTPROTO=dhcp
TYPE=Ethernet
USERCTL=no
PEERDNS=yes
IPV6INIT=no
NM_CONTROLLED=no
DHCP_HOSTNAME=...
```

Please notice that the parameter NM_CONTROLLED is set to no; this way NetworkManager is not able to control the connection. You can use the nmcli command to show the device settings, but you can't use the command to modify those settings:

```
[linvirt@CentOS-01 network-scripts]$ nmcli device show eth0
GENERAL.DEVICE:                 eth0
GENERAL.TYPE:                   ethernet
GENERAL.HWADDR:                 00:0D:3A:3A:E2:7F
GENERAL.MTU:                    1500
GENERAL.STATE:                  10 (unmanaged)
GENERAL.CONNECTION:             --
GENERAL.CON-PATH:               --
WIRED-PROPERTIES.CARRIER:       on
IP4.ADDRESS[1]:                 192.168.1.4/24
IP4.GATEWAY:                    192.168.1.1
IP4.ROUTE[1]:                   dst = 168.63.129.16/32, nh = 192.168.1.1
, mt = 0
IP4.ROUTE[2]:                   dst = 169.254.0.0/16, nh = 0.0.0.0, mt =
 1002
IP4.ROUTE[3]:                   dst = 169.254.169.254/32, nh = 192.168.1
.1, mt = 0
IP6.ADDRESS[1]:                 fe80::20d:3aff:fe3a:e27f/64
IP6.GATEWAY:
```

Changes in the network configuration

As stated before, every network setting is provided by the Azure DHCP server. Everything we learned until now was about the verification of the network settings configured in Azure.

If you changed something in Azure, you'll need to restart the network in Linux.

In SUSE and CentOS, you can do this with the following:

```
sudo systemctl restart network
```

In the latest version of Ubuntu Server, use this:

```
sudo systemctl restart systemd-networkd
```

```
sudo systemctl restart systems-resolved
```

Hostname

The current hostname of the virtual machine can be found with the `hostnamectl` utility:

```
[linvirt@CentOS-01 ~]$ hostnamectl status
   Static hostname: CentOS-01
         Icon name: computer-vm
           Chassis: vm
        Machine ID: e8abe05b1d42472d882942fe2bdfc47e
           Boot ID: 3d2a68fc99a346349fa0656f5184cf0f
    Virtualization: microsoft
  Operating System: CentOS Linux 7 (Core)
       CPE OS Name: cpe:/o:centos:centos:7
            Kernel: Linux 3.10.0-514.26.2.el7.x86_64
      Architecture: x86_64
```

The hostname is provided by the DHCP server in Azure; to view the configured hostname in Azure, you can use the Azure portal, the Azure CLI, or PowerShell. As an example, in PowerShell, use:

```
$myvm=Get-AzureRmVM -Name CentOS-01 `
  -ResourceGroupName MyResource1

$myvm.OSProfile.ComputerName
```

In Linux, you can change the hostname with the `hostnamectl` utility:

```
sudo hostnamectl set-hostname <hostname>

sudo systemctl restart waagent #RedHat & SUSE

sudo systemctl restart walinuxagent  #Ubuntu
```

This should change your hostname. If it doesn't work, check the configuration file of the Azure Linux VM agent, `/etc/waagent.conf`:

```
Provisioning.MonitorHostName=y
```

If it is still not working, edit the file `/var/lib/waagent/ovf-env.xml` and change the `HostName` parameter. Another possible cause is the line `DHCP_HOSTNAME` in the `ifcfg-<interface>` file; just remove it and restart `NetworkManager`.

DNS

The DNS settings are also provided via the Azure DHCP server. In Azure, the settings are attached to the virtual network interface. You can view them in the Azure Portal, PowerShell (`Get-AzureRmNetworkInterface`), or the Azure CLI (`az vm nic show`).

You can, of course, configure your own DNS settings. In PowerShell, declare the virtual machine and identify the network interface:

```
$myvm = Get-AzureRmVM -Name <vm name> `
  -ResourceGroupName <resource group>

$myvm.NetworkProfile.NetworkInterfaces.Id
```

The last command will give you the complete ID of the required network interface; the last part of this ID is the interface name. Let's strip it from the output and request the interface properties:

```
$nicname = $nicid.split("/")[-1]

$nic = Get-AzureRmNetworkInterface `
  -ResourceGroupName <resource group> -Name $nicname

$nic
```

The last step is to update the DNS name server settings. For the purpose of this book, I am using 9.9.9.9, which is a public, freely available DNS service called Quad9. You can also use the DNS service of Google (8.8.8.8 and 8.8.4.4):

```
$nic.DnsSettings.DnsServers.Add("9.9.9.9")

$nic | Set-AzureRmNetworkInterface

$nic | Get-AzureRmNetworkInterface | `
  Select-Object -ExpandProperty DnsSettings
```

The method in the Azure CLI is similar, but involves less steps. Search for the network interface name:

```
nicname=$(az vm nic list \
  --resource-group <resource group> \
  --vm-name <vm name> --query '[].id' -o tsv | cut -d/ -f9)
```

Update the DNS settings:

```
az network nic update -g MyResource1 --name $nicname \
  --dns-servers 9.9.9.9
```

And verify the new DNS settings:

```
az network nic show --resource-group <resource group> \
  --name $nicname --query "dnsSettings"
```

In the Linux virtual machine, you have to renew the DHCP lease to receive the new settings. The settings are saved in the file /etc/resolv.conf.

In Linux distributions that use the network implementation of systemd, such as Ubuntu, the file /etc/resolv.conf is a symbolic link to a file in the /run/systemd/resolve/ directory, and the command sudo systemd-resolve --status shows you the current settings:

```
link 2 (eth0)
      Current Scopes: DNS
       LLMNR setting: yes
MulticastDNS setting: no
      DNSSEC setting: no
   DNSSEC supported: no
         DNS Servers: 9.9.9.9
          DNS Domain: reddog.microsoft.com
```

To test the DNS configuration, you can use dig, or the simpler host utility, for instance:

```
host -t A www.google.com
```

Storage

There are two types of storage available in Azure: virtual disks that are attached to the virtual machine and Azure File Shares. In this chapter, both types will be covered. We will be discussing the following topics:

- Adding a single virtual disk to a virtual machine
- Working with filesystems
- Working with multiple virtual disks using the **Logical Volume Manager** (**LVM**) and RAID software

Storage provided by block devices

Local and remote storage can be delivered by block devices. In Azure, it's almost always a virtual hard disk that is attached to the virtual machine, but it is possible to use iSCSI volumes as well, delivered by Microsoft Azure StorSimple or third parties.

Every disk attached to a virtual machine is identified by the kernel, and after identification, the kernel hands it over to a daemon called `systemd-udevd`. This daemon is responsible for creating an entry in the `/dev` directory, updating `/sys/class/block`, and if necessary loading a driver to access the filesystem.

The device file in `/dev` provides a simple interface to the block device and is accessed by a SCSI driver.

There are multiple methods to identify available block devices. One of the possibilities is using the `lsscsi` command:

```
linvirt@ubuntu02:~$ sudo lsscsi
[0:0:0:0]    disk    Msft    Virtual Disk      1.0    /dev/sda
[1:0:1:0]    disk    Msft    Virtual Disk      1.0    /dev/sdb
[5:0:0:0]    cd/dvd  Msft    Virtual CD/ROM    1.0    /dev/sr0
```

In Azure, by default a DVD drive is available, but for this chapter we're only interested in the virtual disks.

The first available disk is called `sda`—SCSI disk A. This disk is created from the image disk used during the provisioning of the virtual machine and is also known as the root disk. You can access this disk via `/dev/sda` or `/dev/disk/azure/root`.

Another way to identify the available storage is using the `lsblk` command. It can provide more information about the content of the disk:

```
linvirt@ubuntu02:~$ sudo lsblk
NAME      MAJ:MIN RM   SIZE RO TYPE MOUNTPOINT
sda         8:0    0    30G  0 disk
|-sda1      8:1    0  29.9G  0 part /
|-sda14     8:14   0     4M  0 part
`-sda15     8:15   0   106M  0 part /boot/efi
sdb         8:16   0     4G  0 disk
`-sdb1      8:17   0     4G  0 part /mnt
sr0        11:0    1   628K  0 rom
```

In this example, there are two partitions created on `/dev/sda`, `sda1` and `sda2` (or `/dev/disk/azure/root-part1` and `root-part2`). The major number in the second column, `8`, means that this is a SCSI device; the minor part is just numbering. The third column tells us that the device is not removable, indicated by a `0` (it's a `1` if it's removable), and the fifth column tells us that the drives and partitions aren't read-only: again a `1` for read-only and a `0` for read-write.

Another disk is available, the resource disk, `/dev/sdb` (`/dev/disk/azure/resource`), which is a temporary disk. That means that data is not persistent and is gone after a reboot.

Adding a data disk

You can add an extra virtual disk to a virtual machine using the Azure Portal or via PowerShell. Let's add a disk.

First, declare how we want to name our disk and where the disk should be created:

```
$resourcegroup = '<resource group>'
$location = '<location>'
$diskname = '<disk name>'

$vm = Get-AzureRmVM `
  -Name <vm name> `
  -ResourceGroupName $resourcegroup
```

Create the virtual disk configuration—an empty, standard managed disk of 2 GB in size:

```
$diskConfig = New-AzureRmDiskConfig `
  -SkuName 'StandardLRS' `
  -Location $location `
  -CreateOption 'Empty' `
  -DiskSizeGB 2
```

Create the virtual disk using this configuration:

```
$dataDisk1 = New-AzureRmDisk `
  -DiskName $diskname `
  -Disk $diskConfig `
  -ResourceGroupName $resourcegroup
```

Attach the disk to the virtual machine:

```
$vmdisk = Add-AzureRmVMDataDisk `
  -VM $vm -Name $diskname `
  -CreateOption Attach `
```

```
-ManagedDiskId $dataDisk1.Id `
-Lun 1

Update-AzureRmVM `
  -VM $vm `
  -ResourceGroupName $resourcegroup
```

Of course, you can use the Azure CLI as well:

```
az disk create \
  --resource-group <resource group> \
  --name <disk name> \
  --location <location> \
  --size-gb 2 \
  --sku Standard_LRS \
  --lun <lun number>

az vm disk attach \
  --disk <disk name> \
  --vm-name <vm name> \
  --resource-group <resource group>
```

> LUN is the abbreviation of logical unit number, a number used to identify a logical unit, which is a device addressed by the SCSI protocol. You can start the numbering with zero.

After creation, the virtual disk is visible in the virtual machine as `/dev/sdc` (`/dev/disk/azure/scsi1/lun1`).

Look again at the output of `lssci`:

```
[5:0:0:1]    disk   Msft     Virtual Disk    1.0  /dev/sdc
```

The first column is formatted:

```
<hostbus adapter id> :  <channel id> : <target id> : <lun number>
```

The `hostbus adapter` is the interface to the storage and is created by the Microsoft Hyper-V virtual storage driver. The channel ID is always `0`, unless you configured multi-pathing. The target ID identifies an SCSI target on a controller; this one is always zero for direct-attached devices in Azure.

Partitioning

Before you can use the block device, you'll need to partition it. There are multiple tools available for partitioning and some distributions come with their own utilities to create and manipulate partition tables. SUSE, for instance, has one in their YaST Configuration tool.

In this book, I want to use the `parted` utility. It's installed by default on every Linux distribution and can handle all known partition layouts: `msdos`, `gpt`, `sun`, and so on.

You can use `parted` in a scripted way from the command line, but if you're new to `parted` it's easier to use the interactive shell:

```
parted /dev/sdc
  GNU Parted 3.1
  Using /dev/sdc
  Welcome to GNU Parted! Type 'help' to view a list of commands.
```

The first step is to show the available information about this device:

```
(parted) print
  Error: /dev/sdc: unrecognised disk label
  Model: Msft Virtual Disk (scsi)
  Disk /dev/sdc: 2147MB
  Sector size (logical/physical): 512B/512B
  Partition Table: unknown
  Disk Flags:
```

The important line here is `unrecognised disk label`. This means that there was no partition layout created. Nowadays, the most common layout is GPT.

> Parted supports autocompletion after a question mark—press *Ctrl +* i twice.

Change the partition label into GPT:

```
(parted) mklabel
 New disk label type? gpt
```

Verify the result by printing the disk partition table again:

```
(parted) print
  Model: Msft Virtual Disk (scsi)
  Disk /dev/sdc: 2147MB
  Sector size (logical/physical): 512B/512B
  Partition Table: gpt
  Disk Flags:
  Number Start  End  Size File system  Name  Flags
```

The next step is to create a partition:

```
(parted) mkpart
  Partition name?  []? lun1_part1
  File system type?  [ext2]? xfs
  Start? 0%
  End? 100%
```

Filesystems will be covered later in this chapter. For sizing, you can use percentages or fixed sizes. In general, in Azure it makes more sense to use the whole disk.

Print the disk partition table again:

```
(parted) print
  Model: Msft Virtual Disk (scsi)
  Disk /dev/sdc: 2147MB
  Sector size (logical/physical): 512B/512B
  Partition Table: gpt
  Disk Flags:
  Number Start   End    Size   File system  Name      Flags
  1      1049kB 2146MB 2145MB              lun1_part1
```

Please notice that the filesystem column is still empty, because the partition is not formatted.

Use *Ctrl* + *D* or `quit` to exit `parted`.

Filesystems in Linux

Linux supports many filesystems—native Linux filesystems such as `ext4` and XFS and third-party filesystems such as FAT32.

Every distribution supports the native filesystems ext4 and XFS; on top of that, SUSE and Ubuntu have support for a very modern filesystem: BTRFS. Ubuntu is one of the few distributions that has support for the ZFS filesystem.

After formatting the filesystem, you can mount it to the `root` filesystem. The basic syntax of the `mount` command is:

```
mount <partition> <mountpoint>
```

A partition can be named with the device name, label, or UUID. ZFS can be mounted with the `mount` command or via the `zfs` utility.

Another important filesystem is the swap filesystem. Besides the normal filesystems, there are also other special filesystems: `devfs`, `sysfs`, `procfs`, and `tmpfs`.

Let's start with a short description of the filesystems and the utilities around them.

Ext4 filesystem

Ext4 is a native Linux filesystem, developed as the successor to ext3, and it was (and for some distributions still is) the default filesystem for many years. It offers stability, high capacity, reliability, and performance while requiring minimal maintenance. On top of that, you can resize (increase/decrease) the filesystem without a problem.

The good news is that it can offer this with very low requirements. There is of course also bad news: it's very reliable but it cannot completely guarantee the integrity of your data. If data is corrupted while already on disk, ext4 has no way of either detecting or repairing such corruption. Luckily, because of the underlying architecture of Azure, this will not happen.

Ext4 is not the fastest filesystem around, but for many workloads the gap between ext4 and the competition is very small.

The most important utilities are:

- `mkfs.ext4`: Format the filesystem
- `e2label`: Change the label of the filesystem
- `tune2fs`: Change the parameters of the filesystem
- `dump2fs`: Show the parameters of the filesystem
- `resize2fs`: Change the size of the filesystem
- `fsck.ext4`: Check and repair the filesystem
- `e2freefrag`: Report on defragmentation
- `e4defrag`: Defrag filesystem, normally not needed

To create an ext4 filesystem, use:

```
sudo mkfs.ext4 -L <label> <partition>
```

The label is optional but makes it easier to recognize a filesystem.

XFS filesystem

XFS is a highly scalable filesystem. It can scale to 8 EiB, with online resizing; the filesystem can grow as long as there is unallocated space and it can span multiple partitions and devices.

XFS is one of the fastest filesystems around, especially in combination with RAID volumes. But, this comes with a cost: you'll need at least 1 GB of memory in your virtual machine if you want to use XFS. And if you want to be able to repair the filesystem, you'll need at least 2 GB of memory.

Another nice feature of XFS is that you can quiesce the traffic to the filesystem to create consistent backups off, for instance, a database server.

The most important utilities are:

- `mkfs.xfs`: Format the filesystem
- `xfs_admin`: Change the parameters of the filesystem
- `xfs_growfs`: Decrease the size of the filesystem
- `xfs_repair`: Check and repair the filesystem
- `xfs_freeze`: Suspend access to an XFS filesystem; this makes consistent backups easier
- `xfs_copy`: Fast copy the contents of an XFS filesystem

To create an XFS filesystem, use:

```
sudo mkfs.xfs -L <label> <partition>
```

The label is optional but makes it easier to recognize a filesystem.

ZFS filesystem

ZFS is a combined filesystem and logical volume manager developed by SUN, owned by Oracle since 2005. It's very well known for excellent performance and its rich features:

- Volume management and RAID
- Protection against data corruption
- Data compression and deduplication
- Scalable to 16 exabytes
- Able to export filesystems
- Snapshot support

ZFS can be implemented on Linux with a user-space driver (FUSE) or with a Linux kernel module (OpenZFS). In Ubuntu, it's better to use the kernel module; it performs better and doesn't have some of the limitations of the FUSE implementation. For instance, if you use FUSE you can't export the filesystem with NFS.

The main reason why OpenZFS is not widely adopted is licensing. OpenZFS's CDDL license is incompatible with the Linux kernel's General Public License. Another reason is that ZFS can be a real memory hog; your virtual machine needs 1 GB memory extra per TB of storage, meaning 4 TB of storage plus 4 GB memory for applications—8 GB memory needed in total.

The most important utilities are:

- `zfs`: Configures the ZFS filesystem
- `zpool`: Configures the ZFS storage pools
- `zfs.fsck`: Checks and repair the ZFS filesystem

In this book, only the basic functionality of ZFS is covered.

Ubuntu is the only distribution with ZFS support. To be able to use ZFS in Ubuntu, you have to install the ZFS utilities:

```
sudo apt install zfsutils-linux
```

After the installation, you can start using ZFS. Let's assume that you added three disks to the virtual machine. It is a good idea to use RAID 0 to improve performance and allow for improved throughput compared to using just a single disk.

As a first step, let's create a pool with two disks:

```
sudo zpool create -f mydata /dev/sdc /dev/sdd

sudo zpool list mydata

sudo zpool status mydata
```

Let's add the third disk, to show how to extend the pool:

```
sudo zpool add mydata /dev/sde

sudo zpool list mydata

sudo zpool history mydata
```

You can use this pool directly or you can create datasets in it for more fine-grained control over features such quotas:

```
sudo zfs create mydata/finance

sudo zfs set quota=5G mydata/finance

sudo zfs list
```

Last but not least, you'll need to mount this dataset to be able to use it:

```
sudo zfs set mountpoint=/home/finance mydata/finance

findmnt /home/finance
```

This mount will be persistent across reboots.

BTRFS filesystem

BTRFS is a relatively new filesystem, mainly developed by Oracle but with contributions from SUSE and companies such as Facebook.

It's very similar to ZFS in terms of features, but it is in heavy development. This means that not all the features are considered to be stable. Before using this filesystem, please visit `https://btrfs.wiki.kernel.org/index.php/Status`.

The memory requirements are the same as XFS: 1 GB memory in your virtual machine. You don't need extra memory if you want to repair the filesystem.

In this book, only the basic functionality of BTRFS is covered. You can use BTRFS on all distributions but please notice that on RHEL and CentOS, the filesystem is labeled as deprecated (`https://access.redhat.com/solutions/197643`).

The most important utilities are:

- `mkfs.btrfs`: Format devices with this filesystem
- `btrfs`: Manage the filesystem

Let's assume that you added three disks to the virtual machine. It is a good idea to use RAID 0 to improve performance and allow for improved throughput compared to using just a single disk.

As a first step, let's create a BTRFS filesystem with two underlying disks:

```
sudo mkfs.btrfs -d raid0 -L mydata /dev/sdc /dev/sdd
```

Of course, you can extend the filesystem with the third disk, but before you can do that, you have to mount the filesystem:

```
sudo mkdir /srv/mydata

sudo mount LABEL=mydata /srv/mydata

sudo btrfs filesystem show /srv/mydata
```

Now add the third disk:

```
sudo btrfs device add /dev/sde /srv/mydata

sudo btrfs filesystem show /srv/mydata
```

Like ZFS, BTRFS has concept of datasets, but in BTRFS they are called `subvolumes`. To create a `subvolume`, execute:

```
sudo btrfs subvolume create /srv/mydata/finance

sudo btrfs subvolume list /srv/mydata
```

You can mount a subvolume independent of the root volume:

```
sudo mkdir /home/finance

sudo mount -o subvol=finance LABEL=mydata /home/finance
```

```
linvirt@suse01:~> sudo btrfs subvolume list /srv/mydata
ID 258 gen 8 top level 5 path finance
linvirt@suse01:~> findmnt /home/finance
TARGET          SOURCE              FSTYPE OPTIONS
/home/finance /dev/sdc[/finance] btrfs  rw,relatime,space_cache,subvolid=258,sub
```

You can see the ID `258` in the output of the `findmnt` command.

Swap filesystem

Swap is used if there is not enough memory available for your application. It's normal and can be a good thing for Linux systems to use swap, even if there is still available RAM. But, it's not just used if there is not enough memory.

Idle memory is memory that was used before but is not currently needed by an application. If this idle memory is not used for a long time, it will be swapped to make more memory available for more frequently used applications.

By default, there is no swap configured in Azure, but also, to improve the overall performance it's a good idea to add some swap space to your Linux installation. It is a good idea to use the fastest storage available, preferably on the resource disk.

> In Linux, you can use swap files and swap partitions. There is no difference in performance. In Azure, you can't use swap partitions; it will make your system unstable, which is caused by the underlying storage.

Swap in Azure is managed by the Azure Agent. Edit the file `/etc/waagent.conf`:

```
# Create and use swapfile on resource disk.
ResourceDisk.EnableSwap=y
# Size of the swapfile.
ResourceDisk.SwapSizeMB=2048
```

In general, a `swapfile` of 2048 MB memory is more then enough. Restart the Azure Agent in RHEL/CentOS and SUSE/openSUSE LEAP:

```
sudo systemctl restart waagent
```

Or to restart the Azure Agent in Debian / Ubuntu:

```
sudo systemctl restart walinuxagent
```

Verify the result:

```
file /mnt/resource/swapfile

swapon -s
```

Linux software RAID

Microsoft officially states at `https://docs.microsoft.com/en-us/azure/virtual-machines/linux/configure-raid` that you'll need RAID 0 for optimal performance. If your filesystem doesn't support RAID, you can use Linux Software RAID to create a RAID 0 device. You'll need to install the `mdadm` utility; it's available on every Linux distribution, but probably not installed by default.

Let's assume you added three disks to your virtual machine. Let's create a RAID 0 device called `/dev/md127` (just a random number that is not yet in use):

```
sudo mdadm --create /dev/md127 --level 0 \
  --raid-devices 3 /dev/sd{c,d,e}
```

Verify the configuration:

```
cat /proc/mdstat

sudo mdadm --detail /dev/md127
```

```
[linvirt@centos ~]$ cat /proc/mdstat
Personalities : [raid0]
md127 : active raid0 sde[2] sdc[1] sdd[0]
       15716352 blocks super 1.2 512k chunks

unused devices: <none>
[linvirt@centos ~]$ sudo mdadm --detail /dev/md127
/dev/md127:
             Version : 1.2
       Creation Time : Wed Jun  6 15:24:36 2018
          Raid Level : raid0
          Array Size : 15716352 (14.99 GiB 16.09 GB)
        Raid Devices : 3
       Total Devices : 3
         Persistence : Superblock is persistent

         Update Time : Wed Jun  6 15:24:36 2018
               State : clean
       Active Devices : 3
      Working Devices : 3
       Failed Devices : 0
       Spare Devices : 0
```

Make the configuration persistent:

```
mdadm --detail --scan --verbose >> /etc/mdadm.conf
```

Now you can use this device and format it with a filesystem. For instance:

```
mkfs.ext4 -L BIGDATA /dev/md127
```

Systemd

After the Linux kernel boots, the first Linux process starts the first process. This process is known as an `init` process. In modern Linux systems, this process is `systemd`:

```
linvirt@ubuntu01:~$ pstree -p | head -10
systemd(1)-+-accounts-daemon(1113)-+-{accounts-daemon}(1117)
           |                        `-{accounts-daemon}(1128)
           |-agetty(1208)
           |-agetty(1215)
           |-atd(1165)
           |-cron(1166)
           |-dbus-daemon(1116)
           |-hv_kvp_daemon(1092)
           |-hv_vss_daemon(1144)
           |-iscsid(1106)
```

Systemd is responsible for starting all processes in parallel during the boot process, except the processes that are created by their kernel. After that it's activating services among other things on demand. It also tracks and manages mount points, and it manages system-wide settings such as the hostname.

Systemd is an event-driven system. It communicates with the kernel and will react to an event such as a point in time or a user that introduces a new device or presses *Ctrl + Alt + Del*.

Working with units

Systemd works with units, entities that are managed by Systemd and encapsulate information about every object that is relevant for Systemd.

There are unit files in ini-style that contain configuration directives that describe the unit and define its behavior. These files are stored as follows:

File	Description
service	Script or daemon
mount	Mount filesystems
automount	Mount remote NFS or CIFS shares
timer	Scheduled tasks
path	Monitor file or directory; if necessary create one
target	Collection of other units

Units are manageable via the utility `systemctl`. If you want to see all the available types, execute:

```
systemctl --type help
```

To list all installed unit files, use:

```
sudo systemctl list-unit-files
```

To list the active units, use:

```
sudo systemctl list-units
```

Both the `list-unit-files` and `list-units` parameters can be used in combination with `--type`.

Services

The service units are there to manage scripts or daemons. Let's have a look at the SSH service.

> The screenshots are taken from Ubuntu 18.04. Names of services may be different on other distributions.

```
linvirt@ubuntu01:~$ systemctl status sshd.service
● ssh.service - OpenBSD Secure Shell server
   Loaded: loaded (/lib/systemd/system/ssh.service; enabled; vendor preset: enab
led)
   Active: active (running) since Thu 2018-06-07 07:34:44 UTC; 58min
ago
 Main PID: 1291 (sshd)
    Tasks: 1 (limit: 1051)
   CGroup: /system.slice/ssh.service
           └─1291 /usr/sbin/sshd -D

Jun 07 07:34:44 ubuntu01 systemd[1]: Starting OpenBSD Secure Shell server...
Jun 07 07:34:44 ubuntu01 sshd[1291]: Server listening on 0.0.0.0 port 22.
Jun 07 07:34:44 ubuntu01 sshd[1291]: Server listening on :: port 22.
```

Using the status parameter of `systemctl`, you can see that the unit is loaded, enabled at boot, and that it's the default value. If it's not enabled, you can enable it with this:

```
sudo systemctl enable <service name.service>
```

In the output, you can see that the service is running and the last entries in the logging are shown.

To look into the content of the `unit` file, execute:

```
sudo systemctl cat <service name.service>
```

A `unit` file always has two or three sections:

- `[Unit]`: Description and dependency handling
- `[<Type>]`: Configuration of the type
- `[Install]`: Optional section if you want to be able to enable the service at boot time

To handle the dependencies, there are several directives available; the most important ones are these:

- `before`: The specified unit is delayed until this unit is started.
- `after`: The specified unit is started before this unit is started.
- `requires`: If this unit gets activated, the unit listed here will be activated as well. If the specified unit failed, this one will fail as well.
- `wanted`: If this unit gets activated, the unit listed here will be activated as well. There are no consequences if the specified unit fails.

If you don't specify a `before` or `after`, the listed unit or units (comma separated) will be started at the same time as the unit starts.

An example of an `ssh` service is as follows:

```
[Unit]
Description=OpenSSH Daemon After=network.target

[Service]
EnvironmentFile=-/etc/sysconfig/ssh
ExecStartPre=/usr/sbin/sshd-gen-keys-start
ExecStart=/usr/sbin/sshd -D $SSHD_OPTS
ExecReload=/bin/kill -HUP $MAINPID KillMode=process
Restart=always

[Install]
WantedBy=multi-user.target
```

Most options in the `Service` section speak for themselves; if not, just look into the man pages of `systemd.unit` and `systemd.service`. For the `[Install]` section, the `WantedBy` directive states that if you enable this service, it will become a part of the collection `multi-user.target`, which is activated at boot.

Before going into the targets, the last thing to cover is how to create overrides. Systemd units can have many different directives; many are default. To show all possible directives, execute:

```
sudo systemctl show
```

If you want to change one of the defaults, use:

```
sudo systemctl edit <service name.service>
```

An editor is started. Add the entry, for instance:

```
[Service]
ProtectHome=read-only
```

Save the changes. You need to reload the systemd configuration files and restart the service:

```
sudo systemctl daemon-reload
```

```
sudo systemctl restart sshd
```

Review the changes with `systemctl cat sshd.service`. Log in again and try to save something in your home directory.

> **TIP**
>
> If you want another editor for `systemctl edit`, add a variable `SYSTEMD_EDITOR` to the `/etc/environment` file, for instance, `SYSTEMD_EDITOR=/usr/bin/vim`.

Targets

A target is a collection of units. There are two types of targets:

- **Non-isolatable**: A normal collection of units. For instance, the `timers.target` that contains all scheduled tasks.
- **Isolatable**: If you execute `systemctl isolate <target name.target>`, it will shut down all processes that are not a part of the target, and start all that are a part of it. Examples are the `rescue.target` and `graphical.target` units.

To see the content of a target, use:

```
systemctl list-dependencies <target name.target>
```

Scheduled tasks

Systemd can be used to schedule tasks. An example of a timer unit file follows:

```
[Unit]
Description=Scheduled backup task

[Timer]
OnCalendar=*-*-* 10:00:00

[Install]
WantedBy=timers.target
```

If you save the content of this file to `/etc/systemd/system/backup.timer`, you'll need a corresponding file `/etc/systemd/system/backup.service`, for example, with the following content:

```
[Unit]
Description = backup script

[Service]
```

```
Type = oneshot
ExecStart = /usr/local/bin/mybackup.sh
```

Enable and activate the timer:

```
sudo systemctl enable --now backup.timer
```

To find about the scheduled tasks, use:

```
sudo systemctl list-timers
```

> Read `man 7 systemd.time` to learn more about the syntax of the
> calendar events. There is a special section on this man-page for it.

If the scheduled task is not a recurring one, you can use:
```
sudo systems-run --on-calendar <event time> <command>
```

Mounting local filesystems

The mount unit is available to mount filesystems. There is something special about the name of the mount unit: it must correspond with the mount point. For instance, if you want to mount on /home/finance, the mount unit file becomes /etc/systemd/system/home-finance.mount:

```
[Unit]
Description = Finance Directory

[Mount]
What = /dev/sdc1
Where = /home/finance
Type = xfs
Options = defaults

[Install]
WantedBy = local-fs.target
```

Use `systemctl start` to start mounting, and `systemctl enable` to mount at boot time.

Mounting remote filesystems

If a filesystem is not local but remote, for instance, an NFS share, the best way to mount it is using automount. It will mount the share, and if you lose the connection to the share, it will try to automount the share on demand.

You have to create two files. Let's take a NFS mount on /home/finance as an example. First create /etc/systemd/system/home-finance.mount with the following content:

```
[Unit]
Description = NFS Finance Share

[Mount]
What = 192.168.122.100:/share
Where = /home/finance
Type = nfs
Options = vers=4.2
```

Create a file /etc/systemd/system/home-finance.automount:

```
[Unit]
Description = Automount NFS Finance Share

[Automount]
Where = /home/finance

[Install]
WantedBy = remote-fs.target
```

Start the automount unit, not the mount unit. Of course, you can enable it at boot.

Summary

In this chapter, we deep dived into Linux, explaining the fundamental tasks of every Linux system administrator: managing software, the network, storage, and services.

Of course, as a Linux system administrator, this is not something you're going to do on a daily base. Most likely, you're not going to do it manually but automate or orchestrate it. But to be able to orchestrate it, you'll need to understand how it works and be able to verify and troubleshoot the configuration. This will be covered in the Chapter 8, *Exploring Continuous Configuration Automation*.

In the next chapter we will explore the options available in Linux that limits the access to the system:

- Mandatory Access Control
- Network Access Control Lists
- Firewall

And cover the integration with the Azure Active Directory Service.

Questions

1. Who is responsible for the recognition of the hardware?
2. Who is responsible for device naming?
3. What are the methods to identify network interfaces?
4. Who maintains the network configuration?
5. What are the methods to identify locally attached storage?
6. Why do we use RAID 0 in Azure?
7. What are the options to implement RAID 0 in Azure?
8. Try to implement a RAID 0 device using three disks; format it with XFS. Mount it, and make sure that it's mounted at boot time.

Further reading

In one way, this chapter was a deep dive, but there is much more to learn about all the topics in this chapter. I strongly suggest that you read the man pages of all the used commands.

For storage, besides the documentation on the Azure website, some filesystems have their own websites:

- **XFS**: https://xfs.org
- **BTRFS**: https://btrfs.wiki.kernel.org
- **ZFS**: http://open-zfs.org

Lennart Poettering, one of the main developers of systemd, has a nice blog with lots of tips and background information: `http://0pointer.net/blog`. And on top of that, documentation is available at `https://www.freedesktop.org/wiki/Software/systemd`.

After this chapter, I strongly suggest you visit `Chapter 11`, *Troubleshooting and Monitoring Your Workloads* to read about logging in Linux, because often the `systemctl status` command doesn't provide you with enough information.

Managing Linux Security and Identities

6

This chapter is about security, the protection of your workload at operating system level. Of course, Azure already provides you with services to protect your virtual machine in many ways and at many levels. The following are a few of the services:

- Azure Resource Manager, which provides security, auditing, and tagging features
- The web application firewall, which protects against many attacks, such as SQL injection
- The stateful packet filtering feature of Network Security Groups
- The Azure Firewall service, which provides a stateful firewall tightly integrated with the monitoring functions of Azure

And you can subscribe to the Azure Security Center service for unified security management with nice features such as continuous security assessment.

With all these possibilities, do we still need protection at the OS level? In my opinion, multi-level protection is a good idea. It will cost the hacker more effort and more time, and this will make it easier to detect the hacker. And there is no such thing as bug-free software: if an application is vulnerable, at least the OS should be protected.

In `Chapter 5`, *Advanced Linux Administration*, systemd was covered as a system and service manager. In systemd, there are several options to add an extra layer of protection to your daemons and filesystem.

Identity management is a topic that is certainly related to security. You can integrate Linux with Azure AD to centralize your login accounts, fine-grain access using role-based access control, revoke them, and enable multi-factor authentication.

This chapter will cover the following topics:

- Linux security tips
- Linux security modules
- Systemd security
- Azure Active Directory Domain Services

Linux security tips

Before we deep dive into all the great security measures you can take, here are some some tips and advice regarding security.

Security implementation on multiple levels is, in general, a good idea. This way, a hacker needs different approaches to gain access, and this costs time. Because of this time, and hopefully also because of logging and monitoring, you have greater chance of detecting them.

But, and there is always a but, don't take that too far. If you can't access a service, it's difficult to troubleshoot where the problem is. And if it's too complex, it's more likely that you are going to make mistakes.

For files and directories, the **Discretionary Access Control** (**DAC**) is still a very good foundation. Make the permissions on files and directories as strict as possible. Check the owner and group ownership, use **access control lists** (**ACLs**) instead of the permission for others. Try to avoid using the `suid`/`sgid` bit as much as possible. Are there users who need to change their own password? No? Remove that bit from the `passwd` command.

Use partitioning, especially for directories such as `/tmp`, `/var`, `/var/tmp`, and `/home`, and mount them with the `noexec`, `nodev`, and `nosuid` flags:

- In general, it's not a good idea that a user can execute programs from these locations. Luckily, you can't set the owner to root if you copy a program with the `suid` bit to your own directory as normal user.
- The `suid` and `sgid` permissions on files in this directories are very, very dangerous.
- Do not allow the creation or existence of character or special devices on this partition.

To access the virtual machine, use SSH key-based authentication, not passwords. Limit access to certain IPs, using the ACLs or firewall. Limit users and allow no remote access for root (use the `PermitRootLogin no` parameter and `AllowUsers` to only allow one or two accounts). Use `sudo` to execute commands as root. Maybe create special users of groups of users for special tasks in the `sudo` configuration.

Do not install too much software on a virtual machine, especially when it comes to network services, such as web servers, email servers, and so on. Use the `ss` command from time to time to review the open ports and compare them with the ACLs and/or firewall rules.

Keep your system up to date; there is a reason why Linux vendors provide you with updates. Do it manually or with an automation/orchestration tool, just do it!

Technical requirements

For the purposes of this chapter, you'll need to deploy a CentOS 7 and a Ubuntu 18.04 virtual machine. It is possible to use SUSE SLE 12 or openSUSE Leap instead of the CentOS and Ubuntu virtual machines. SUSE supports all options discussed in this chapter.

For the section about the Linux firewall, make sure that the firewalld software is installed and other firewall software is removed from the system to avoid conflicts. In RHEL/CentOS 7 based distributions, this is already the case. In Ubuntu, use the following commands:

```
sudo apt remove ufw

sudo apt install firewalld
```

In SUSE-based distributions, use the following commands:

```
sudo zypper install susefirewall2-to-firewalld

sudo susefirewall2-to-firewalld -c
```

Linux firewall

To be honest, in my opinion it really makes sense to use the Azure Firewall on top of the Azure Network Security Groups. It is easy to set up, provides central administration, and requires almost no maintenance. It provides security between virtual machines, virtual networks, and even different Azure subscriptions.

> There is an additional cost if you want to use this firewall.

The choice between the Azure service and Linux Firewall depends on many things:

- Cost
- Deployment and orchestration of your virtual machines and applications
- Different roles: is there one administrator for everything?

I hope that after covering one of the Linux firewall implementations, it becomes clear that the Linux firewall is in no way a complete replacement for the Azure Firewall, it only can provide security for incoming traffic to the virtual machine, and yes, it is possible to configure this firewall to block outgoing traffic as well, but that's quite complex. On the other hand, if it's configured on top of the Azure Network Security Groups, in many cases that is more than enough.

There are multiple firewall implementations for Linux; some of them are even developed for a specific distribution, such as the SuSEfirewall2. In this chapter, I'll cover firewalld, which is available on every distribution.

Firewalld consists of a daemon that manages all the components of the firewall:

- Zones
- Interfaces
- Sources
- Direct rules for iptables and ebtables (not covered in this book)

It utilizes two kernel modules: IP tables/IP6 tables for IPv4 and IPv6 traffic, and ebtables for filtering of network traffic passing through a Linux bridge.

To configure the firewalld rules, there is a command-line utility available: `firewall-cmd`. Rules can be runtime-only or persistent. There are two important reasons for this behavior: this way, it's not necessary to reload all the rules implying a temporary security risk, you can dynamically add and remove them, and if you made a mistake, and you are not able to log in again because of this, just reboot as a quick solution. We can also use the `systemd-run ˙--oncalendar` command to create a scheduled task that executes `firewall-cmd --reload`, which is an even better solution:

```
sudo systemd-run --on-calendar='2018-08-20 13:00:00' \
  firewall-cmd --reload

sudo systemctl list-timers
```

Don't forget to stop and disable the timer, if it was done correctly.

You can also configure the daemon with orchestration tools that talk to the daemon or push XML files to the host.

> The ports are only open for the virtual machines connected to the virtual machine network, unless you open the ports in the network security group!

It is important to know that the Azure Fabric (infrastructure) will add, if needed, extra rules to your firewall configuration. You can see that if you search in the logging database with the `journalctl` command:

```
sudo journalctl | grep "Azure fabric firewall"
```

Use the `iptables-save` command to view all the active firewall rules.

Firewalld zones

One of the most important concepts of firewalld is the zone. A zone consist of a default rule, called a target, a network interface or network source, and additional services, ports, protocols, and rich rules.

A zone is only active if a network interface is attached to the interface or a network source.

To list the available zones, use the following command:

```
sudo firewall-cmd --get-zones
```

These zones are configured in /usr/lib/firewalld/zones. You should not make changes to these files. New zones or changes to a zone are written into the /etc/firewalld/zones directory.

The default zone is, by default, the public zone:

```
sudo firewall-cmd --get-default-zone
```

To list the zone configuration of the public zone, use the following command:

```
sudo firewall-cmd --zone public --list-all
```

The public zone has the target policy default, which means that everything incoming is blocked by default, except the configured services, ports, and protocols. There are also options to configure masquerading and port-forwarding. Rich rules are advanced firewall rules, as described in the man page firewalld.richlanguage:

```
public
  target: default
  icmp-block-inversion: no
  interfaces:
  sources:
  services: ssh dhcpv6-client
  ports:
  protocols:
  masquerade: no
  forward-ports:
  source-ports:
  icmp-blocks:
  rich rules:
```

The corresponding /lib/usr/firewalld/zones/public.xml file of this zone:

```
<?xml version="1.0" encoding="utf-8"?>
<zone>
 <short>Public</short>
 <description>For use in public areas. You do not trust the other computers
on networks to not harm your computer. Only selected incoming connections
are accepted.</description>
 <service name="ssh"/>
 <service name="dhcpv6-client"/>
</zone>
```

The target is the default behavior. The possible values are as follows:

- `default`: Don't do anything, accept every ICMP packet, and reject everything else.
- `%%REJECT%%`: It sends a reject response to the client via the ICMP protocol.
- `DROP`: It sends a TCP SYN/ACK as on an open port, but all other traffic is dropped. No ICMP message to inform the client.
- `ACCEPT`: Accept everything.

In Ubuntu, by default there is no network interface attached. Please don't reboot the virtual machine before an interface is attached! Execute the following:

```
sudo firewall-cmd --add-interface=eth0 --zone=public

sudo firewall-cmd --add-interface=eth0 --zone=public --permanent

sudo firewall-cmd --zone=public --list-all
```

If you modify a zone, the file is copied from `/usr/lib/firewalld/zones` to `/etc/firewalld/zones`. The next modification will create a backup of the zone with the file extension `.old` and create a new file with the modifications in it.

Firewalld services

A service is an application-centric configuration to allow one or more ports. To receive a list of the available services, use the following command:

```
sudo firewall-cmd --get-services
```

If you want to add a service, for instance, MySQL, use the following commands:

```
sudo firewall-cmd --add-service=mysql --zone=public

sudo firewall-cmd --add-service=mysql --zone=public \
   --permanent
```

If you want to remove a service from a zone, use the `--remove-service` parameter.

The services are configured in the `/usr/lib/firewalld/services` directory. Again, you shouldn't modify these files. You can change them or create your own by copying them to the `/etc/firewalld/service` directory.

It is possible to add single ports as well, but in general that's not a good idea: can you still remember after a while which ports are in use by which application? Instead, if the service is not already defined, create your own service.

Let's create a service file for the Microsoft PPtP firewall protocol, /etc/firewalld/service/pptp.xml:

```
<?xml version="1.0" encoding="utf-8"?>
<service>
 <short>PPtP</short>
 <description>Microsoft VPN</description>
 <port protocol="tcp" port="1723"/>
</service>
```

You can add as many port rules as you want.

After reloading the firewall with firewalld-cmd --reload, the service is available. This is not enough: the GRE protocol is not allowed. To allow the protocol, use the following commands:

```
sudo firewall-cmd --service=pptp --add-protocol=gre \
  --permanent

sudo firewall-cmd --reload
```

This will add the following line to the service file:

```
<protocol value="gre"/>
```

You can remove the protocol using the --remove-protocol parameter.

Firewalld network sources

A zone is only active when a network interface is attached to it, or a network source. It doesn't make sense to add a network interface to the drop zone. But, it makes sense to add a network source. A source consist of one or more entries: MAC addresses, IP address, or IP ranges.

For instance, for whatever reason you want to block all traffic from Bermuda. The website `http://ipdeny.com` can provide you with a list of IP addresses:

```
cd /tmp
```

```
wget http://www.ipdeny.com/ipblocks/data/countries/bm.zone
```

There are several types of ipsets, to view the possibilities:

```
sudo firewall-cmd --get-ipset-types
```

In our scenario, we want the type for ip ranges, `hash:net`:

```
sudo firewall-cmd --new-ipset=block_bermuda --type=hash:net --permanent
```

```
sudo firewall-cmd --reload
```

Now we can add entries to the `ipset` using the downloaded file:

```
sudo firewall-cmd --ipset=block_bermuda --add-entries-from-file=/tmp/bm.zone
```

```
sudo firewall-cmd --ipset=block_bermuda --add-entries-from-file=/tmp/bm.zone \
  --permanent
```

```
sudo firewall-cmd --reload
```

The last step involves adding the `ipset` as a source to the zone:

```
sudo firewall-cmd --zone=drop --add-source=ipset:block_bermuda
```

```
sudo firewall-cmd --zone=drop --add-source=ipset:block_bermuda --permanent
```

```
sudo firewall-cmd --reload
```

The purpose of the zone `drop` is to drop all traffic, without letting the client know that the traffic is dropped. Adding the `ipset` to this zone makes it active and all the traffic coming from Bermuda will be dropped:

```
sudo firewall-cmd --get-active-zones
```

```
drop
  sources: ipset:block_bermuda
public
  interfaces: eth0
```

Linux Security Modules

Linux Security Modules (**LSM**) is a framework to provide an interface for adding MAC on top of DAC. This extra layer of security can be added with SELinux (Red Hat-based distributions and SUSE), AppArmor (Ubuntu and SUSE), or the lesser-known Tomoyo (SUSE). In this section, I'll cover SELinux and AppArmor.

DAC is a model that provides access control based on users who are a member of a group and permissions on files and devices. MAC restricts access on resource objects such as the following:

- Files
- Processes
- TCP/UDP ports
- Users and their roles

MAC, as implemented by SELinux, works by assigning a classification label, also known as context label, to every resource object, whereas AppArmor is path-based. In either case, if one resource object needs access to another object, it needs clearance. So, even if a hacker makes it into, for instance, your web application, the other resources are still protected!

SELinux

SELinux was developed by the NSA and Red Hat in 1998. It can be used on every Red Hat based distribution and SUSE. This book will cover the implementation on Red Hat. If you want to use it on SUSE, visit the SUSE documentation at `https://doc.opensuse.org/documentation/leap/security/html/book.security/cha.selinux.html` to install and enable SELinux. After that, the procedures are the same. In the past, there were some efforts to make it work on Ubuntu but, at the moment, there is no active development and the packages are broken.

All access must be explicitly granted, but on the distributions that utilize SELinux, many policies are already in place. It covers almost every resource object. On top of the list already mentioned, it covers the following:

- Complete network stack including IPsec
- Kernel capabilities
- **Inter-process communication (IPC)**
- Memory protection
- File descriptor (communication channels) inheritance and transfer

For container virtualization solutions such as Docker, it can protect the host and offers protection between containers.

SELinux configuration

SELinux is configured via the file `/etc/selinux/config`:

```
#   This file controls the state of SELinux on the system.
#   SELINUX= can take one of these three values:
#   enforcing - SELinux security policy is enforced.
#   permissive - SELinux prints warnings instead of enforcing.
#   disabled - No SELinux policy is loaded.

SELINUX=enforcing
```

The status should be in `enforcing` mode in a production environment. Policies are enforced and, if access is restricted, auditing can be done to be able to fix the problems caused by SELinux. The permissive mode can become handy if you are a software developer or packager and you need to create SELinux policies for your software.

It's possible to switch between the enforcing and permissive mode using the `setenforce` command. Use `setenforce 0` to switch to the permissive mode and `setenforce 1` to go back to the enforcing mode. The `getenforce` command is available to view the current status:

```
#   SELINUXTYPE= can take one of these three values:
#   targeted - Targeted processes are protected ,
#   minimum - Modification of targeted policy.
#   Only selected processes are protected.
#   mls - Multi Level Security protection.

SELINUXTYPE=targeted
```

`Targeted` is the default policy and protects all resources; this will provide enough protection for most workloads. **Multi Level Security** (**MLS**) offers additional security by using levels of clearance provided by categories and sensitivities (such as confidential, secret, and top secret) together with SELinux users and roles. It can be very useful for file servers that offers file shares.

If the `minimum` type is selected then only the bare minimum is protected; you need to configure everything else yourself, if you want more protection. This type can be useful if there are difficulties to protect an multi-process application (typically very old applications) and a generated policy removes too many restrictions. In this scenario, it's better to leave the specific application unprotected, and protect the rest of the system. In this section, I'll only discuss the `SELINUXTYPE=targeted` option. It is the most widely used option.

To show the state of SELinux, you can use the `sestatus` command:

```
[root@server1 ~]# sestatus
SELinux status:                 enabled
SELinuxfs mount:                /sys/fs/selinux
SELinux root directory:         /etc/selinux
Loaded policy name:             targeted
Current mode:                   enforcing
Mode from config file:          enforcing
Policy MLS status:              enabled
Policy deny_unknown status:     allowed
Max kernel policy version:      28
```

Before we explore SELinux, you'll need to add the necessary packages to your system to be able to audit SELinux. Please execute the following:

```
sudo yum install setroubleshoot
```

After this, you'll need to reboot the virtual machine:

```
sudo systemctl reboot
```

After the reboot, we're ready to use and troubleshoot SELinux.

SELinux context on ports

Let's start with an easy example with the SSH service. As stated earlier, all processes are labeled with a context label. To make this label visible, many utilities, such as `ls`, `ps`, and `lsof`, have the `-Z` parameter. First, you have to find the main process ID of this service:

```
systemctl status sshd | grep PID
```

Using this process ID, we can ask for the context label:

```
ps -q <PID> -Z
```

The context label is `system_u, system_r, sshd_t, s0-s0, c0.c1023`. Because we're using the targeted SELinux type, we only take care of the SELinux type part: `sshd_t`.

SSH is running on port `22`; let's investigate the label on the port:

```
ss -ltn sport eq 22 -Z
```

You will find out that the context label is `system_u, system_r, sshd_t, s0-s0, c0.c1023`, so exactly the same. It's not difficult to understand that the process `sshd` has indeed the permission to run on this port with the same label.

It's not always that simple, but before going into a more complex scenario, let's modify the port that the SSH server is listening on to port `44`. To do so, edit the file `/etc/ssh/sshd_config`. Find the following line:

```
#Port 22
```

Change the preceding line to the following:

```
Port 44
```

And restart the SSH server:

```
sudo systemctl restart sshd
```

This will fail:

```
Job for sshd.service failed because the control process exited with error
code.
See "systemctl status sshd.service" and "journalctl -xe" for details.
```

If you execute the command `journalctl -xe`, you can see the following message:

```
SELinux is preventing /usr/sbin/sshd from name_bind access
on the tcp_socket port 44.
```

There are multiple methods to troubleshoot SELinux. You can use the log file `/var/log/audit/audit.log` directly or with the `sealert -a /var/log/audit/audit.log` command , or use the `journalctl` command:

```
journalctl --identifier setroubleshoot
```

The logging entry also states the following:

```
For complete SELinux messages run: sealert -l <audit id>
```

Execute this command (and maybe redirect the output to a file or pipe it through less or more), and it will not only show you the same SELinux message again, but will also come with a suggestion for how to fix it:

```
If you want to allow /usr/sbin/sshd to bind to network port 44
Then you need to modify the port type.
Do
# semanage port -a -t PORT_TYPE -p tcp 44
where PORT_TYPE is one of the following: ssh_port_t, vnc_port_t,
xserver_port_t.
```

Before going into this solution, SELinux works with multiple databases that contain the resource object, and the context label, that is, /, should be applied to the resource object. The `semanage` tool is available to modify the database and add entries to it, in our scenario, the database port. The output of the logging suggests adding a context label for TCP port 44 to the database. There are three possible contexts; all of them will fix your problem.

Another important thing that there are sometimes more possible solutions. There is a confidence rating to make the choice easier for you. But even then, you still have to read carefully. Especially with files, sometimes you want to add a regular expression instead of doing it for every file over and over again.

You can take a pragmatic approach and state "I am not using `vnc` and `xserver`, so I choose `ssh_port_t`" or you can use the `sepolicy` utility, part of the `policycoreutils-devel` package:

```
sepolicy network -a /usr/sbin/sshd
```

Search in the output for TCP `name_bind`, because SELinux access is preventing `/usr/sbin/sshd` from `name_bind` access on the `tcp_socket` port 44

Now you know where the suggestion comes from. Look into the current label of port 22:

```
sepolicy network -p 22
```

The label is `ssh_port_t`.

> You can use `semanage port -l` and `grep` on port 22.

It really makes sense to use the same label. Not convinced? Let's generate man pages:

```
sepolicy manpage -a -p /usr/share/man/man8/

mandb
```

The man page `ssh_selinux` tells you in the **PORT TYPES** section that the correct label is `ssh_port_t`.

Finally, let's fix the problem:

```
semanage port -a -t ssh_port_t -p tcp 44
```

You don't have to restart the `sshd` service, systemd will restart this service automatically within 42 seconds. By the way, the `sshd_config` file has already a comment that describes this fix. It is explicitly stated in the line before `#Port 22`:

```
If you want to change the port on a SELinux system, you have to tell
# SELinux about this change.
# semanage port -a -t ssh_port_t -p tcp #PORTNUMBER
```

It's a good idea to undo the configuration change and configure it back to port `22`, otherwise you might be locked out of the test system.

SELinux context on files

After our first meeting with SELinux, investigating the context labels on ports, it's time to investigate context labels on files. As an example, we're going to use an FTP server and client. Install the `vsftpd` and an FTP client:

```
sudo yum install vsftpd ftp
```

Create a directory called `/srv/ftp/pub`:

```
sudo mkdir -p /srv/ftp/pub

chown -R ftp:ftp /srv/ftp
```

And create a file in `/srv/ftp`:

```
echo WELCOME > /srv/ftp/README
```

Edit the configuration file `/etc/vsftpd/vsftpd.conf` and add the following beneath the line `local_enable=YES`:

```
anon_root=/srv/ftp
```

This makes `/srv/ftp` the default root directory for the `vsftpd` service for anonymous users. Now you are ready to start the service:

```
sudo systemctl start vsftpd.service
```

```
sudo systemctl status vsftpd.service
```

Using the `ftp` utility, try to log in on the FTP server with the user `anonymous`, without a password:

```
ftp localhost

Trying ::1...
Connected to localhost (::1).
220 (vsFTPd 3.0.2)
Name (localhost:root): anonymous
331 Please specify the password.
Password:
230 Login successful.
Remote system type is UNIX.
Using binary mode to transfer files.
ftp> ls
229 Entering Extended Passive Mode (|||57280|).
150 Here comes the directory listing.
-rw-r--r-- 1 14 50 8 Jul 16 09:47 README
drwxr-xr-x 2 14 50 6 Jul 16 09:44 pub
226 Directory send OK.
```

Try to get the file:

```
get README
```

And it works! Why is this possible? Because there is already an entry in the database for `/srv/ftp/README` with the correct label:

```
semanage fcontext -l | grep /srv
```

The preceding command shows the following line:

```
/srv/([^/]*/)?ftp(/.*)? all files system_u:object_r:public_content_t:s0
```

And it's applied while creating a new file:

```
stat -c %C /srv/ftp/README
```

```
ls -Z /srv/ftp/README
```

Both commands tell you that the type is `public_content_t`. The man page of `ftpd_selinux` has two sections that are important here: **STANDARD FILE CONTEXT** and **SHARING FILES**. The man page states that the `public_content_t` type only allows you to read (download) files, but that you are not allowed to write (upload) files with this type. You need another type, `public_content_rw_t`, to be able to upload files.

Create an upload directory:

```
mkdir -m 2770 /srv/ftp/incoming
```

```
chown -R ftp:ftp /srv/ftp/incoming
```

View the the current label and change it:

```
ls -dZ /srv/ftp/incoming
```

```
semanage fcontext -a -t public_content_rw_t "/srv/ftp/incoming(/.*)?"
```

```
restorecon -rv /srv/ftp/incoming
```

```
ls -dZ /srv/ftp/incoming
```

First, you have to add the policy to the `fcontext` database; after that, you can apply the policy to the already existing directory.

> Read the man page of `selinux-fcontext`. It not only describes all the options, there are also some nice examples.

SELinux Boolean

Connect anonymous to the FTP server again and try to upload a file:

```
ftp> cd /incoming
250 Directory successfully changed.
ftp> put /etc/hosts hosts
local: /etc/hosts remote: hosts
229 Entering Extended Passive Mode (||||12830|).
550 Permission denied.
```

The command `journalctl --identifier setroubleshoot` makes it very clear to you:

SELinux is preventing vsftpd from write access on the directory ftp.

And the `sealert` command will provide you with the necessary information to fix the problem:

```
setsebool -P allow_ftpd_anon_write 1
```

So, what's happening here? Sometimes, simple rules for a port or file are not enough, for instance, if an NFS share must be exported with Samba as well. In this scenario, it is possible to create your own complex SELinux policy, or use the Boolean database with easy-to-use on/off switches. To do so, you can use the older `setsebool` utility or `semanage`:

```
semanage boolean --list | grep "ftpd_anon_write"

semanage boolean --modify ftpd_anon_write --on
```

> Using `setsebool` without `-P` makes the change, but not persistent. The `semanage` utility doesn't have the option to change it non-permanently.

AppArmor

In Debian, Ubuntu, and SUSE distributions, AppArmor is available to implement MAC. Please notice that there are some minor differences between the distributions, but in general a distribution can add less or more profiles and some extra tooling. In this section, I use Ubuntu 18.04 as an example.

Please note that you must make sure you keep your distribution up to date, especially with AppArmor; the packages in Debian and Ubuntu were plagued by bugs, which sometimes led to unexpected behavior.

Make sure that the necessary packages are installed:

```
sudo apt install apparmor-utils apparmor-easyprof \
   apparmor-profiles apparmor-profiles-extra apparmor-easyprof
```

There are some fundamental differences with SELinux:

- By default, only a bare minimum is protected. You have to apply security per application.
- You can mix enforcing and complaining modes; you can decide per application.
- When AppArmor development started, the scope was quite limited: processes and files. Nowadays, you can use it for **role-based access control** (**RBAC**), MLS, login policies, and so on.

In this chapter, I'll cover the initial scope: processes that need access to files.

AppArmor status

The first thing to do is check whether the AppArmor service is up and running:

```
sudo systemctl status apparmor
```

Alternatively, execute the following:

```
sudo aa-enabled
```

And after that, view the status more in detail with the following:

```
sudo apparmor_status
```

Alternatively, you can use the following command:

```
sudo aa-status
```

```
linvirt@ubuntu01:~$ sudo apparmor_status
apparmor module is loaded.
15 profiles are loaded.
15 profiles are in enforce mode.
   /sbin/dhclient
   /usr/bin/lxc-start
   /usr/bin/man
   /usr/lib/NetworkManager/nm-dhcp-client.action
   /usr/lib/NetworkManager/nm-dhcp-helper
   /usr/lib/connman/scripts/dhclient-script
   /usr/lib/snapd/snap-confine
   /usr/lib/snapd/snap-confine//mount-namespace-capture-helper
   /usr/sbin/tcpdump
   lxc-container-default
   lxc-container-default-cgns
   lxc-container-default-with-mounting
   lxc-container-default-with-nesting
   man_filter
   man_groff
0 profiles are in complain mode.
0 processes have profiles defined.
0 processes are in enforce mode.
0 processes are in complain mode.
0 processes are unconfined but have a profile defined.
```

Generating AppArmor profiles

Each application you want to protect needs a profile, provided by the packages `apparmor-profiles` or `apparmor-profiles-extra`, the application package, or you. The profiles are stored in `/etc/apparmor.d`.

Let's install the nginx web server as an example:

```
sudo apt install nginx
```

If you browse through the `/etc/apparmor.d` directory, there is no profile for nginx. Create a default one:

```
sudo aa-autodep nginx
```

A profile is created: `/etc/apparmor.d/usr.sbin.nginx`. This file is almost empty, and only includes some basic rules and variables, called abstractions, and the following line:

```
/usr/sbin/nginx mr,
```

The value `mr` defines the access mode: `r` means read-mode and `m` allows a file to be mapped into memory.

Let's enforce the mode for nginx:

```
sudo aa-enforce /usr/sbin/nginx
```

```
sudo systemctl restart nginx
```

nginx will not start. The output of the commands is as follows:

```
sudo journalctl --identifier audit
```

It points very clearly in the direction of AppArmor:

```
sudo journalctl -k | grep audit
```

To fix the problem, set the complain mode for this profile. This way, it doesn't enforce the policy, but complains about every violation of the security policy:

```
sudo aa-complain /usr/sbin/nginx
```

```
sudo systemctl start nginx
```

Make an `http` request, using a browser or an utility, for instance `curl`:

```
curl http://127.0.0.1
```

The next step is to scan the `logfile` and approve or reject every action:

```
sudo aa-logprof
```

Read very carefully and select the correct option with the arrow keys (if needed):

```
Profile:    /usr/sbin/nginx
Capability: dac_override
Severity:   9

  1 - #include <abstractions/lxc/container-base>
  2 - #include <abstractions/lxc/start-container>
 [3 - capability dac_override,]
(A)llow / [(D)eny] / (I)gnore / Audi(t) / Abo(r)t / (F)inish
```

LXC is a container technology, and we are just configuring the profile for a web server, something to fix with the DAC seems to be a good choice:

```
Profile:   /usr/sbin/nginx
Path:      /var/log/nginx/error.log
New Mode: w
Severity: 8

  1 - #include <abstractions/lxc/container-base>
  2 - #include <abstractions/lxc/start-container>
 [3 - /var/log/nginx/error.log w,]
```

The audit suggests a new mode: w means write access to the file
`/var/log/nginx/error.log`.

It goes further:

- Read access to `/etc/ssl/openssl.conf`. Difficult one, but the abstraction for `ssl` sounds right.
- Read access to `/etc/nginx/nginx.conf`. Again, not a container, so the owner of the file must be OK.
- In general, the owner of the file is a good choice.

Time to save the changes and try again:

```
sudo aa-enforce /usr/sbin/nginx

sudo systemctl restart nginx

curl http://127.0.0.1
```

Everything seems to work now, at least for a request to a simple website. As you can see, it's all based more or less on educated guesses. The alternative is a deep-dive into all the suggested abstractions.

The created file, `/etc/apparmor.d/usr.sbin.nginx`, is relatively easy. It starts with all tuneable variables that should be available for every profile:

```
#include <tunables/global>
```

Followed by other abstractions such as:

```
#include <abstractions/nameservice
```

To know what they are doing, just view the file. For instance, the file `/etc/apparmor.d/abstractions/nameservice` states the following:

> Many programs wish to perform name service-like operations, such as looking up users by name or ID, groups by name or ID, hosts by name or IP, and so on. These operations may be performed through files, DNS, NIS, NIS+, LDAP, hesiod, wins, and so on. Allow them all here.

```
/usr/sbin/nginx flags=(complain) {
#include <abstractions/base>
#include <abstractions/nameservice>
#include <abstractions/openssl>
#include <abstractions/web-data>
```

The next section is about Posix capabilities, see `man 7 capabilities` for more information:

```
capability dac_override,
```

The last section are the permissions; for a complete list, see the **Access Mode** section in `man 5 apparmor.d`:

```
/var/log/nginx/error.log w,
 owner /etc/nginx/modules-enabled/ r,
 owner /etc/nginx/nginx.conf r,
 owner /run/nginx.pid w,
 owner /usr/lib/nginx/modules/ngx_http_geoip_module.so mr,
 owner /usr/share/nginx/modules-available/mod-http-geoip.conf r,
 owner /usr/share/nginx/modules-available/mod-http-image-filter.conf r,
 owner /var/log/nginx/access.log w,
}
```

The `aa-logprof` in particular can be a little bit overwhelming if you start using it. But the profile is not that difficult to read; every option is in the two man pages and the included abstractions are documented by comments.

Systemd security

The systemd units can also provide an extra layer of security. You can add several options to your unit file to make your unit more secure.

Just edit the unit file using `systemctl --edit` and add the security measures. For instance, execute the following:

```
sudo systemctl --edit sshd
```

Add the following lines:

```
[Service]
ProtectHome=read-only
```

Save the file, reread the `systemctl` configuration, and restart `sshd`:

```
sudo systemctl daemon-reload
```

```
sudo systemctl restart sshd
```

Now log in again with your SSH client and try to save a file in your home. It will fail because it's a read-only filesystem:

```
linvirt@ubuntu01:~$ echo test > ~/test
-bash: /home/linvirt/test: Read-only file system
linvirt@ubuntu01:~$ findmnt -T ~
TARGET SOURCE           FSTYPE OPTIONS
/home  /dev/sda1[/home] ext4   ro,relatime,discard,data=ordered
```

Restricting access to the filesystem

The `ProtectHome` parameter is a very interesting one. The following values are available:

- `true`: The directories `/home`, `/root`, and `/run/user` are not accessible by the unit, and show empty for processes starting within the unit
- `read-only`: These directories are read-only

Another very similar parameter is `ProtectSystem`:

- `true`: /usr and /boot are mounted read-only.
- `full`: Same as "true" + /etc
- `strict`: Full filesystem is read-only, except /proc, /dev, and /sys.

Instead of `ProtectHome` and `ProtectSystem`, or additionally, you can use the following parameters: `ReadWritePaths` to whitelist directories, `ReadOnlyPaths`, and `InaccessiblePaths`.

Some daemons use the /tmp directory for temporary storage. The problem with this directory is that its world-readable. The `PrivateTmp=true` parameter sets up a new temporary filesystem for the process, which is only accessible by the process.

There are also kernel-related parameters: the `ProtectKernelModules=true` parameter makes it impossible to load modules, and the `ProtectKernelTunables=true` parameter makes it impossible to change kernel parameters with the `sysctl` command or manually in the /proc and /sys directory structure.

Last but not least, the `SELinuxContext` and `AppArmorProfile` parameters force the context for the unit.

Restricting network access

Newer versions of systemd (>235), as in use by Ubuntu 18.04, also support IP accounting and access lists to restrict network access.

`IPAccounting=yes` allows the unit to collect and analyze network data. To view the results, you can use the `systemctl` command:

```
systemctl show <service name> -p IPIngressBytes \
 -p IPIngressPackets \
 -p IPEgressBytes -p IPEgressPackets
```

As with every parameter, you can use this with `systemd-run` as well, for instance:

```
root@ubuntu01:~# systemd-run -p IPAccounting=yes ping -c5 9.9.9.9
Running as unit: run-rfd0ca0d359ee4f77aefa7b6e1fcfe43f.service
root@ubuntu01:~#
root@ubuntu01:~# systemctl show run-rfd0ca0d359ee4f77aefa7b6e1fcfe43f.service -p
 IPIngressBytes -p IPIngressPackets \
> -p IPEgressBytes -p IPEgressPackets
IPIngressBytes=18446744073709551615
IPIngressPackets=18446744073709551615
IPEgressBytes=18446744073709551615
IPEgressPackets=18446744073709551615
```

You can use `IPAddressDeny` to deny an IP address or an IP range. An exception can be made with `IPAddressAllow`. It's even possible to deny everything system-wide and whitelist per service:

```
sudo systemctl set-property ssh.service IPAddressAllow=any

sudo systemctl set-property waagent.service IPAddressAllow=10.0.0.1

sudo systemctl set-property system.slice IPAddressAllow=localhost

sudo systemctl set-property system.slice IPAddressAllow=10.0.0.1

sudo systemctl set-property system.slice IPAddressDeny=any
```

The changes are saved in the `/etc/systemd/system.control` directory structure:

```
[linvirt@centos01 ~]$ timedatectl
      Local time: Tue 2018-07-17 14:51:20 UTC
  Universal time: Tue 2018-07-17 14:51:20 UTC
        RTC time: Tue 2018-07-17 14:51:20
       Time zone: Etc/UTC (UTC, +0000)
     NTP enabled: yes
 NTP synchronized: yes
 RTC in local TZ: no
     DST active: n/a
```

Here are some remarks:

- Of course, you have to change the IP range to your virtual subnet, and you have to allow access to the first IP address of your subnet for the Azure Agent and network service, such as DHCP

- It's also a very good idea to restrict SSH access to the IP address of your own network
- View the systemd journal very carefully, to know whether you need more ports to open

The systemd access list feature is maybe not as advanced as firewalld, but it is a very good alternative for restrictions on the application level (host allow directives in the configuration files of the daemon or `/etc/hosts.allow` and `/etc/hosts.deny` for applications that are compiled with `libwrap` support). And, in my opinion, in Azure you don't need more than this. If only all distributions had a recent version of systemd.

> I don't cover the `libwrap` library in this book, because more and more applications are not using this option any longer, and some vendors, like SUSE, are very busy to remove the complete support for this library.

Azure Active Directory Domain Service

The **Azure Active Directory Service** (**AADS**) is a domain controller as a service to provide you with a DNS service and identity management. Central identity management is always an important part of security solutions. It enables the user to access the resources. On top of that, you can enforce policies and enable multi-factor authentication.

In the near future, it will be possible to use the **Azure AD** (**AAD**) as well. This is a completely different identity management system, without LDAP and Kerberos. In Linux, AAD will allow you to use your Azure credentials to log in to your virtual machine, but has no support on application level. So for now, AADS is a better idea.

In this section, we will focus on how to create the service and how to join the domain.

Setting up AADS

The easiest way to set up AADS is via the Azure portal. In the left bar, select **Create a resource** and search for `Domain Services`. Select the AADS service and click on the **Create** button.

During the wizard, you will be asked for some settings:

- **Domain name**: You can use your own or use a built-in domain name that ends with `.onmicrosoft.com`. For the purposes of this book, it's enough.
- **Virtual network**: It's a good idea to create a new virtual network and a new subnet. Labeling doesn't matter.
- **Administrators**: A group will be made called `AAD DC Administrators`. To be able to join a domain with a user, the user must be a member of this group and have the `Global administrator` role. Of course, you can add users and modify this later on, using the **Active Directory** section in the left bar in the Azure portal.

Now you are ready to deploy the service. It will take a while; in my personal experience, it can take 20 to 30 minutes.

When you are finished, go to the **Virtual Networks** section in the left bar, and enter the newly created virtual network. You will find two newly created network interfaces and their IP addresses. You'll need this information.

It is a good idea to create a new subnet in this virtual network, but it's not necessary.

Linux configuration

You have to deploy the Linux virtual machine in the same virtual network as the AADS service. As stated, it is a good idea to attach to another subnet.

NTP configuration

You have to set up an NTP client to synchronize the time with the AADS. There are multiple clients available, one of them is chrony. In almost every image, it's already installed and running, only in Ubuntu do you have to install it:

```
sudo apt-get install chrony
```

Verify it with the `timedatectl` utility:

```
[linvirt@centos01 ~]$ timedatectl
        Local time: Tue 2018-07-17 14:51:20 UTC
    Universal time: Tue 2018-07-17 14:51:20 UTC
          RTC time: Tue 2018-07-17 14:51:20
         Time zone: Etc/UTC (UTC, +0000)
       NTP enabled: yes
  NTP synchronized: yes
   RTC in local TZ: no
        DST active: n/a
```

To use the AADS NTP service, edit `/etc/chrony.conf` (in Ubuntu: `/etc/chrony/chrony.conf`).

Remove existing server and/or pool entries and replace them with the following:

```
server <ip address of AD Network interface 1> iburst
server <ip address of AD Network interface 2> iburst
```

Restart the daemon:

```
sudo systemctl restart chronyd
```

In Ubuntu, the services is named `chrony`. Verify the results with the help of the `chronyc` utility:

```
chronyc sources
```

```
[linvirt@centos01 ~]$ chronyc sources
210 Number of sources = 2
MS Name/IP address         Stratum Poll Reach LastRx Last sample
===============================================================================
^* 10.1.0.4                      2   6    17     57  -1846us[+1943us] +/-   49ms
^+ 10.1.0.5                      2   6    17     57  +1398us[+5186us] +/-   49ms
```

Hostname

Change the hostname with the `hostnamectl` utility into the correct `fqdn`, for instance:

```
sudo hostnamectl set-hostname ubuntu01.frederikvoslinvirt.onmicrosoft.com
```

And edit the `/etc/hosts` file. Add an entry like this:

```
127.0.0.1 ubuntu01.frederikvoslinvirt.onmicrosoft.com ubuntu01
```

DNS servers

In the left-bar navigation of the Azure portal, go to **Virtual Networks** and navigate to the subnet where the AADS network interfaces are. Select `DNS servers` and use the custom options to set the IP addresses of the AADS network interfaces.

Normally, it should be enough to restart the network in the virtual machine, but it's a better idea to reboot now. From time to time, the old and new settings both survive.

In Red Hat and SUSE, view the content of the `/etc/resolv.conf` file to verify the result. In Ubuntu, execute the following:

```
systemd-resolve --status
```

Then look into the settings for `eth0`.

Installing dependencies

There are some important components, dependencies, required to be able to use AADS:

- Kerberos client, for authorization
- SSSD, a backend that is responsible for the configuration and utilization of features such as using and caching credentials
- Samba libraries, to be compatible with Windows features/options
- Some utilities to join and manage the domain, such as `realm`, `adcli`, and the `net` command

Install the necessary software to be able to join the domain.

For RHEL/CentOS-based distributions, execute the following:

```
sudo yum install realmd sssd krb5-workstation krb5-libs samba-common-tools
```

In Ubuntu, execute the following:

```
sudo apt install krb5-user samba sssd sssd-tools libnss-sss libpam-sss realmd adcli
```

In SLE/OpenSUSE LEAP, dependencies will be handled by YaST.

Joining the domain – Ubuntu and RHEL/CentOS

In Ubuntu and RHEL/CentOS based distributions, the `realm` utility is available to join the domain. First, discover the domain:

```
sudo realm discover <your domain>
```

The output should be similar to this:

```
linvirt@ubuntu01:~$ sudo realm discover frederikvoslinvirt.onmicrosoft.com
frederikvoslinvirt.onmicrosoft.com
  type: kerberos
  realm-name: FREDERIKVOSLINVIRT.ONMICROSOFT.COM
  domain-name: frederikvoslinvirt.onmicrosoft.com
  configured: no
  server-software: active-directory
  client-software: sssd
  required-package: sssd-tools
  required-package: sssd
  required-package: libnss-sss
  required-package: libpam-sss
  required-package: adcli
  required-package: samba-common-bin
```

Now you are ready to join the domain:

```
sudo realm join <your domain> -U <username>
```

Use the username you added earlier on as a member of the AADS administrator group. Don't add the domain name. If you get a message saying `Necessary packages are not installed` but you are sure that they are installed, add the `--install=/` parameter to the `realm` command.

To verify the result, execute the following:

```
sudo realm list
```

The output should be similar to this:

```
frederikvoslinvirt.onmicrosoft.com
  type: kerberos
  realm-name: FREDERIKVOSLINVIRT.ONMICROSOFT.COM
  domain-name: frederikvoslinvirt.onmicrosoft.com
  configured: kerberos-member
  server-software: active-directory
  client-software: sssd
  required-package: sssd-tools
  required-package: sssd
  required-package: libnss-sss
  required-package: libpam-sss
  required-package: adcli
  required-package: samba-common-bin
  login-formats: %U@frederikvoslinvirt.onmicrosoft.com
  login-policy: allow-realm-logins
```

And you should be able to do things such as the following:

```
id <user>@<domain>
```

```
su <user>@<domain>
```

Log in remotely with `ssh` with this user.

> If this doesn't work, and the join was successful, reboot the virtual machine.

Joining the domain – SUSE

In SUSE SLE and LEAP, the best way to join the domain is using YaST.

Start the YaST utility:

```
sudo yast
```

From the YaST main window, start the module **User Logon Management** and click on **Change Settings**. Click on **Join Domain** and fill in the domain name. After that, you will be able to enroll in the domain successfully. If necessary, dependencies will be installed.

A new window appears to manage the domain user logons. You need at least the following: **Allow Domain User Logon** and **Create Home Directory**. All the other options are not possible in AADS yet.

Summary

Security is a very important topic nowadays. Many reports, books and so on are written on this subject. In this chapter, I covered several options in Linux to increase the security level. All of them come on top of the basic security already provided by Azure through network security groups. They are relatively easy to implement and it already makes a big difference!

Central identity management is not only a way to provide users access to the virtual machine, but it's also a part of the reducing the security risks. Azure Directory Services provides, via LDAP and Kerberos, an identity management solution for all operating systems and applications that have support for these protocols.

Chapter 8, *Exploring Continuous Configuration Automation*, will cover automation and orchestration. Please note that all the security measures covered in this chapter can be easily orchestrated. Orchestration makes central configuration management possible. One of the big advantages is preventing mistakes and unmanageable configurations. This way, even orchestration is a part of your security plan!

And it would be nice, if you are going to create your own virtual machines, especially if you're going to build your own images, as I will discuss in the next chapter, that you also keep security in mind before you upload them and release them in your environment.

Questions

1. If you are going to implement firewalld, what are the methods to configure this firewall?
2. What is the reason for the `--permanent` parameter of `firewall-cmd`?
3. What other options are available to restrict network access?
4. Explain the difference between DAC and MAC.
5. Why is it important to utilize Linux Security Modules in a virtual machine running on Azure?

6. Which MAC is available for which distribution?
7. What is the main difference between AppArmor and SELinux?
8. What are the requirements to be able to join the Azure Active Directory Service in terms of dependencies and Linux configuration?

Further reading

Similar to the previous chapter, I strongly suggest you visit Chapter 11, *Troubleshooting and Monitoring Your Workloads* to read about logging in Linux, because often the `systemctl status` command doesn't provide you with enough information. I also already pointed to the blog by Lennart Poettering, and the systemd website.

For Linux security in general, you can start reading the book *Mastering Linux Security and Hardening* by Donald A. Tevault. Many of the topics covered in this chapter and many more are explained with a great eye for detail.

The firewalld daemon has a project website, `https://firewalld.org`, with a blog and excellent documentation. For older distributions, the Wiki of ArchLinux is a good start to learn more: `https://wiki.archlinux.org/index.php/iptables`. And since iptables is utilized by firewalld, it's a good start before diving into the man page of **firewalld.richlanguage**.

All the details about SELinux are covered in guides provided by Red Hat: `https://access. redhat.com/documentation/en-us/red_hat_enterprise_linux/7/html/selinux_users_ and_administrators_guide/`. And although it's slightly out of date, it's a very good idea to watch a video of a Red Hat Summit on YouTube about SELinux: `https://www.youtube. com/watch?v=MxjenQ31b70`.

It's more difficult to find good information about AppArmor. There is project documentation on `https://gitlab.com/apparmor/apparmor/wikis/Documentation` and the Ubuntu server guide is a good start, available on `https://help.ubuntu.com/lts/ serverguide/apparmor.html.en`.

Deploying Your Virtual Machines

7

It's easy to deploy a single virtual machine in Azure, but as soon you want to deploy more workloads in a single, reproducible way, you need some sort of automation.

In Azure, you can use the Azure Resource Manager to deploy virtual machines using template configuration files together with Bash, PowerShell, Ruby, and C#. Other deployment methods are available using third-party tools such as Packer and Vagrant.

All the methods described are using available images, but it's also possible to create your own custom virtual machines.

Before going into the configuration of all the possible options available, it is important to be aware of the different deployment options and why you want or don't want to use them. You have to ask yourself some questions first:

- When are you going to deploy your application?
- What parts of the workload should be reproducible?
- Which parts of the configuration of the workload should be done during deployment?

Deployment scenarios

The last three questions are very important; the answers can differ per company, per application, and during the development stage. Here are a few examples:

- Applications are developed in-house, maybe even locally; when it's finished, the application is deployed in Azure. Updates will be applied to the running workload.
- This is the same scenario, but now the updates will be done by deploying a new virtual machine.
- An application is delivered by another vendor.

These three examples are very common and can affect the way you want to deploy your workload.

What do you need?

What do I actually need in Azure, before I am even able to start deploying my virtual machine?

- Resource group
- Storage account
- Network Security Group
- Virtual network
- Subnet for the virtual network
- Network interface attached to the virtual machine

Regarding the virtual machine, I need to specify and think about the following:

- Virtual machine sizing
- Storage
- Virtual machine extensions
- Operating system
- Initial configuration
- Deployment of your application

If you look into these lists, you have to ask yourself, as stated in the introduction of this chapter: *Do I need automation or orchestration and do I need to reproduce it*? And the answer is not easy to find. Let's look again into the scenarios and try to find an answer. It is imaginable that you could look into it and make the following decisions:

- Create a script in PowerShell or Bash to prepare the Azure environment for the workload
- Create a second script to deploy the virtual machine based on an offer in Azure and use a virtual machine extension to configure the initial configuration
- Deploy the application with a software manager such as Yum

There is nothing wrong if you make this decision; it can be the best solution for you! But, whether you like it or not, there are dependencies:

- You deploy your operating system based on an offer. This offer is made available by a publisher. What happens if the offer is updated, even for the same version?
- How much initial configuration is already done in this offer? How much is needed, and who is in control of the image?
- Is this image compliant to my policy standards regarding security?
- If I want to leave Azure, for whatever reason, can I move my application to somewhere else?

Automated deployment options

After this long introduction, it's time to have a look into the available options that make it possible to automate the deployment of your workload:

- Scripting
- Azure Resource Manager
- Initial configuration with the Custom Script Extension
- Initial configuration with cloud-init

Scripting

Automation can be done with scripts. In Azure, there are many options supported by Microsoft:

- Bash with Azure CLI
- PowerShell with the AzureRM module
- Python, with a complete SDK available (https://azure.microsoft.com/en-us/develop/python)
- Ruby, with an SDK available (preview) (https://azure.microsoft.com/en-us/develop/ruby)
- Go, with a complete SDK available
- And there are libraries available for Node.js

Besides that, you can use programming languages such as Java (libraries available) and C#. There are community projects as well, for instance, https://github.com/capside/azure-sdk-perl is an attempt to build a full Azure SDK for Perl.

All languages are valid options; choose the language you are already familiar with. Please be aware that the Ruby SDK was in a preview phase at the time that this book was written. During this preview state, the syntax can change.

Scripting is especially good for preparing the Azure environment. You can also use scripting to deploy your virtual machines and can even include initial configuration using virtual machine extensions. The question of whether it's a good idea is dependent on your scripting abilities; the base image offered in Azure is good enough to use and can determine how dependent your application is on the OS and versions of software installed in it.

The biggest argument against using scripts is that it is time consuming to write them. Here are some tips:

- Use as many variables as possible. This way, you have more changes that you can reuse the script.
- Use recognizable variable names, not something like *for i in*.
- Especially for bigger scripts, declare functions that you can reuse.
- Sometimes, it makes sense to put variables (such as the one that provides authentication) and functions in separate files. One task per script is often a good idea.

- Include the time stamp of modification in your code, or, even better, use a version control system such as Git.
- Include tests, for instance, only create this resource if it doesn't already exist. Use human readable exit codes, using the variables *not able to create $resource*
- Include many comments; if you need to debug or reuse the script after some time, you'll still know what it's doing. Don't forget to include a description in the header as well.
- Spend some time on the layout; use indentation to keep the code readable. Use two spaces for indentation, not tabs!
- Don't go beyond initial configuration via virtual machine extensions.

It's time for a little example. The purpose of this example is to give you an idea of how to create scripts to provide the things you need in Azure before deploying a virtual machine.

First, create a file with variables, for instance, with the name `azvariable.ps1`:

```
$myResourceGroup = "LinuxOnAzure"
$myLocation = "West Europe"
$myNSG = "NSG_WebApp"
$mySubnet = "10.0.0.0/24"
$myVnet= "VNET_WebApp"
```

Next, create a script to create a resource group. Note for the purpose of readability, I added line breaks with `` ` ``. Try to avoid that in your script, especially if you add an indentation to the next line; it will break the script:

```
<#
 The purpose of this script is to a resource group in Azure.
 This script is created by Frederik Vos,
 last updated: 08-06-2018
 #>

# include variables
$ScriptDirectory = Split-Path -Path $MyInvocation.MyCommand.Definition -
Parent
try {
  . ("$ScriptDirectory/azvariable.ps1")
}
```

```
catch {
    Write-Host "Error while loading supporting variables"
}

# test if the Resource Group already exist, if not: create it.
Get-AzureRmResourceGroup -Name $myResourceGroup `
  -ErrorVariable notPresent -ErrorAction SilentlyContinue `
  | out-null

if ($notPresent)
  {
    # ResourceGroup doesn't exist, create it:
    New-AzureRmResourceGroup -Name $myResourceGroup -Location`
      $myLocation
    Write-Host "The Resource Group $myResourceGroup is created in`
      the location $myLocation"
  }

else

  {
    Write-Host "The Resource Group $myResourceGroup already existed`
      in the location $myLocation"
  }
```

Create the virtual network and configure the subnet:

```
<#
    The purpose of this script is to provide vm networking in Azure.
    This script is created by Frederik Vos,
    last updated: 08-06-2018
                            #>

$ScriptDirectory = Split-Path -Path $MyInvocation.MyCommand.Definition -
Parent
try {
    . ("$ScriptDirectory/azvariable.ps1")
}

catch {
    Write-Host "Error while loading supporting variables"
}

# Test if the vnet name not already exist:
```

```
get-AzureRmVirtualNetwork -Name $myVnet `
  -ResourceGroupName $myResourceGroup -ErrorVariable notPresent`
  -ErrorAction SilentlyContinue | out-null
if ($notPresent)
  {
    # vnet doesn't exist, create the subnet configuration first:
    $subnetConfig = New-AzureRmVirtualNetworkSubnetConfig `
      -Name $myVnet -AddressPrefix $mySubnet

    # create the actual vnet
    $vnet = New-AzureRmVirtualNetwork `
      -ResourceGroupName $myResourceGroup -Location $myLocation `
      -Name $myVnet -AddressPrefix $mySubnet -Subnet $subnetConfig

    Write-Host "The virtual network $myVnet with $mySubnet `
      configured is created in the location $myLocation"
  }
```

Here is another one for the network security group:

```
<#
 The purpose of this script is to create a NSG in Azure.
 This script is created by Frederik Vos,
 last updated: 08-06-2018
 #>

$ScriptDirectory = Split-Path -Path $MyInvocation.MyCommand.Definition -
Parent
try {
 . ("$ScriptDirectory/azvariable.ps1")
}

catch {
 Write-Host "Error while loading supporting variables"
}

# Test if the Network Security Group not already exist:

Get-AzureRmNetworkSecurityGroup -ResourceGroupName $myResourceGroup`
 -Name $myNSG -ErrorVariable notPresent `
 -ErrorAction SilentlyContinue | out-null

if ($notPresent)
 {
 # NSG doesn't exist, create the rules
```

```
$NSGSSH = New-AzureRmNetworkSecurityRuleConfig -Name "SSHRule" `
-Protocol "Tcp" -Direction "Inbound" -Priority 1000 `
-SourceAddressPrefix * -SourcePortRange * `
-DestinationAddressPrefix * -DestinationPortRange 22 `
-Access "Allow"
$NSGHTTP = New-AzureRmNetworkSecurityRuleConfig `
-Name "HTTPRULE" -Protocol "Tcp" -Direction "Inbound" `
-Priority 1001 -SourceAddressPrefix * -SourcePortRange *`
-DestinationAddressPrefix * -DestinationPortRange 80 `
-Access "Allow"

# create the NSG
$NSG = New-AzureRmNetworkSecurityGroup `
-ResourceGroupName $myResourceGroup -Location $myLocation`
-Name $myNSG -SecurityRules $NSGSSH,$NSGHTTP

Write-Host "The NSG: $myNSG is configured is created with rules`
for SSH and HTTP in the resource group $myResourceGroup"
}

else
{
Write-Host "The NSG $myNSG already existed in the `
resource group $myResourceGroup"

Write-Host "Configured Rules:"
Get-AzureRmNetworkSecurityGroup -Name $myNSG`
-ResourceGroupName $myResourceGroup | `
Get-AzureRmNetworkSecurityRuleConfig
}
```

By now, you should have a pretty good picture of how you can do it.

Azure Resource Manager

In `Chapter 2`, *Getting Started with the Azure Cloud*, I gave a definition of the Azure Resource Manager:

> "Basically, the Azure Resource Manager enables you to work with resources, such as storage and virtual machines. To do so, you have to create one or more resource groups, so you can execute life-cycle operations, such as deploy, update and delete all the resources in the resource group in a single operation."

After that, I covered the concept of the resource group. The definition was already true; from the Azure portal or with scripting, you were able to do all of the things stated. But that's only a small part of it. You can deploy Azure resources through the Azure Resource Manager by using templates. There are hundreds of them available as Azure Quickstart Templates on `https://azure.microsoft.com/en-us/resources/templates`.

When you create a virtual machine via the Azure portal, you can download that virtual machine as a template, even before you create it:

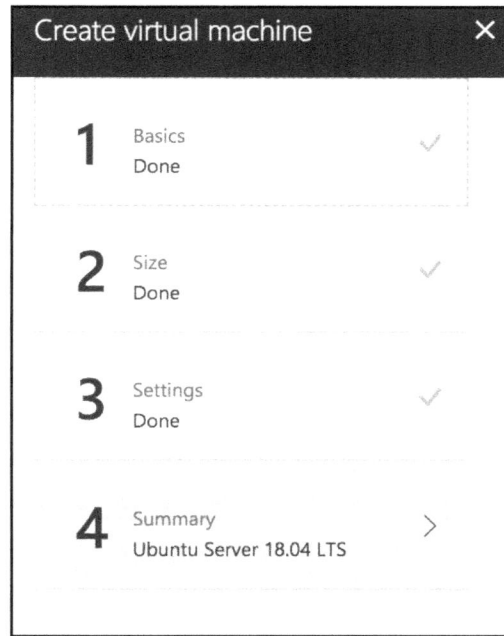

If you click on **Download template and parameters**, you'll get the next screen:

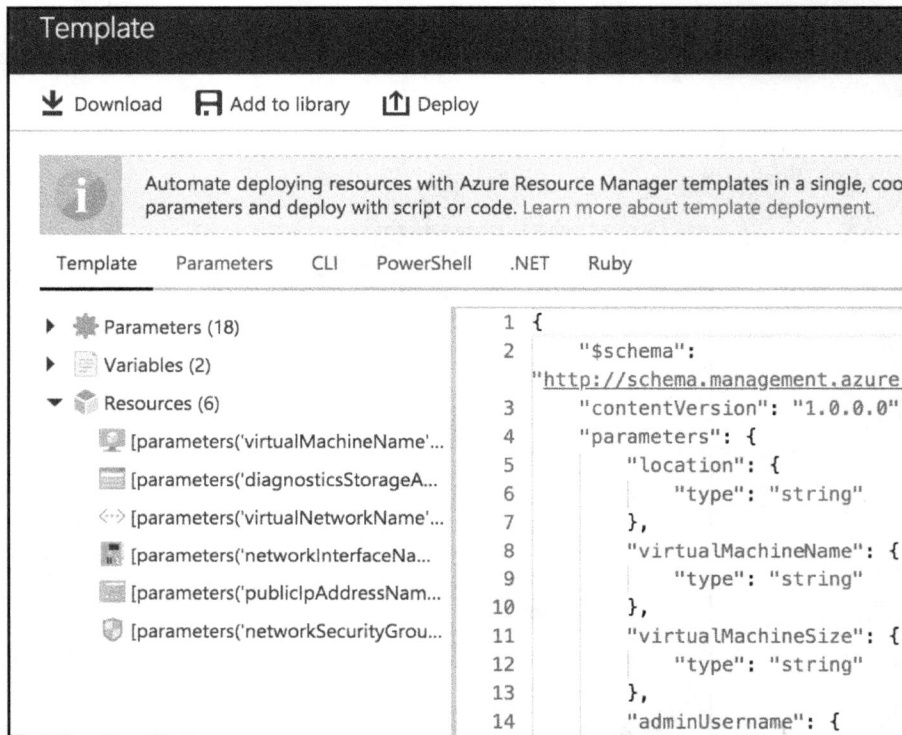

As you can see, you can preview all the parameters, change them, and click on **Deploy**, but you can also save them to a library or download them to your local disk.

The download contains:

- A Bash script for usage with Azure CLI
- A PowerShell script for usage with the AzureRM module
- A Ruby script
- A C# version

- A `template.json` file that contains expressions which can be used to construct values for your deployment
- All the virtual machine parameters in a `parameters.json` file; these are the answers to the statements in the `template.json` file

You can easily change the parameters and deploy a new virtual machine, or redeploy exactly the same. It is not that different than using your own scripts, but less time-consuming in development terms.

This is not the only thing you can do with ARM; you can configure every aspect of Azure, many resources. It's not that difficult to create your own ARM template. You'll need the ARM reference guide that can be found at `https://docs.microsoft.com/en-us/azure/templates`. Together with these examples it's a great resource to get started.

Another way of getting started is by using the Visual Studio Code editor, which is available for Windows, Linux, and macOS on `https://code.visualstudio.com`. The **Azure Resource Manager Tools** extension is a must-have if you are going to start using ARM, together with some other extensions, such as the **Azure Account and Sign-In**, **Azure Resource Manager snippets**, and the **Azure CLI Tools**. You can start using existing templates, even upload them to the cloud shell, execute and debug them:

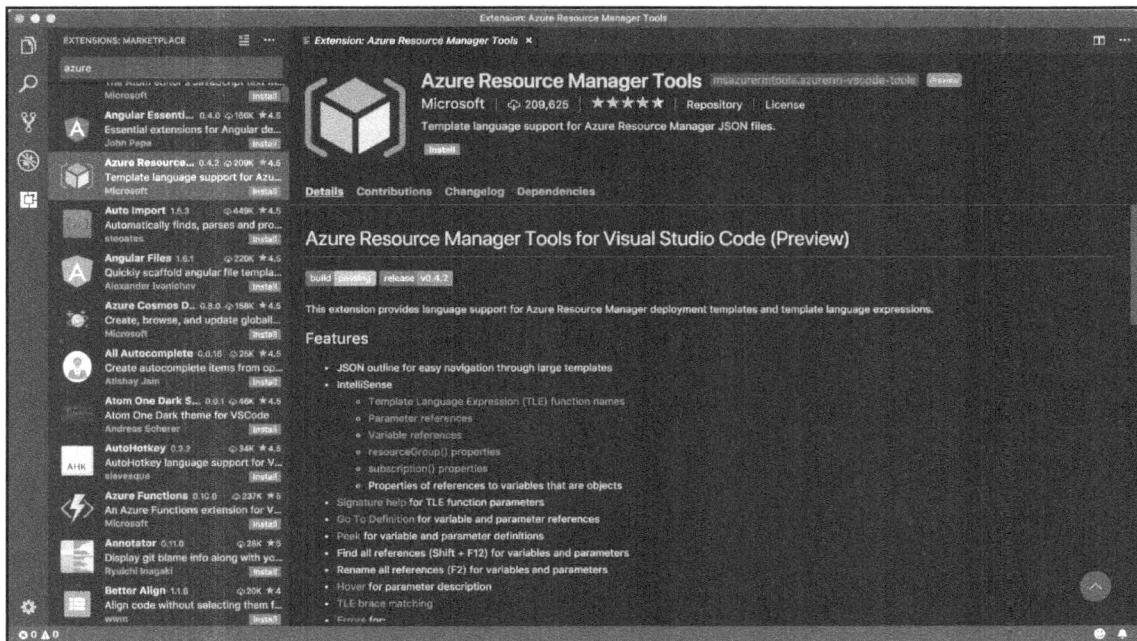

Another nice feature in Azure is the ARM Visualizer, which you can find at `http://armviz.io`. It's still in an early state of development. It's a tool that especially can help to get a quick insight into the purpose of the ARM template you downloaded from the Quickstart Templates website.

Instead of downloading the templates, it's also possible to save them to a library:

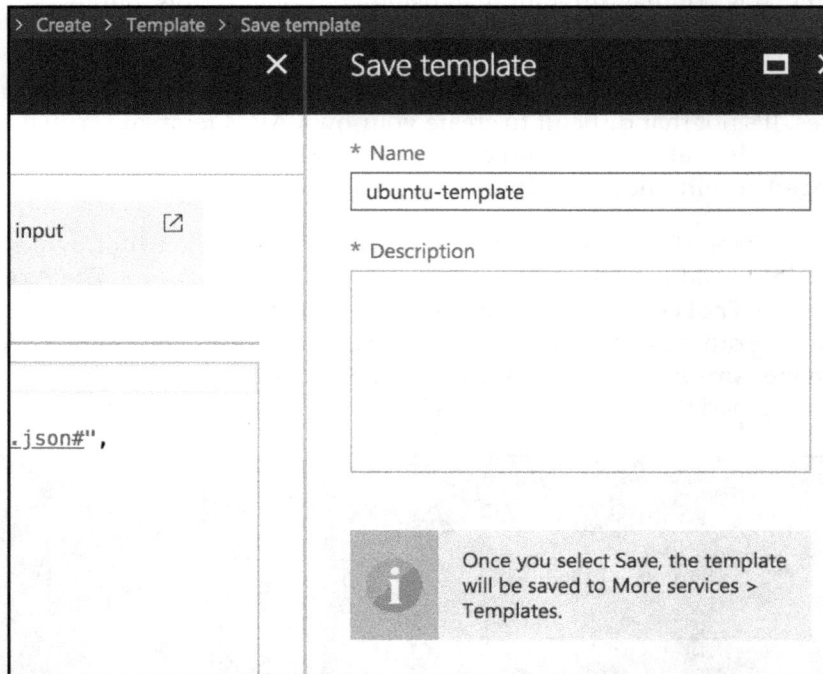

As stated in this pane, you can easily navigate in the Azure portal, using **All Service** in the left-hand navigation bar and search for templates. You still have the possibility to edit the template here! Another nice feature is that you can share the template with other users of your tenant. This can be very useful, as you can create a user who is only allowed to use this template for deployments.

Let's go back to what we downloaded and have a look into the versions for Bash and PowerShell.

First, a remark about the Bash version is that there is a little problem with the Bash version if you execute it from Linux or macOS. The file is created in the DOS version of ASCII that has other line-ends than the Unix version. You have to convert it with a little utility: `dos2unix`:

```
dos2unix deploy.sh
```

Now, make it executable:

```
chmod +x deploy.sh
```

The script needs some Azure parameters; it can ask for these interactively, or you can provide them using the options:

```
./deploy.sh -i <subscriptionId> -g <resource group name> \
  -n <vm name> -l <location>
```

The subscription ID can be found using the `az account list` command.

If you want to use the PowerShell version, `deploy.ps1` has the following options:

```
./deploy.ps1 -subscriptionId <subscriptionId> `
  -resourceGroupName `
  <resource group> -resourceGroupLocation <location> `
  -deploymentName <vm name>
```

In both PowerShell and Shell script, the parameter for the `vm name` overrules the default parameter in `virtualMachineName`.

Initial configuration

After the deployment of your workload, post-deployment configuration is needed. If you want to do this as a part of your automation solution, then there are two solutions for you:

- The Custom Script Extension that can be used at any time after the deployment
- cloud-init is available during boot

Initial configuration with the Custom Script Extension

After the deployment of the virtual machine, it is possible to execute post-deployment scripts using the Custom Script Extension. This extension will work on all Microsoft-endorsed Linux operating systems, except CoreOS and OpenSUSE LEAP.

You can use PowerShell to configure it:

```
$myResourceGroup = "<resource group name>"
$myLocation = "<location>"
$myVM = "<vm name>"
$Settings = @{ "commandToExecute" = "apt-get -y install nginx";};

Set-AzureRmVMExtension -VMName $myVM -ResourceGroupName $myResourceGroup `
  -Location $myLocation `
  -Name "CustomscriptLinux" -ExtensionType "CustomScript" `
  -Publisher "Microsoft.Azure.Extensions" `
  -typeHandlerVersion "2.0" -InformationAction SilentlyContinue `
  -Verbose -Settings $Settings
```

Change the `apt-get` command in another command if you are using another distribution than Debian or Ubuntu. Instead of a command, you can also provide a script.

Let's create a very simple script:

```
#!/bin/sh
apt-get install -y nginx firewalld
firewall-cmd --add-service=http
firewall-cmd --add-service=http --permanent
```

Now the script must be encrypted using the `base64` command:

```
cat nginx.sh| base64
```

> On some versions of base64, you have to add the parameter -w0 to disable word wrapping. Just make sure that it is one line!

The `$Settings` variable will be as follows:

```
$Settings = @{"script" = "<base64 string>";};
```

Scripts can be compressed or uploaded to a storage blob if you want.

Of course, you can use the Azure CLI as well. In that scenario, you have to provide a JSON file, similar to this one:

```
{
    "autoUpgradeMinorVersion": true,
    "location": "<location>",
    "name": "CustomscriptLinux",
    "protectedSettings": {},
    "provisioningState": "Failed",
    "publisher": "Microsoft.Azure.Extensions",
    "resourceGroup": "<resource group>",
    "settings": {
      "script": "<base64 string>"
    },
    "tags": {},
    "type": "Microsoft.Compute/virtualMachines/extensions",
    "typeHandlerVersion": "2.0",
    "virtualMachineExtensionType": "CustomScript"
}
```

Then, execute the following `az` command:

```
az vm extension set --resource-group <resource group> \
   --vm-name <vm name> \
   --name customScript --publisher Microsoft.Azure.Extensions \
   --settings ./nginx.json
```

The JSON file can be included in an ARM template.

If you are using PowerShell or Azure CLI for debugging purposes, the directory `/var/log/azure/custom-script` contains the log of your actions.

Initial configuration with cloud-init

A problem with the custom VM extension is that scripts can be very distribution specific. You can already see that in the examples used. If you use different distributions, you'll need multiple scripts or you'll have to include distribution checks.

Another way to do some initial configuration after the deployment of your virtual machine is by using cloud-init.

cloud-init is a project of Canonical, which is created to have a cloud-solution and a Linux distribution agnostic approach for customizing cloud images. In Azure, it can be used in images, to prepare the operating system during the first boot, or while creating the virtual machine.

Not every Microsoft-endorsed Linux distribution is supported; Debian and SUSE are not supported at all and it always takes some time before the latest version of a distribution can be used.

cloud-init can be used to run Linux commands and create files. There are modules available to configure the system, for instance to install software or do some user and group management. If a module is available, then it's the best way to do it. It is not only easier (the hard work is done for you), but also distribution agnostic.

cloud-init uses YAML; please be aware that indentation is important! Create a YAML file with the following content, and name it `cloudinit.txt`:

```
#cloud-config
groups: users
users:
  - default
  - name: azureuser
  - groups: users
  - shell: /bin/bash
package_upgrade: true
packages:
  - nginx
  - nodejs
  - npm
write_files:
  - owner: www-data:www-data
  - path: /etc/nginx/sites-available/default
    content: |
      server {
        listen 80;
        location / {
          proxy_pass http://localhost:3000;
          proxy_http_version 1.1;
          proxy_set_header Upgrade $http_upgrade;
          proxy_set_header Connection keep-alive;
          proxy_set_header Host $host;
          proxy_cache_bypass $http_upgrade;
        }
```

```
      }
  - owner: azureuser:users
  - path: /home/azureuser/myapp/index.js
    content: |
      var express = require('express')
      var app = express()
      var os = require('os');
      app.get('/', function (req, res) {
        res.send('Hello World from host ' + os.hostname() + '!')
      })
      app.listen(3000, function () {
        console.log('Hello world app listening on port 3000!')
      })
runcmd:
  - systemctl restart nginx
  - cd "/home/azureuser/myapp"
  - npm init
  - npm install express -y
  - nodejs index.js
```

If you look into this configuration files, you can use some of the modules in action:

- `users` and `groups`: User management
- `packages` and `package_upgrade`: Software management
- `write_files`: Create files
- `runcmd`: Run commands that are not possible with modules.

You can also create the virtual machine, for instance:

```
az vm create --resource-group <resource group> \
  --name <vm name> --image UbuntuLTS \
  --admin-username linuxadmin \
  --generate-ssh-keys --custom-data cloudinit.txt
```

After deployment, it will take some time before everything is done. Logging is done in the virtual machine in the files `/var/log/cloud-init.log` and `/var/log/cloud-init-output.log`.

Change the network security group rules, to permit traffic on port 80. After that, open your browser to the IP address of the virtual machine. If everything is OK, it shows: `Hello World from host ubuntu-web!`

> There is no support for cloud-init in the AzureRM cmdlets.

Vagrant and Packer

Until now, we used solutions provided by Microsoft; maybe we should call them native solutions. That's not the only way to deploy your workload in Azure. Many vendors have created solutions to automate deployments in Azure. In this section, I want to cover a solution from a company called HashiCorp (`https://www.hashicorp.com`). Later on in this chapter, I'll cover another product from this company: Packer. There are several reasons why I have chose these products:

- The products are very popular and well-known.
- There is an excellent relationship between Microsoft and HashiCorp; they work very hard together to implement more and more features.
- And, the most important reason: they have different products that you can use for different implementation scenarios. This will make you think again about what method you want to choose in different use cases.

Vagrant is a tool you can use for deployment if you are a developer. It helps you to set up an environment in a standardized way that you can redeploy over and over again.

Installing and configuring Vagrant

Vagrant is available for several Linux distributions, Windows and macOS and can be downloaded from `https://www.vagrantup.com/downloads.html`. To install the software in Ubuntu, use the following commands:

```
cd /tmp

wget https://releases.hashicorp.com/vagrant/2.1.2/\
  vagrant_2.1.2_x86_64.deb

sudo apt install vagrant_2.1.2_x86_64.deb
```

In RHEL/CentOS use the following command:

```
sudo yum install \
 https://releases.hashicorp.com/vagrant/2.1.2/\
 vagrant_2.1.2_x86_64.rpm
```

If you deploy it on a separate virtual machine or workstation, make sure that you installed Azure CLI as well.

Log in to Azure:

```
az login
```

Create a service principle account that Vagrant can use to authenticate:

```
az ad sp create-for-rbac --name vagrant
```

From the output you need the `appID`, also known as the **Client ID**, and the password, which is the same as the **Client Secret**.

Execute the command:

```
az account show
```

In the output of this command, you can see your tenant ID and your subscription ID.

Create a file with the following content:

```
AZURE_TENANT_ID="<tenant id>"
AZURE_SUBSCRIPTION_ID="<account id>"
AZURE_CLIENT_ID="<app id>"
AZURE_CLIENT_SECRET="<password>"

export AZURE_TENANT_ID AZURE_SUBSCRIPTION_ID AZURE_CLIENT_ID\
  AZURE_CLIENT_SECRET
```

Save the file, for instance in Linux to `~/.azure/vagrant.sh`. These variables must be exported before you can use Vagrant. In a macOS and Linux, you can do that by executing the following:

```
source <file>
```

An SSH key pair must be available. If it's not already done, create them with this:

```
ssh-keygen
```

The last step involves the installation of the Azure plugin for Vagrant:

```
vagrant plugin install vagrant-azure
```

Verify the installation:

```
vagrant version
```

```
student@azure01:~$ vagrant version
Installed Version: 2.1.2
Latest Version: 2.1.2

You're running an up-to-date version of Vagrant!
```

Deploying a virtual machine with Vagrant

To deploy a virtual machine with Vagrant, you'll need a working directory and a file called Vagrantfile:

```
# Require the Azure provider plugin
require 'vagrant-azure'

# Create and configure the Azure VMs
Vagrant.configure('2') do |config|

  # Use dummy Azure box
  config.vm.box = 'azure-dummy'

  # Specify SSH key
  config.ssh.private_key_path = '~/.ssh/id_rsa'

  # Configure the Azure provider
  config.vm.provider 'azure' do |az, override|
    # Pull Azure AD service principal information from environment
variables
    az.tenant_id = ENV['AZURE_TENANT_ID']
    az.client_id = ENV['AZURE_CLIENT_ID']
    az.client_secret = ENV['AZURE_CLIENT_SECRET']
    az.subscription_id = ENV['AZURE_SUBSCRIPTION_ID']
```

```
    # Specify VM parameters
    az.vm_name = 'aztest'
    az.vm_size = 'Standard_B1s'
    az.vm_image_urn = 'Canonical:UbuntuServer:18.04-LTS:latest'
    az.resource_group_name = 'vagrant'
  end # config.vm.provider 'azure'
end # Vagrant.config
```

The configuration file starts with a statement that the Azure plugin for Vagrant that we installed before is needed. After that, the configuration of the virtual machine starts. To be able to provide a workload with Vagrant, a dummy virtual machine is needed; it's almost an empty file: it only registers Azure as a provider. To get this dummy virtual machine, execute the following command:

```
vagrant box add azure-dummy \
   https://github.com/azure/vagrant-azure/raw/v2.0/dummy.box\
   --provider azure
```

This provider is configured using the environment variables and settings for the virtual machine, such as the resource group name and the size. The az.vm_image_urn is the actual image offered by Azure with the syntax:

```
<publisher>:<image>:<sku>:<version>
```

Besides using standard images, it is possible to use custom VHD files using these directives:

- vm_vhd_uri
- vm_operating_system
- vm_vhd_storage_account_id

Later in this chapter, we will discuss more about this custom VHD files.

Another important value is the name of the virtual machine; it's also used as a DNS prefix. This must be unique! Otherwise, you'll get this error: DNS record `<name>.<location>.cloudapp.azure.com is already used by another public IP.`

Deploy the Vagrant box, the virtual machine:

vagrant up

```
student@azure01:~/ubuntu_lts$ vagrant up
Bringing machine 'default' up with 'azure' provider...
==> default: Launching an instance with the following settings...
==> default:    -- Management Endpoint: https://management.azure.com
==> default:    -- Subscription Id:
==> default:    -- Resource Group Name: vagrant
==> default:    -- Location: westus
==> default:    -- Admin Username: vagrant
==> default:    -- VM Name: linvirt001
==> default:    -- VM Storage Account Type: Premium_LRS
==> default:    -- VM Size: Standard_B1s
==> default:    -- Image URN: Canonical:UbuntuServer:18.04-LTS:latest
==> default:    -- DNS Label Prefix: linvirt001
==> default:    -- Create or Update of Resource Group: vagrant
==> default:    -- Starting deployment
==> default:    -- Finished deploying
==> default: Waiting for SSH to become available...
Enter passphrase for /home/student/.ssh/id_rsa:
==> default: Machine is booted and ready for use!
```

When the machine is ready to use, you can log in using this:

vagrant ssh

The contents of your work directory is copied to /vagrant in the virtual machine. This can be a very nice way to have your some files available in the virtual machine.

Clean up your work with this:

vagrant destroy

> It's possible to create multi-machine boxes as well.

Vagrant provisioners

An easy way to deploy a virtual machine is not the most important feature of Vagrant. The main reason to use Vagrant is to have a complete environment up-and-running; after the deployment, the virtual machines needs configuration. There are provisioners to do to the after-work. You can use the shell provisioner and the file provisioner to be able to run commands and copy files in the virtual machine.

Another possibility is to use Vagrant provisioners for orchestration tools, such as Ansible and Salt. Our next chapter will discuss these tools. This chapter together with the provisioners documentation on the website of Vagrant will help you to configure it. In this section, I want to show you the shell provisioner.

Add this to the bottom of the file:

```
# Configure the Shell Provisioner
config.vm.provision "shell", path: "provision.sh"
end # Vagrant.config
```

Create a little `provision.sh` script, with some simple commands:

```
#!/bin/sh
touch /tmp/done
touch /var/lib/cloud/instance/locale-check.skip
```

Deploy the virtual machine again. Verify whether the file `/tmp/done` is created in the virtual machine:

```
Enter passphrase for key '/home/student/.ssh/id_rsa':
==> default: Running provisioner: shell...
    default: Running: /tmp/vagrant-shell20180807-2269-1i5pqjq.sh
```

Execute this code:

```
vagrant ssh -c "ls -al /tmp/done"
```

Packer (part 1)

It's important for a developer, especially if there are more people working on the same application, to have a standardized environment. If you are not using container technology (see the `Chapter 9`, *Container Virtualization in Azure* and `Chapter 10`, *Working with Azure Kubernetes Service* to read more about this technology), Vagrant is a great tool that helps the developer with this and manage the life cycle of a virtual machine to get things running very fast in a reproducible way. It provisions the setup based on image offerings or a custom VHD. It's everything you need, if you want to develop your application in the cloud.

But if you want more complex environments, building your own images, multi-machine deployments, cross-cloud environments, and so on, it's not completely impossible, but as soon as you try, you really can see that Vagrant is not made for these scenarios.

This is where another product of HashiCorps becomes handy: Packer. In this section, we're going to use Packer with a very similar configuration as we used before with Vagrant.

Installing and configuring Packer

Packer is available for macOS, Windows, several Linux distributions, and FreeBSD. Packages are available to download at `https://www.packer.io/downloads.html`.

Download the package, unzip it, and you're ready to go. In Linux, it's a good idea to create a directory `~/.bin` and unzip it there:

```
mkdir ~/bin

cd /tmp

wget wget https://releases.hashicorp.com/packer/1.2.5/\
  packer_1.2.5_linux_amd64.zip

unzip /tmp/packer*zip
```

Log out, and log in again. Almost every distribution adds the `~/bin` directory to the `PATH` variable as soon it's available, but you have to log out and log in again. Verify the installation:

```
packer version
```

```
student@azure01:~$ packer version
Packer v1.2.5
```

For the configuration of Packer, we'll need the same information as for Vagrant:

- Azure tenant ID (`az account show`)
- Azure subscription ID (`az account show`)
- ID of the service principal account (if you want to use the same one as in Vagrant: `az app list --display-name vagrant`)
- The secret of this account (if needed, you can use `az ad sp reset-credentials` to generate a new one)
- Existing (!) resource group in the correct location; in this example, I'm using Linux on Azure as a resource group name and West Europe as the location (created with the command: `az group create --location "West Europe" --name "LinuxOnAzure"`)

Create a file, for instance `/packer/ubuntu.json` with the following content:

```
{
  "builders": [{
    "type": "azure-arm",

    "client_id": "<app id>",
    "client_secret": "<secret>",
    "tenant_id": "<tenant id>",
    "subscription_id": "<subscription id>",

    "managed_image_resource_group_name": "LinuxOnAzure",
    "managed_image_name": "myPackerImage",

    "os_type": "Linux",
    "image_publisher": "Canonical",
    "image_offer": "UbuntuServer",
    "image_sku": "18.04-LTS",
    "location": "West Europe",
    "vm_size": "Standard_B1s"
  }],

  "provisioners": [{
  "type": "shell",
  "inline": [
  "touch /tmp/done",
  "sudo touch /var/lib/cloud/instance/locale-check.skip"
  ]
  }]
}
```

Validate the syntax:

```
packer validate ubuntu.json
```

Build it:

```
packer build ubuntu.json
```

There are two stages in the build process:

```
==> azure-arm: Running builder ...
    azure-arm: Creating Azure Resource Manager (ARM) client ...
==> azure-arm: Creating resource group ...
==> azure-arm:  -> ResourceGroupName : 'packer-Resource-Group-vhcm2t1rdf'
==> azure-arm:  -> Location          : 'West Europe'
==> azure-arm:  -> Tags             :
==> azure-arm: Validating deployment template ...
==> azure-arm:  -> ResourceGroupName : 'packer-Resource-Group-vhcm2t1rdf'
==> azure-arm:  -> DeploymentName    : 'pkrdpvhcm2t1rdf'
==> azure-arm: Deploying deployment template ...
==> azure-arm:  -> ResourceGroupName : 'packer-Resource-Group-vhcm2t1rdf'
==> azure-arm:  -> DeploymentName    : 'pkrdpvhcm2t1rdf'
==> azure-arm: Getting the VM's IP address ...
==> azure-arm:  -> ResourceGroupName  : 'packer-Resource-Group-vhcm2t1rdf'
==> azure-arm:  -> PublicIPAddressName : 'pkripvhcm2t1rdf'
==> azure-arm:  -> NicName            : 'pkrnivhcm2t1rdf'
==> azure-arm:  -> Network Connection  : 'PublicEndpoint'
==> azure-arm:  -> IP Address          : '40.114.202.106'
==> azure-arm: Waiting for SSH to become available...
==> azure-arm: Connected to SSH!
==> azure-arm: Provisioning with shell script: /tmp/packer-shell859779849
==> azure-arm: Querying the machine's properties ...
==> azure-arm:  -> ResourceGroupName : 'packer-Resource-Group-vhcm2t1rdf'
==> azure-arm:  -> ComputeName        : 'pkrvmvhcm2t1rdf'
==> azure-arm:  -> Managed OS Disk    : '/subscriptions/88525bff-081c-45ad-bc
2t1rdf/providers/Microsoft.Compute/disks/pkrosvhcm2t1rdf'
==> azure-arm: Querying the machine's additional disks properties ...
==> azure-arm:  -> ResourceGroupName : 'packer-Resource-Group-vhcm2t1rdf'
==> azure-arm:  -> ComputeName        : 'pkrvmvhcm2t1rdf'
```

And then another process starts, something with capturing image. It all ends with this:

```
==> Builds finished. The artifacts of successful builds are:
--> azure-arm: Azure.ResourceManagement.VMImage:

ManagedImageResourceGroupName: LinuxOnAzure
ManagedImageName: myPackerImage
ManagedImageLocation: westeurope
```

For sure, Packer deployed something, but not a running virtual machine.

For now, clean everything up with this:

```
az resource delete --resource-group LinuxOnAzure --resource-type images \
  --namespace Microsoft.Compute --name myPackerImage
```

Custom images and VHDs

In the previous section, we used standard VM offerings in Azure and used two different methods to do some configuration work afterward. However, as stated before, there can be reasons that a default image is not the solution for you. Let's summarize the reasons one more time.

There is nothing wrong with using standard images; it's a good starting point for all your deployments in Azure:

- Created and supported by Linux distribution vendors or a trusted partner
- Fast to deploy, both manually and orchestrated, and of course you can customize them afterward
- Easy to extend functionality and options with Azure Extensions

But, sometimes there are problems:

- Standard image is not hardened enough
- Standard image is not compliant with, for example, company standards, especially when it comes to partitioning
- Standard image is not optimized for a certain application
- Non-supported Linux distributions
- Questions about reproducible environments: how long is a certain image version available?

But sometimes it's not good enough: In this section, we will explore possibilities to build your own custom image in Azure.

Creating a managed image

In the previous section, we looked a little bit into Packer. What happened there is that a virtual machine was created, some customization were done, and after that it was transformed into an image. This image can be used to deploy a new virtual machine. This technique is also called *capturing a VM image*.

Let's find out if we can do it, step by step, the manual way, using the Azure CLI:

1. Create a resource group:

   ```
   myRG="capture"
   myLocation="westus"

   az group create --name $myRG--location $myLocation
   ```

2. Create a virtual machine:

   ```
   myVM="ubuntudevel"
   AZImage="UbuntuLTS"
   admin="linvirt"

   az vm create --resource-group $myRG  --name $myVM \
     --image $AZImage \
     --admin-username $admin  --generate-ssh-keys
   ```

3. Log in to the virtual machine and deprovision the virtual machine using the Azure Virtual Agent. It generalizes the virtual machine by removing user-specific data:

   ```
   sudo waagent -deprovision+user
   ```

   ```
   linvirt@ubuntudevel:~$ sudo waagent -deprovision+user
   WARNING! The waagent service will be stopped.
   WARNING! Cached DHCP leases will be deleted.
   WARNING! root password will be disabled. You will not be able to login as root.
   WARNING! /etc/resolvconf/resolv.conf.d/tail and /etc/resolvconf/resolv.conf.d/original will be deleted.
   WARNING! linvirt account and entire home directory will be deleted.
   Do you want to proceed (y/n)y
   ```

   Type `exit` to leave the SSH session.

4. Deallocate the virtual machine:

```
az vm deallocate --resource-group $myRG --name $myVM
```

5. Mark it as being generalized:

```
az vm generalize --resource-group $myRG --name $myVM
```

6. Create an image from the virtual machine in this resource group:

```
destIMG="customUbuntu"

az group create --name $destRG --location $myLocation

az image create --resource-group $myRG --name $destIMG --source
$myVM
```

7. Verify the result:

```
az image list
```

```
student@azure01:/etc/grub.d$ az image list --output table
Location     Name           ProvisioningState     ResourceGroup
----------   -------------  --------------------  ----------------
westus       customUbuntu   Succeeded             CAPTURE
```

8. You can deploy a new virtual machine with this image:

```
az vm create --resource-group <resource group> \
  --name <vm name> \
  --image $destIMG \
  --admin-username <username> \
  --generate-ssh-key
```

If you want to use the manual method in PowerShell, it is also possible. Let's go very quickly through the first steps:

```
$myRG="capture"
$myLocation="westus"
$myVM="ubuntudevel"
$AZImage="UbuntuLTS"

New-AzureRMResourceGroup -Name $myRG -Location $myLocation

New-AzureRmVm `
 -ResourceGroupName $myRG `
 -Name $myVM `
 -ImageName $AZimage `
```

```
-Location $myLocation `
-VirtualNetworkName "$myVM-Vnet" `
-SubnetName $myVM-Subnet `
-SecurityGroupName "$myVM-NSG" `
-PublicIpAddressName $myVM-pip
```

For now, don't bother about the script asking for credentials and let's start at *step 4*:

```
Stop-AzureRmVM -ResourceGroupName <resource group>`
  -Name <vm name>
```

Now convert the VM to a managed disk:

```
ConvertTo-AzureRmVMManagedDisk `
  -ResourceGroupName <resource group> `
  -VMName <vm name>
```

This new cmdlet, makes the process much easier then before!

Alternative method using snapshots

If you want to keep the original virtual machine, you can also create a image from a snapshot. A snapshot in Azure is actually a complete virtual machine!

1. First take the snapshot. In PowerShell:

   ```
   $vm = get-azurermvm -ResourceGroupName <resource group> `
     -Name $vmName

   $snapshot = New-AzureRmSnapshotConfig `
     -SourceUri $vm.StorageProfile.OsDisk.ManagedDisk.Id `
     -Location <location> -CreateOption copy

   New-AzureRmSnapshot `
     -Snapshot $snapshot -SnapshotName <snapshot name> `
     -ResourceGroupName <resource group>
   ```

   Or using the Azure CLI:

   ```
   disk=$(az vm show --resource-group <resource group>\
     --name <vm name> --query "storageProfile.osDisk.name" \
     -o tsv)

   az snapshot create --resource-group <resource group>\
     --name <snapshot name> --source $disk
   ```

2. The last step involves creating the image from the snapshot. In PowerShell, you have to get the configuration of the image first:

```
$imageConfig = New-AzureRmImageConfig -Location <location>

$imageConfig = Set-AzureRmImageOsDisk -Image $imageConfig `
  -OsState Generalized -OsType Linux -SnapshotId $snapshot.Id
```

3. Finally, create the image:

```
New-AzureRmImage -ImageName <image name> `
  -ResourceGroupName <resource group> -Image $imageConfig
```

In Azure CLI, it's easier, just get the id of the snapshot and convert it to a disk:

```
snapshotId=$(az snapshot show --name <snapshot name>\
  --resource-group <resource group> --query "id" -o tsv)

az image create --resource-group <resource group> --name myImage \
  --source $snapshotID --os-type linux
```

Don't forget to generalize the virtual machine, before you snapshot it. If you don't want to do that, create a disk from the snapshot and use that as `--attach-os-disk` disk parameter in Azure CLI or `Set-AzureRmVMOSDisk` in PowerShell.

Packer (part 2)

The JSON file that I provided earlier in this chapter was not complete. It was very similar to what we did with Vagrant, but to make it into a deployable image, we have to add the generalize part. Replace the following code:

```
"provisioners": [{
   "type": "shell",
   "inline": [
     "touch /tmp/done",
     "sudo touch /var/lib/cloud/instance/locale-check.skip"
   ]
```

With the following one:

```
"provisioners": [{
   "type": "shell",
   "execute_command": "echo '{{user `ssh_pass`}}' | {{ .Vars }} sudo -S -E
sh '{{ .Path }}'",
   "inline": [
      "touch /tmp/done",
      "touch /var/lib/cloud/instance/locale-check.skip"
      "/usr/sbin/waagent -force -deprovision+user & export HISTSIZE=0 &&
sync"
   ]
```

The `execute_command` is actually a better way to make sure that everything is started using `sudo` under the correct user.

Build the image again.

Custom VHDs

You can completely build your own image from scratch. In this scenario, you have to build your own VHD file. There are multiple ways to do so:

- Create a virtual machine in HyperV or in the free hypervisor VirtualBox. Both products support VHD natively.
- Create your virtual machine in VMware Workstation or KVM and use in Linux `qemu-img` to convert the image. For Windows the Microsoft Virtual Machine Converter is available at `https://www.microsoft.com/en-us/download/details.aspx?id=42497`. It includes a PowerShell cmdlet `ConvertTo-MvmcVirtualHardDisk` to make the conversion.

> Azure only supports type-1 VHD files and should have a virtual size aligned to 1 MB.

It's almost impossible to describe every available option for each Linux distribution and each hypervisor. In general, these are the things you need to do:

1. Configure the virtual machine the way you want it.
2. Make sure that there is no swap configured/created.
3. Make sure that everything is updated, including the kernel.

4. You'll need to install the HyperV integration services (`https://www.microsoft.com/en-us/download/details.aspx?id=55106`). This possibly involves recreating the `initrd`, using the `mkinitrd --preload=hv_storvsc --preload=hv_vmbus -v -f initrd-`uname -r`.img `uname -r`` command.

5. Install the Microsoft Azure Linux Agent (`https://github.com/Azure/WALinuxAgent`). Don't forget to enable the service.

6. Add the parameters `console=ttyS0,115200n8 earlyprintk=ttyS0,115200 rootdelay=300` to your grub configuration in `/etc/default/grub` and `/boot/grub/grub.cfg`.

7. Generalize using `sudo waagent -force -deprovision;  export HISTSIZE=0`.

8. Shut down the system; if necessary, convert the disk to the correct format.

For the purpose of this book, we're going to cheat, because the most important part is the upload of the image to Azure. Download the cloud image of Ubuntu that is already in VHD format: `http://cloud-images.ubuntu.com/releases/18.04/release/ubuntu-18.04-server-cloudimg-amd64.vhd.zip`.

Now we have to upload the VHD to Azure to start; it's a good idea to have a separate storage account available for images:

```
az storage account create --location <location> \
  --resource-group <resource group> --sku Premium_LRS \
  --name <account name> --access-tier Cool --kind StorageV2
```

Save the output for later use. List the access keys:

```
az storage account keys list --account-name <storage account name>\
  --resource-group <resource group>
```

Save the output again. The next thing we need is a container to store the files:

```
az storage container create \
  --account-name <storage account>\
  --account-key <storage account key 1>
  --name <container name>
```

Now you can upload the VHD:

```
az storage blob upload --account-name <storage account>\
  --account-key <storage account key> \
  --container-name <container name> \
  --type page --file ./bionic-server-cloudimg-amd64.vhd \
  --name bionic.vhd
```

> You can also upload the file using the Azure Portal or PowerShell. Other available methods are the Azure Storage Explorer (https://azure.microsoft.com/en-us/features/storage-explorer/) or the Azure VHD utils (https://github.com/Microsoft/azure-vhd-utils). The last one is amazingly fast!

Receive the blob URL:
```
az storage blob url --account-name <storage account> \
  --account-key <storage account key> \
  --container-name <container name> \
  --name bionic.vhd
```

It's now possible to create a disk from the upload:
```
az disk create --resource-group <resource group> \
  --name bionic --source <blob url> --Location <location>
```

Create a virtual machine image with this disk:

```
az image create --resource-group <resource group> \
  --name bionic --source <blob url> --os-type linux
  --location <location>
```

Create a virtual machine based on this image:

```
az vm create --resource-group <resource group> \
  --name <vm name> \
  --image bionic \
  --admin-username <username> \
  --generate-ssh-key \
  --location <location>
```

> You can make your VHD images public, a nice example of this is a, lesser known, Linux distribution named NixOS. On their website https://nixos.org/nixos/download.html they described a way to deploy their operating system in Azure!

Summary

In this chapter, we started questioning ourselves about why and when you should use automation in Azure. Later on, we added questions around using the images offered by Azure.

With these questions in mind, we explored the options to automate our deployments:

- Scripting
- ARM templates
- Vagrant
- Packer
- Building and using your own images

Vagrant and Packer are examples of third-party solutions that are very popular tools that make it possible to easily create and recreate environments as an important part of your development process.

It's important to know that all the techniques described in this chapter can be combined into a complete solution. For instance, you use cloud-init together with ARM but also with Vagrant.

Automation and orchestration are closely related. In this chapter, we covered automation, especially as a part of development environments, to automate the deployment of virtual machines. Automation is often a difficult solution to maintain your workload after the development and deployment. Here is where orchestration kicks in, as covered in the next chapter.

There is one product of the HashiCorp company that is not mentioned in this chapter, but which is worth investigation: **Terraform**. It crosses the borders between development and production, between automation and orchestration. Configuration files contain everything you need to run your workload. Based on this configuration file, it generates an execution plan describing what it will do to reach the desired state, and then executes it to build the complete infrastructure in Azure. After that, Terraform takes care of the change-management process as well.

Questions

1. What are the main reasons to use automated deployments in Azure?
2. What is the purpose of automation in development environments?
3. Can you describe the differences between scripting and automation?
4. Can you name some of the automated deployment options available in Azure?
5. What is the difference between Vagrant and Packer?
6. Why should you use your own image instead of an image offered by Azure?
7. What options are available to create your own image?

And maybe you can find some time to finish the example script in the section *Scripting*, in the language of your choice.

Further reading

Especially regarding Azure CLI, PowerShell, and ARM, the Azure documentation contains so much valuable information, with many examples. And everything I wrote in the *Further reading* section of the `Chapter 2`, *Getting Started with the Azure Cloud* is important in this chapter as well.

Another resource of Microsoft that provides are their blogs. If you visit `https://blogs.msdn.microsoft.com/wriju/category/azure/` you'll find many interesting postings about automation, including more detailed examples.

Michael S Collier provides on his blog at `https://michaelcollier.wordpress.com` a lot of information regarding Azure, almost every posting includes scripting and automation possibilities.

There are not many recent books about Vagrant. I really enjoined the *Infrastructure as Code (IAC) Cookbook* from Stephane Jourdan and Pierre Pomes, published already one year ago. This book is not only about Vagrant, but covers also other solutions such as cloud-init and Terraform. The authors created a book that is not only a great introduction, but managed to make it useable as a reference guide as well.

Can I suggest a book that is not published at the time of writing? I do think so: *Hands-On DevOps with Vagrant: Implement end to end DevOps and infrastructure management using Vagrant* from Alex Braunton. His postings on YouTube regarding this topic are worth looking for.

James Turnbull is the author of a book about Packer, available as an EBook on Amazon. He also wrote a book about Terraform. Both books are really good introductions if you are completely new to these topics. He is using the Amazon Cloud as an example in his books, but thanks to the way he explains everything, it's easy to make it work in Azure.

Already, the second edition of the book *Getting Started with Terraform* from the author Kirill Shirinkin is on the market. It's a pleasure to read, and, before you know it, you gain a lot of knowledge. This author is also using Amazon; similar to the books of James Turnbull, this shouldn't be a problem. Time for a third edition though!

8
Exploring Continuous Configuration Automation

Until now, we have worked with single virtual machines, deploying and configuring them manually. This is nice for labs and very small environments. But if you have to manage bigger environments, this is a very time-consuming and even a boring job. And it's too easy to make mistakes and forget things, such as the slight differences between virtual machines and so on. Not to mention stability and security risks because of that.

It's time to automate deployment and configuration management using scripts. But after a while, you will notice some problems with that approach. There are so many reasons why. To name a few:

- The script fails because something changed, caused by, for instance, a software update
- There is a newer version of a base image that is slightly different
- The scripts can be hard to read and difficult to maintain
- Scripts are dependent on other components: for instance, the operating system, script language, available internal and external commands
- And, there is always that one colleague—the script works for you but for some reason it always fails if he executes it...

Of course, things have improved over time:

- Many script languages are multi-platform now, such as Bash, Python, and PowerShell. They are available on Windows, macOS, and Linux.
- The systemd utility `systemctl -H` parameter can execute commands remotely, and it works even if the remote host is another Linux distribution. (Little problem: newer systemd version has more features.)
- FirewallD and systemd work with easy-to-deploy configuration files and overrides.

Automation is most likely not the answer in our search to deploy, install, configure, and manage your workload. Luckily there is another way: orchestration.

In musical terms, orchestration is the study of how to write music for an orchestra. You have to understand each instrument and know what sounds they can make. Then you can start writing the music; to do this, you have to understand how they sound together. Most of the time you start with a single instrument, for instance a piano. After that you scale up to include the other instruments. Hopefully, the result will be a masterpiece and members of the orchestra can start playing it. It's not that important how the members start, but in the end the conductor makes sure that the results count.

There are many similarities for orchestration in compute. Before you can start, you have to understand how all components work, how they fit together, and what the components do so you can get the job done. After that, you can start writing the code to receive the ultimate goal: a manageable environment.

One of the biggest advantages of a cloud environment is that really, every component of the environment is written in software. Yes, I know, at the end of the line there is still a data center with many hardware components, but as a cloud user, you don't care about that. Everything you need is written in software and has APIs to talk to. So, it's not only possible to automate the deployment of your Linux workloads, but you can automate and orchestrate the configuration of the Linux operating system and the installation and configuration of applications and keep everything up to date. You can also use orchestration tools to configure the Azure resources, and it's even possible to create Linux virtual machines using these tools.

In orchestration, there are two different approaches:

- Imperative: Tell the orchestration tool what to do to reach this goal
- Declarative: Tell the orchestration tool what the goal you want to achieve is

Some orchestration tools can do both, but, in general, the declarative approach is a better approach in a cloud environment, where things start changing often and where there are too many things you can't be sure of. The good news is that, if it's becoming too complex for this method, for instance when the orchestration tool is not able to understand the goal, you can always extend this method with a little bit of the imperative method, using scripts.

A big part of this chapter is about Ansible, but I'll also cover PowerShell DSC and SaltStack as examples of a declarative implementation. The focus in this chapter is to understand orchestration and know enough to get started. And, of course, I'll discuss the integration with Azure.

Technical requirements

In practice, you'll need at least one virtual machine as a control machine and one as a node. It doesn't matter which Linux distribution you're using. The examples in this section to orchestrate the node are for an Ubuntu node, but it's easy to translate them to other distributions.

In this chapter, multiple orchestration tools are explored. For every tool, you'll need a clean environment. So, when you are finished with the Ansible section in this chapter, remove the virtual machines and deploy new ones before going into SaltStack.

Ansible

In 1993, Mark Burgess made CFEngine, the first big open source config management tool, to make the management of the workstations at the the Department of Theoretical Physics at the Oslo University much easier. In 2009, the company CFEngine Enterprise was founded. CFEngine, which uses an imperative approach, is still in use today. Luke Kaines, one of the developers of CFEngine, got frustrated with CFEngine given the inflexibility and usability problems mostly caused by the imperative approach—it's very similar to scripting in that subtle changes in the environment can break the automation. That's why he created Puppet in 2005.

The founder of Ansible, Michael deHaan, started the development of Ansible in 2006. He had many experiences with deployment tooling. He was the main developer of Cobbler (an automated deployment tool), was working at Puppet Enterprise, and was a senior engineer at rPath, a company that created tooling to create repeatable images for cloud environments. Development of Ansible started slowly, but, in 2013, the company Ansible Inc. was founded, later on acquired by Red Hat.

Ansible is minimal in nature, has almost no dependencies, and it doesn't deploy agents to the nodes. Only OpenSSH and Python are required there. It's also highly reliable: changes can be applied multiple times without changing the result beyond the initial application and there shouldn't be any side effects on the rest of the system (unless you write really bad code). There is a strong focus on the reuse of code, which makes it even more reliable.

Ansible doesn't have a very high learning curve. You can just start with a few lines of code and scale up afterwards without breaking anything. In my personal opinion, if you want to try an orchestration tool, start with Ansible and if you want to try another, the learning curve will be much lower.

Installation of Ansible

In the Azure virtual machine market, a ready-to-go virtual machine is available for purpose. This product contains the Enterprise version of Ansible, including their management software called Ansible Tower. In this book, we concentrate on the open source product that is freely available; it's more than enough to learn and get started with Ansible. After that, you can go to the Ansible website to explore the differences, download the trial version of Ansible, and decide if you need the Enterprise version.

There are multiple ways to install Ansible:

- Using the repository of your distribution
- Using the Ansible repository: `https://releases.ansible.com/ansible`
- Using GitHub: `https://github.com/ansible`
- Using the Python Installer, the preferred method, which works on every operating system:

```
pip install ansible[azure]
```

The Python install pip is not available in the standard repositories of Red Hat and CentOS. You have to use the extra EPEL repository:

```
sudo yum install epel-release
```

```
sudo yum install python-pip
```

After the installation of Ansible, check the version:

```
ansible --version
```

You don't have to install Ansible if you don't want to: Ansible is pre-installed in the Azure Cloud Shell. However, it's better to install Ansible yourself, because the version in the Azure Cloud Shell is pretty old. For integration with Azure, you also need to install the Azure CLI to get the information you'll need to provide to Ansible.

SSH configuration

The machine where you installed Ansible is now called the Ansible or control machine. There is no master-client relationship. It's just a machine with Ansible, the Ansible configuration file, and the instructions on where and what to orchestrate. Communication with the nodes is done with a so-called transport. For Linux, SSH is used as communication protocol. To make Ansible able to communicate in a secure way with the nodes, use key-based authentication. If not already done, generate an SSH keypair and copy the key to the virtual machine you want to orchestrate:

```
ssh-copy-id <user>@<ip address>
```

To make authentication easier, set up the SSH agent:

```
eval $(ssh-agent)

ssh-add
```

Add the following code to your ~/.bash_profile:

```
#SSH
exec ssh-agent $BASH -s 10<&0 << EOF
  ssh-add ~/.ssh/id_rsa &> /dev/null
  exec $BASH <&10-
EOF
```

You can use as many keys as you want; just generate new ones and add the filenames separated by spaces as parameters to ssh-add.

Bare-minimum configuration

To configure Ansible, you'll need an ansible.cfg file. There are three possible locations:

- System-wide configuration in /etc/ansible/ansible.cfg
- ~/.ansible.cfg
- A working directory with all your Ansible stuff

To keep things simple, I suggest you use ~/.ansible.cfg. Create this file and add the following lines to it:

```
[defaults]
inventory = ~/Ansible/hosts
```

Now create a directory, `~/Ansible/`, and create the file hosts and add a line into it with only the IP address of the node you want to manage (which typically is another VM in Azure Cloud). With everything in place, we should be able to communicate with the node.

Let's try:

```
ansible all -a "systemctl status sshd"
```

This command, called an **ad-hoc command**, executes `systemctl status sshd` to all hosts listed in the inventory. Unfortunately, it is possible that it will fail, because it tries to log in with the same username as on your local machine. You'll need a user with administrative (sudo) privileges that is available on the remote host. Edit the inventory file `~/Ansible/hosts` and modify it:

```
<ip address>   ansible_ssh_user='<ansible user>'
```

Try again. Instead of your local username, the remote user is used. You're able to log in and execute the command.

Inventory file

The inventory file is the file that contains the nodes with, if needed, some parameters.

You can use just IP addresses or hostnames, line by line, or group them:

```
[webservers]
 web-01.example.com
 web-02.example.com
```

Instead of using all in our example, you can use web servers. It's also possible to use generic variables that are valid for every host and override them per server. For instance:

```
[all:vars]
ansible_ssh_user='student'

[webservers]
<ip address> ansible_ssh_user='other user'
```

Sometimes, you'll need privileges to execute a command.

```
ansible webservers -a "systemctl restart sshd"
```

It gives the following error message:

```
Failed to restart sshd.service: Interactive authentication required.
 See system logs and 'systemctl status sshd.service' for details.non-zero
return code
```

For ad-hoc commands, just add the -b option as an Ansible parameter to enable privilege escalation. It will use the `sudo` method by default. In Azure images, you don't need to give your root password if you are using `sudo`. This is why the -b option works without a problem. If you configured `sudo` to prompt for a password, use -K.

Ansible playbooks and modules

Using ad-hoc commands is an imperative method and is not any better than just using the SSH client to execute commands remotely.

There are two components that you need to make it into real, imperative orchestration: a playbook and modules. The playbook is the basis for the deployment, configuration, and maintenance of your system. It can orchestrate everything, even between hosts! A playbook is there to describe the state you want to reach. Playbooks are written in the YAML language and can be executed with the `ansible-playbook` command:

```
ansible-playbook <filename>
```

The second component is the module. The best way to describe a module is: the task to be executed to reach the desired state. They are also known as **task plugins** or **library plugins**.

All the available modules are documented; you can find the documentation online and on your system.

To list all the available plugin documentation, execute:

```
ansible-doc -l
```

This will take a while. I suggest that you redirect the result to a file. This way, it takes less time and it's easier to search for a module.

As an example, let's try to create a playbook that will create a user using the user module if the user doesn't already exist. In other words, the desired state is that a specific user exists.

Start by reading the documentation:

```
ansible-doc user
```

Create a file in the Ansible directory, for instance, `example1.yaml`, with the following content. Verify the parameters in the user documentation:

```
---

- hosts: all

  tasks:

  - name: Add user Jane Roe
    become: yes
    become_method: sudo
    user:
      state: present
      name: jane
      create_home: yes
      comment: Jane Roe
      generate_ssh_key: yes
      group: users
      groups:
        - sudo
        - adm
      shell: /bin/bash
      skeleton: /etc/skel
```

Make sure that the indentation is , YAML, is a very strict language when it comes to indentation and white space. Using an editor such as VI, Emacs, or Visual Studio Code Editor with YAML support really helps.

Two parameters are added, become and become_method, as an alternative for the -b parameter, to invoke privilege escalation.

To check the Ansible syntax, use:

```
ansible-playbook --syntax-check Ansible/example1.yaml
```

Finally, execute the playbook:

```
ansible-playbook Ansible/example1.yaml
```

Please note the output:

```
ok=2      changed=1
```

Execute the playbook again; the output is now as follows:

```
ok=2      changed=0
```

Log in to the node; verify if everything is done:

```
sudo gentent passwd jane

sudo id jane

ls /home/jane/.ssh/

ls -ha /etc/skel

ls -ha /home/jane
```

Conditionals – when statement

Let's create a new playbook with another example:

```
---

- hosts: webservers

  tasks:

---

- hosts: webservers

  tasks:

  - name: Install Apache Web Server
    become: yes
    become_method: sudo
    apt:
      name: apache2
      install_recommends: yes
      state: latest
      update-cache: yes
```

If you look into this example, there is a big problem. As we learned in the Chapter 5, *Advanced Linux Administration*, every distribution has its own software management solution. Ansible doesn't have an agnostic approach for every module; for several tasks, a distribution-specific module is needed.

To fix this problem, you can use a conditional: a `when` statement, based on so-called facts. To gather all facts from the listed hosts in your inventory and save them into a file per host, you can use the setup module:

```
ansible all -m setup --tree /tmp/facts
```

It will create files beneath /tmp/facts for every host per file.

Of course, you can do it for one host or group as well:

```
ansible <host or group> -m setup > filename
```

Do it for one of your hosts, and grep on some facts:

- os_family
- distribution

We can use this information for a `when` statement:

```
---
- hosts: webservers

  tasks:

  - name: Install Apache Web Server
    become: yes
    become_method: sudo
    apt:
      name: apache2
      install_recommends: yes
      state: latest
      update-cache: yes
    when:
      - ansible_distribution == "Ubuntu"
      - ansible_distribution_version == "18.04"
```

You can also use >, <, >=, and <= to make your selection or include the and/or keywords:

```
(ansible_distribution == "CentOS" and ansible_distribution_major_version ==
"6") or (ansible_distribution == "Debian" and
ansible_distribution_major_version == "7")
```

Loops

When installing software packages, and with many other tasks as well, using a loop to do multiple tasks at once can be handy.

Create a new playbook with the following content:

```
---
- hosts: webservers
tasks:
- name: Install LAMP
  become: yes
  become_method: sudo
  apt:
    name: "{{ item }}"
    install_recommends: yes
    state: present
    update-cache: yes
    with_items:
      - apache2
      - mysql-server
      - php
      - libapache2-mod-php
      - php-mysql
  when:
    - ansible_distribution == "Ubuntu"
    - ansible_distribution_version == "18.04"
```

Handlers

If the playbook is executed and a task actually changes something on the node, it is possible to trigger an handler. You'll need a notify directive in the task and a handler with the same name as specified in the notify directive.

If nothing has changed, the handler is not executed.

Create a new playbook:

```
---

- hosts: webservers

  tasks:

  - name: Install the Very Secure FTP Server and Client software
    become: yes
```

```
            become_method: sudo
            apt:
              name: "{{ item }}"
              install_recommends: yes
              state: present
              update-cache: yes
            with_items:
              - vsftpd
              - ftp
              - lftp
            when:
              - ansible_distribution == "Ubuntu"
              - ansible_distribution_version == "18.04"
            notify: Start VSFTPD

        handlers:
        - name: Start VSFTPD
            systemd:
              state: started
              name: vsftpd.service
              enabled: yes
```

Log in to the node, and verify:

```
sudo systemctl status vsftpd
```

Now, stop the service:

```
sudo systemctl stop vsftpd
```

Go back to the controller and execute the playbook again. The service will not start again, because the task describes a state that is already reached.

Working with variables

In Ansible, working with variables can make your playbook more readable, flexible, and easier to reuse code. Earlier on, we already used variables in a `for` loop; the variable was used in the task.

Now, we're going to use the `vars` directive. Let's create a new playbook:

```
---

- hosts: webservers
  become: yes
```

```
vars:
  gitrepo: https://github.com/Bash-it/bash-it.git
  gitremote: origin
  gitversion: master
  gitdest: /etc/skel/.bash_it
  gitdepth: 1

tasks:
  - name: deploy from repository
    git:
      repo: "{{ gitrepo }}"
      dest: "{{ gitdest }}"
      remote: "{{ gitremote }}"
      version: "{{ gitversion }}"
      depth: "{{ gitdepth }}"
```

It would be nice to combine this with the creation of a user and execute the `install.sh` script of `bash_it`. One reason is that a handler can't take the `with_items` directive from the task.

Remove the users and the corresponding home directories from the system and create a new playbook:

```
---

- hosts: webservers
  become: yes

  vars:
    users:
      - name: "testuser1"
      - name: "testuser2"

  tasks:
    - name: add users
      user:
        name: "{{ item.name }}"
        state: present
      with_items: "{{ users }}"
      register: users_created

    - debug:
        var: users_created
```

The register directive is added; it saves the result of the task in a variable. The debug directive shows what is in this variable:

```
ok: [Ubuntu02] => {
    "users_created": {
        "changed": true,
        "msg": "All items completed",
        "results": [
            {
                "_ansible_ignore_errors": null,
                "_ansible_item_label": {
                    "name": "testuser1"
                },
                "_ansible_item_result": true,
                "_ansible_no_log": false,
                "_ansible_parsed": true,
                "changed": true,
                "comment": "",
                "create_home": true,
                "failed": false,
                "group": 1002,
                "home": "/home/testuser1",
```

You can select the values of the content with `users_created.results`. The complete playbook is as follows:

```
---

- hosts: webservers
  become: yes

  vars:
    gitrepo: https://github.com/Bash-it/bash-it.git
    gitremote: origin
    gitversion: master
    gitdest: /etc/skel/.bash_it
    gitdepth: 1
    users:
      - name: "testuser1"
      - name: "testuser2"

  tasks:
    - name: deploy from repository
      git:
        repo: "{{ gitrepo }}"
        dest: "{{ gitdest }}"
        remote: "{{ gitremote }}"
```

```
          version: "{{ gitversion }}"
          depth: "{{ gitdepth }}"

      - name: add users
        notify: bash it
        user:
          name: "{{ item.name }}"
          state: present
        with_items: "{{ users }}"
        register: users_created

    handlers:
      - name: bash it
        command: "systemd-run --uid {{ item.name }}
{{item.home}}/.bash_it/install.sh"
        with_items: "{{ users_created.results }}"
```

Working with templates

Deployment of configuration files can be done using the git module and the file module. This method can be used for many different applications, such as the configuration of systemd, FirewallD, and daemons. Ansible can use Jinja2 (http://jinja.pocoo.org/) templating to enable dynamic expressions and access variables. Jinja2 uses filters to transform the data in the variables. After that, the modified data can be used; for instance, it can be written to a file. Jinja2 is in use by many open source projects, including SaltStack.

Let's start with an example:

```
- hosts: webservers
  become: yes
  vars:
    - greeting: 'Hello'
  tasks:
    - name: Ansible Template Example
      template:
        src: Ansible/modt.j2
        dest: /etc/motd
        force: yes
```

The content of modt.j2 is:

```
{{ greeting }} to {{ ansible_hostname }}.
```

The first variable is coming from the playbook; the second one is an Ansible fact.

Execute the playbook and review the contents of the node. Actually, if you log in to the machine, you'll notice that it will greet you with the new message.

This is just a simple example, but it should already give you an idea of what you can do with templates. It can become very powerful using loops in your template file:

```
{% for x in range(3)%}
  This is the {{ x }}th variable
{% endfor %}
```

Using a list of items coming from the `vars` in your playbook:

```
{% for username in users %}
  {{ username }}
{% endfor %}
```

The `vars` in your playbook can also be used to render different templates, each with different sources and destinations:

```
tasks:
    - name: Ansible template with_items example.
      template:
        src: "{{ item.src }}"
        dest: "{{ item.dest }}"
        mode: 0700
      with_items:
        - {src: 'ex.j2',dest: '/tmp/ex1.txt'}
        - {src: 'ex2.j2',dest: '/tmp/ex2.txt'}
        - {src: 'ex3.j2',dest: '/tmp/ex3.txt'}
```

Authenticating to Microsoft Azure

To integrate Ansible with Microsoft Azure, you need to create a configuration file to provide the credentials for Azure to Ansible.

The credentials must be stored in your home directory, in the file `~/.azure/credentials`. First, we have to collect the necessary information with the Azure CLI. Authenticate to Azure:

```
az login
```

```
[
  {
    "cloudName": "AzureCloud",
    "id": "88525bff-_81c-_5ad-ba_1-4e79cc539_F9",
    "isDefault": true,
    "name": "Pay-As-You-Go",
    "state": "Enabled",
    "tenantId": "                                                ",
    "user": {
      "name": "frederik.vos@linvirt.nl",
      "type": "user"
    }
  }
]
```

This is already a part of the information you'll need. If you were already logged in, execute:

```
az account list
```

Create a service principal:

```
az ad sp create-for-rbac --name <principal> --password <password>
```

The app ID is your `client_id`, and the password is your secret.

Create the `~/.azure/credentials` file with the following content:

```
[default]
subscription_id=xxxxxxx-xxxx-xxxx-xxxx-xxxxxxxxxxxx
client_id=xxxxxxx-xxxx-xxxx-xxxx-xxxxxxxxxxxx
secret=xxxxxxxxxxxxxxxx
tenant=xxxxxxx-xxxx-xxxx-xxxx-xxxxxxxxxxxx
```

Use `ansible-doc -l | grep azure` to find out which Ansible modules are available for Azure. Redirect the content to a file for reference.

Resource group

Let's find out if everything works as expected. Create a new playbook with the following content:

```
---

- hosts: localhost
```

```
    tasks:

    - name: Create a resource group
      azure_rm_resourcegroup:
        name: TestingLOA
        location: westus
```

Please notice that the hosts directive is localhost! Execute the playbook and verify:

```
    az group show --name TestingLOA
```

The output should be very similar to the following:

```
{
 "id": "/subscriptions/xxxx/resourceGroups/TestingLOA",
 "location": "westus",
 "managedBy": null,
 "name": "TestingLOA",
 "properties": {
 "provisioningState": "Succeeded"
 },
 "tags": null
 }
```

Virtual machine

Let's create a simple virtual machine. We don't use the resource group created in the previous example, but use a resource group that already exists:

```
    ---

    - hosts: localhost

      tasks:

      - name: Create a CentOS VM
        azure_rm_virtualmachine:
          resource_group: MyLab1
          name: CentOS03
          vm_size: Standard_DS1_v2
          admin_username: student
          admin_password: welk0mITG!
          image:
            offer: CentOS
            publisher: OpenLogic
            sku: '7.5'
            version: latest
```

If you want to create a virtual machine in the `TestingLOA` resource group, you'll need the following Ansible modules to create the necessary resources:

- `azure_rm_storageaccount`
- `azure_rm_virtualnetwork`
- `azure_rm_subnet`
- `azure_rm_publicaddress`
- `azure_rm_securitygroup`
- `azure_rm_networkinterface`

You can find a full example in the Microsoft Azure Guide in the Ansible documentation (`https://docs.ansible.com/ansible/2.5/scenario_guides/guide_azure.html`).

Azure inventory management in Ansible

We have learned two ways to use Ansible in Azure:

- Using Ansible within a inventory file to connect to Linux machines. In fact, it doesn't matter if it's running in Azure or somewhere else.
- Using Ansible to manage Azure resources.

In this section, we're going one step further. Instead of using a static inventory, we will ask Azure what is running in your environment using Dynamic Inventory Scripts.

The first step is to download the Dynamic Inventory Script for Azure:

```
cd ~/Ansible
```

```
wget
https://raw.githubusercontent.com/ansible/ansible/devel/contrib/inventory/azure_rm.py
```

```
chmod +x ~/Ansible/azure_rm.py
```

Edit the file `~/.ansible.cfg` and remove the line `inventory=~/Ansible/hosts`.

Let's do the first step:

```
ansible -i ~/Ansible/azure_rm.py azure -m ping
```

It will probably fail because of authentication problems:

```
[student@centos01 ~]$ ansible -i ~/Ansible/azure_rm.py azure -m ping
 [ERROR]: No handlers could be found for logger
"msrestazure.azure_active_directory"

ubuntu01 | UNREACHABLE! => {
    "changed": false,
    "msg": "Failed to connect to the host via ssh: Permission denied (publickey,
password).\r\n",
    "unreachable": true
}
CentOS03 | SUCCESS => {
    "changed": false,
    "ping": "pong"
}
```

If you have a different login for different virtual machines, you can always use the `remote_user` directive per task.

By creating an `azure_rm.ini` file in the same directory as the `azure_rm.py` directory, you can modify the behavior of the inventory script. Here is an example `ini` file:

```
[azure]
include_powerstate=yes
group_by_resource_group=yes
group_by_location=yes
group_by_security_group=yes
group_by_tag=yes
```

It works very similar to the hosts file. The section [azure] means all virtual machines. You can also provide sections for the following:

- Location name
- Resource group name
- Security group name
- `key` tag
- `key_value` tag

Another method to select one or more virtual machines is using tags. To be able to tag a virtual machine, you'll need the ID:

```
az vm list --output tsv
```

Now you can tag the virtual machine:

```
az resource tag --resource-group <resource group> \
  --tags webserver --id </subscriptions/...>
```

You can also tag the virtual machine in the Azure Portal:

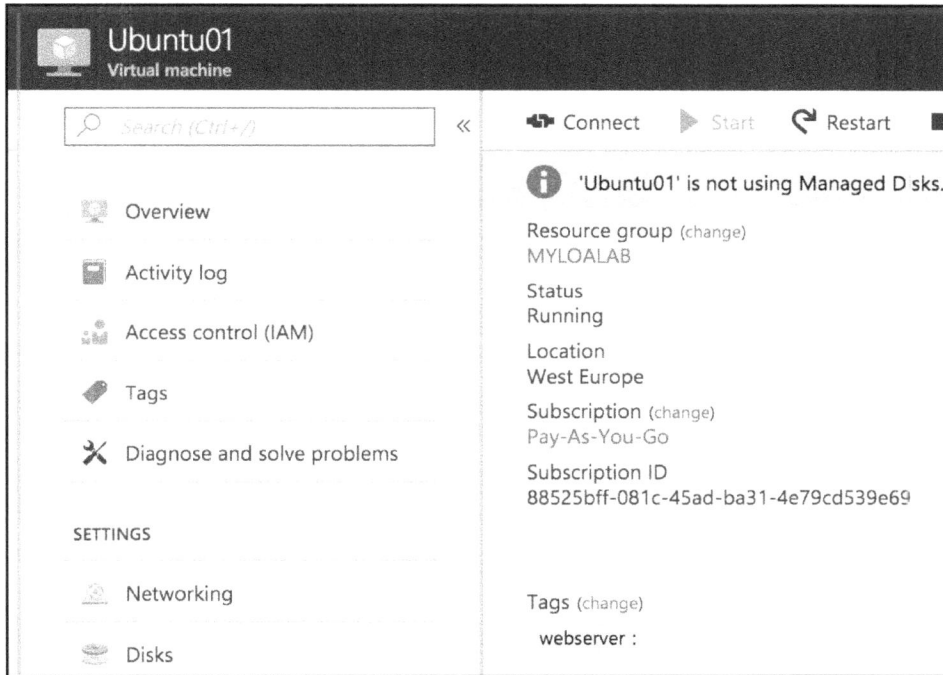

Click on **change** and add a tag, with or without a value (you can use the value to filter the value too). To verify, use the tag name host:

```
ansible -i ~/Ansible/azure_rm.py webserver -m ping
```

Only the tagged virtual machine is pinged. Let's create a playbook for this tagged virtual machine, for instance ~/Ansible/example9.yaml. The tag is, again, used in the hosts directive:

```
---

- hosts: webserver

  tasks:
```

```
   - name: Install Apache Web Server
     become: yes
     become_method: sudo
     apt:
       name: apache2
       install_recommends: yes
       state: present
       update-cache: yes
     when:
       - ansible_distribution == "Ubuntu"
       - ansible_distribution_version == "18.04"
```

Execute the playbook:

```
ansible-playbook -i ~/Ansible/azure_rm.py Ansible/example9.yaml
```

SaltStack

Salt started as a tool to provide a method to execute remote commands. Nowadays, it's a complete open source solution for infrastructure management maintained by the company SaltStack. It's often referred to as SaltStack Platform.

Salt is easy enough to get running in minutes, scalable enough to manage tens of thousands of servers, and fast enough to communicate with them in seconds.

Salt is different from Ansible in terms of architecture. It is a client-server model; communication between the master and the slave is secured by the ZeroMQ transport method using keys for authentication. If you want to use SSH (agentless), it's possible, but the client-server model is chosen because that scales much better than working with many SSH clients at the same time. It is also different in the way you provide the configuration. You can push the configuration to the nodes (push model), or the node can ask for the changes (pull model).

Some Salt terminology

Salt is somewhat special in terms of terminology; before we start installing and using Salt, it will be handy to get familiar with the terms:

- As stated, Salt uses a master/client architecture model, or if you want master/agent. The master is called SALT Master. SALT minions are the nodes the Salt agents installed.
- Configuration description is done using SALT state descriptions.

- SALT execution modules are used by Salt state descriptions to describe the desired state of a resource, for example, installing packages, creating users, and so on.
- GRAINS are configuration information (both inventory and user-defined variables) that are stored on the minions themselves. You can compare them more or less with the facts from Ansible.
- For storing sensitive information, Pillars can be used, which are stored on the SALT Master only.

SaltStack installation

In the Azure marketplace, you can purchase SaltStack Enterprise; it includes a graphical user interface, reporting and audit functions, user-based controls and permissions, a database, and integration with and support for proprietary third-party technologies. In this book, we're going to use the open source version without all the fancy stuff and install the software on a Linux distribution of your choice.

Again, there are multiple ways to install Salt; using the bootstrap method is a very good way to install the software. It installs everything you need and it works the same for every distribution.

On the virtual machine that you want to use as a Salt Master, execute:

```
curl -L https://bootstrap.saltstack.com -o install_salt.sh

sudo sh install_salt.sh -M
```

In the Salt minion virtual machine, execute:

```
curl -L https://bootstrap.saltstack.com -o install_salt.sh

sudo sh install_salt.sh
```

If you are using a firewall, make sure that TCP ports 4505 and 4506 are open.

We're not going to go deep into the configuration; normally all defaults are good to start with. The only thing that is important is that the minion is going to search for the hostname salt for the Salt Master. The easiest way to fix that is by adding an entry into /etc/hosts:

```
<private ip> salt
```

It also makes sense to add an entry for your minion on the Salt Masters' host file. Normally, you should configure your DNS server to make this all happen, but for our lab environment it will do.

Authorization

On the Salt minion, run the following command:

```
sudo salt-call state.apply
```

The `salt-call` command is used to run module functions locally on a minion instead of executing them from the master. It can also be used for stand-alone configurations or if you want to use the pull model. `state.apply` means just apply all configured states:

```
[ERROR   ] The Salt Master has cached the public key for this node, this salt mi
nion will wait for 10 seconds before attempting to re-authenticate
Minion failed to authenticate with the master, has the minion key been accepted?
```

Now log in to the Salt Master and execute:

```
sudo salt-key
```

To find out that the key is indeed in an unaccepted state, execute:

```
sudo salt-key -a <hostname>
```

Let's execute again:

```
sudo salt-call state.apply
```

```
local:
----------
          ID: states
    Function: no.None
      Result: False
     Comment: No Top file or master_tops data matches found.
     Changes:

Summary for local
------------
Succeeded: 0
Failed:    1
------------
Total states run:     1
Total run time:    0.000 ms
```

SALT using states to apply configuration management on the Minions using state files in YAML format or another structured format. And it seems that there is something missing...

Execution modules

Before configuring our first state, log in to the Salt Master and run a final test:

```
salt '*' test.ping
```

In this example, we use the execution module test, one of the state modules with the function ping and apply it to all minions. There are hundreds of other modules available.

To list them all, run:

```
salt '*' sys.doc
```

Let's try one:

```
sudo salt '*' ip.get_interface
```

```
        Passed invalid arguments to ip.get_interface: get_interface() takes exactl
1 argument (0 given)

        Return the contents of an interface script

        CLI Example:

        .. code-block:: bash

            salt '*' ip.get_interface eth0
```

Salt is very helpful in correcting your mistake:

```
salt '*' ip.get_interface eth0
```

The output clearly suggests that this is maybe what you wanted.

In Ubuntu-based distributions this is not going to work, because there is no network interface script, but a `systemd-networkd` configuration instead. The command `salt * network.interfaces` is more useful.

Salt states

Running ad-hoc commands is especially nice to test a module or to receive some information when you're writing state files. Time to write your first state file. Create a file `/srv/salt/example1.sls`:

```
mc:
  pkg.installed
```

Push the state:

```
salt '*' state.apply example1
```

Don't mention the file extension! It will install the mc package on the minions.

Another state is example2.sls:

```
john:
  user.present:
    - fullname: John Tester
    - home: /home/testuser1
    - shell: /bin/bash
    - groups:
      - staff
      - sudo
      - webmaster
```

Applying the state will fail, because the webmaster group doesn't exist. Modify the file:

```
john:
  user.present:
    - fullname: John Tester
    - home: /home/testuser1
    - shell: /bin/bash
    - groups:
      - staff
      - sudo
      - webmaster
    - require:
      - group: webmaster

webmaster:
  group.present
```

Try again. Salt allows for the building of relationships between states with requisite statements.

Top file

Until now, we have applied the state to all minions. To include all the state files at once, you'll need at least one environment. Most of the time, it's called the base environment. Create a file, `/srv/salt/file_root`:

```
file_roots:
  base:
    - /srv/salt
```

This means all files for the base environment are stored in `/srv/salt`. To include the different files for `base`, create a `top.sls` file:

```
base:
  '*':
    - example1
    - example2
```

With everything in place, let's try the pull model now. Go back to the minion and execute:

```
sudo salt-call state.apply
```

The previous error messages are gone.

Salt grains

Salt provides an interface to the underlying system. It is very similar to that of Ansible facts. A list of the available grains can be received by executing:

```
salt '*' grains.ls
```

It can also be received using the item function, for instance:

```
salt '*' grains.item osfullname
```

This information can be used in a state file:

```
apache:
  pkg.installed:
    {% if grains['os'] == 'RedHat' %}
    - name: httpd
    {% elif grains['os'] == 'Ubuntu' %}
    - name: apache2
    {% endif %}
```

State conditions

In the previous example, an *if - then* construction was shown. You can use a *for i in* construction as well:

```
{% for member in ['john','jane','linda'] %}
{{ member }}:
  user.present
{% endfor %}
```

Additionally, a `watch` directive is available, similar to Ansible's handlers:

```
vsftpd:
  pkg.installed: []
  service.running:
    - watch:
      - file: /etc/vsfpd/vsftpd.conf
    - require:
      - pkg: vsftpd
```

This state makes sure that `vsftpd` is installed and that when the configuration file is changed, the service restarts. The `watch` is a part of the service declaration. Note: not every state supports it. There are some exceptions, such as the module run. Luckily, there is an alternative available. The following example is taken from the manual (`https://docs.saltstack.com/en/latest/ref/states/requisites.html`):

```
myservice:
  pkg.installed:
    - name: myservice
  file.managed:
    - name: /etc/myservice/myservice.conf
    - source: salt://myservice/files/myservice.conf
    - mode: 600
  cmd.run:
    - name: /usr/libexec/myservice/post-changes-hook.sh
    - onchanges:
      - file: /etc/myservice/myservice.conf
```

The source can be `http://` or a subdirectory of `/srv/salt`.

Working with variables and templates

We already worked with variables using *if - then* and *for i in* conditionals. If you want to use variables to make your state file more readable and flexible, you can do so using statements such as:

```
{% set remote_user = 'testuser1' %}
```

You can use this variable later on, for instance:

```
- user: {{ remote_user }}
```

The conditionals and variables are all in the Jinja language. The same language as is used in Ansible. You can use Jinja for templating as well:

```
/etc/motd.conf:
  file.managed:
    - source: salt://motd.conf
    - template: jinja

# greetings.sls {% set greeting = "Hello" %}

# motd.conf
{% from 'greetings.sls' import greeting %}
{{ greeting }} from {{ grains['os'] }}
```

Integration with Azure

Salt support with Azure is a work in progress (as stated in their documentation at `https://docs.saltstack.com/en/latest/topics/cloud/azure.html`); on top of that the documentation about Salt and Azure is not always up to date and accurate.

The support for Azure is somewhat limited if you compare it to Ansible. The resources that you can manage are:

- Virtual machines
- Virtual networks
- Certificates
- Endpoints such as load-balancers
- Storage accounts and Blob storage
- Affinity groups

To install the cloud support, you have to rerun the bootstrap script:

```
sh install_salt.sh -LM
```

The support for Azure is not completely up to date in the current release, but it's not very difficult to make it work. First of all, you need the Azure libraries from Python; the easiest method is to install azure-cli with pip.

Receive your Azure account settings:

```
az account list
```

Create a service principal:

```
az ad sp create-for-rbac --name <principal> --password <password>
```

Create a file, `/etc/salt/cloud.providers.d/azure.provider.conf`, with the following content:

```
azure:
  driver: azure
  minion:
    master: salt
  certificate_path: /etc/salt/azure.pem
  subscription_id: <azure subscription id>
  tentant: <azure tenant id>
  client_id: <service principal>
  secret:
  resource_group: <resource group>
```

Create a certificate set:

```
cd /etc/salt

openssl req -x509 -nodes -days 365 -newkey rsa:1024 \
  -keyout azure.pem -out azure.pem

openssl x509 -inform pem -in azure.pem -outform der -out azure.cer
```

Go to the Azure Portal. In the left bar, select **All Services** and search for `Subscriptions`. Go to **Management certificates** and upload your `azure.cer` certificate:

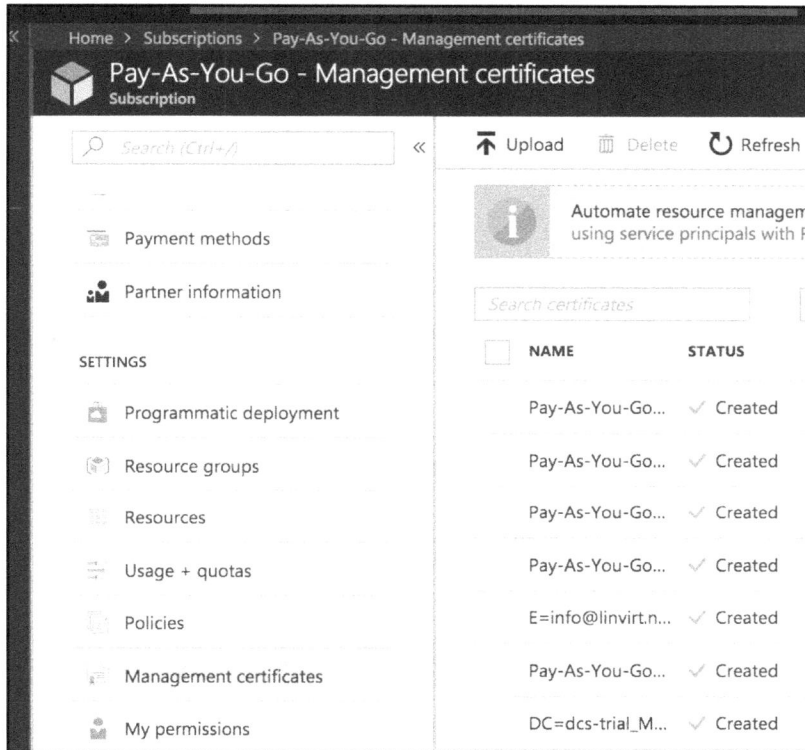

List the images that are available:

```
salt-cloud --list-images azure
```

List their sizes:

```
salt-cloud --list-sizes azure
```

The Blob management in salt-cloud is not complete yet. You can create a storage account and a container, but it is not possible to create a Blob. You have to do this with the Azure Portal. Afterwards, you can review the URL with `azure-cloud`:

```
salt-cloud -f make_blob_url azure container=<container> blob=<blob>
```

Now you can create a profile for virtual machines, for instance, `/etc/salt/cloud.profiles.d/azure.profiles.conf`:

```
azure-ubuntu:
  provider: azure
  image: 'b39f27a8b8c64d52b05eac6a62ebad85__Ubuntu-18_04-LTS-amd64-
server-20180517-en-us-30GB'
  size: Small
  location: 'West US'
  ssh_username: student
  ssh_password: welk0mITG!
  media_link: 'https://storageaccount.blob.core.windows.net/vhds'
  slot: production
```

Create a new virtual machine instance named `Ubuntu04`:

```
salt-cloud -p azure-ubuntu ubuntu04 -l debug
```

The first time, especially, it's necessary to add the debugging parameter. The error message shown is most of the time not the real error message, but the latest one.

PowerShell desired state configuration

Like Bash, PowerShell is a shell with strong scripting possibilities. Although I do believe that PowerShell is more in use as a scripting language in script files than as an interactive Shell. But PowerShell is more: it is a task automation and configuration management framework.

Desired State Configuration (DSC) is an important, but lesser known, part of PowerShell that instead of automating scripts in the PowerShell language, provides declarative orchestration in PowerShell.

If you compare it to Ansible, the support for Linux is very limited. But it is very usable for common administration tasks and missing features can be compensated with PowerShell scripts. Microsoft is very focused on getting it on par with the possibilities for Windows Server. At that time, it will be replaced with PowerShell DSC core, a move very similar to what they did before with PowerShell | PowerShell Core. This will be finished by the end of 2019.

Another important note is that for some reason the Python scripts coming with DSC don't work—from time to time, you'll get a `401` error or even an undefined one. First make sure that you have the latest version of the OMI server and DSC and just try again; sometimes you have to try two or three times.

Azure automation DSC

One way to use DSC is to use Azure Automation DSC. This way, you don't have to use a separate machine as a controller node. To be able to use AADSC, you'll need an Azure automation account.

Automation account

In the **Azure Portal**, select in the left bar **All Services**, navigate to the **Management Tools**, and choose automation accounts. Create an automation account and make sure that you choose **Run As Account**.

Navigate again to **All Services** then **Management Tools**, and select the just-created account:

Here you can manage your nodes, configurations, and so on.

Please note that this service is not exactly free. Process automation is priced per job execution minute, while configuration management is priced per managed node.

To be able to use this account, you'll need the registration URL and corresponding key of your **Run As Account**. Both values are available under **Account** and **Key Settings**.

Or in PowerShell:

```
Get-AzureRmAutomationRegistrationInfo `
  -ResourceGroup <resource group> -AutomationAccountName <automation acc>
```

There is a virtual machine extension available for Linux; this way you can deploy virtual machines, including their configuration, fully orchestrated.

For more information, visit `https://github.com/Azure/azure-linux-extensions/tree/master/DSC` and `https://docs.microsoft.com/en-us/azure/virtual-machines/extensions/dsc-linux`.

Because we're going to play with Linux and DSC, we'll need a DSC module called `nx`. In the settings of your Automation Account, select **Shared Resources and Modules**. In the tab **Browse Gallery**, search for `nx` and import the module.

Installing PowerShell DSC on Linux

To be able to use PowerShell DSC on Linux, you'll need the Open Management Infrastructure Server.

The software is available for download at `https://github.com/Microsoft/omi`. Installation on Red Hat-based distributions:

```
sudo yum install \
  https://github.com/Microsoft/omi/releases/download/\
  v1.4.2-3/omi-1.4.2-3.ssl_100.ulinux.x64.rpm
```

In SUSE, replace yum with `zypper`. For Ubuntu, use:

```
sudo dpkg -i omi-1.4.2-3.ssl_110.ulinux.x64.deb
```

After the installation, the service is automatically started. Verify:

```
sudo systemctl status omid.service
```

To show product and version information including the used configuration directories, use:

```
/opt/omi/bin/omicli id
```

```
[root@centos01 bin]# /opt/omi/bin/omicli id
instance of OMI_Identify
{
        [Key] InstanceID=2FDB5542-5896-45D5-9BE9-DC04430AAABE
        SystemName=centos01
        ProductName=OMI
        ProductVendor=Microsoft
        ProductVersionMajor=1
        ProductVersionMinor=4
        ProductVersionRevision=2
        ProductVersionString=1.4.2-3
        Platform=LINUX_X86_64_GNU
        OperatingSystem=LINUX
        Architecture=X86_64
        Compiler=GNU
        ConfigPrefix=GNU
        ConfigLibDir=/opt/omi/lib
        ConfigBinDir=/opt/omi/bin
        ConfigIncludeDir=/opt/omi/include
        ConfigDataDir=/opt/omi/share
        ConfigLocalStateDir=/var/opt/omi
        ConfigSysConfDir=/etc/opt/omi/conf
        ConfigProviderDir=/etc/opt/omi/conf
        ConfigLogFile=/var/opt/omi/log/omiserver.log
        ConfigPIDFile=/var/opt/omi/run/omiserver.pid
        ConfigRegisterDir=/etc/opt/omi/conf/omiregister
        ConfigSchemaDir=/opt/omi/share/omischema
        ConfigNameSpaces={root-omi, root-Microsoft-DesiredStateConfiguration, root-M
icrosoft-Windows-DesiredStateConfiguration}
```

PowerShell DSC packages are available at `https://github.com/Microsoft/PowerShell-DSC-for-Linux/releases`. Installation on Red Hat-based distributions:

```
sudo yum install \
  https://github.com/Microsoft/PowerShell-DSC-for-\
  Linux/releases/download/v1.1.1-294/dsc-1.1.1-294.ssl_100.x64.rpm
```

In SUSE, again use zypper instead of yum. Ubuntu:

```
sudo dpkg -i dsc-1.1.1-294.ssl_100.x64.deb
```

Check the websites of PowerShell DSC and OMI regularly to see if newer versions are available.

Use the command `openssl version` to verify which OpenSSL version is installed on your system.

Check if everything went well:

```
sudo /opt/microsoft/dsc/Scripts/GetDscLocalConfigurationManager.py
```

In PowerShell, install the `nx` module:

```
Install-Module nx
```

Creating a desired state

PowerShell DSC is not just executing a script, or like in Ansible, a program with parameters. You start with a configuration file that must be compiled into a **Management Object Format** (**MOF**) file.

But, first things first. Let's create a file, `example1.ps1`, with the following content:

```
Configuration webserver {
Import-DscResource -ModuleName PSDesiredStateConfiguration,nx

Node "ubuntu01"{
    nxPackage apache2
    {
        Name = "apache2"
        Ensure = "Present"
        PackageManager = "apt"
    }
  }
}
webserver
```

Let's investigate this configuration. As stated, it's very similar to a function declaration. The configuration gets a label and is executed at the end of the script. The necessary modules are imported, the hostname of the virtual machine declared, and the configuration starts.

PowerShell DSC Resources

In this configuration file, a resource is used, called `nxPackage`. There are several built-in resources available:

- `nxArchive`: Provides a mechanism to unpack archive (`.tar`, `.zip`) files at a specific path.
- `nxEnvironment`: Manages environment variables.
- `nxFile`: Manages Linux files and directories.
- `nxFileLine`: Manages individual lines in a Linux file.
- `nxGroup`: Manages local Linux groups.
- `nxPackage`: Manages packages on Linux nodes.
- `nxScript`: Runs scripts. Most of the time, this is used to switch temporarily to a more imperative orchestration approach.
- `nxService`: Manages Linux services (daemons).
- `nxUser`: Manages local Linux users.

You can also write your own resources in the MOF language, C#, Python, or C/C++

There is no help available; you have to visit the documentation available at `https://docs.microsoft.com/en-us/powershell/dsc/lnxbuiltinresources`.

Save the script and execute the script:

```
pwsh -file example1.ps
```

As a result of the script, a directory is created with the same name as the configuration name. In it is a localhost file in the MOF format. It is the language used to describe CIM classes, where CIM stands for **Common Information Model**. It's an open standard for management of a complete environment, including hardware (build-in software or not). In the CIM model, every element is represented as a part of similar objects and it describes the relationship with other elements.

I do think that only this description is enough to understand that Microsoft chooses this model and the corresponding language file for orchestration!

You can also upload the configuration file to Azure, under **DSC Configurations**. Press the **Compile** button to generate the MOF file in Azure.

Applying the resources in Azure

If you want, you can apply the desired state locally, using scripts in `/opt/microsoft/dsc/Scripts`, which is, in my opinion, not as easy as it should be. And because this chapter is about orchestration in Azure, we'll just go straight ahead to Azure.

Register the virtual machine:

```
sudo /opt/microsoft/dsc/Scripts/Register.py \
  --RegistrationKey <automation account key> \
  --ConfigurationMode ApplyOnly \
  --RefreshMode Push --ServerURL <automation account url>
```

Check the configuration again.

```
sudo /opt/microsoft/dsc/Scripts/GetDscLocalConfigurationManager.py
```

The node is now visible in the DSC nodes pane under your Automation Account settings. Now you can link the uploaded and compiled DSC configuration. The configuration is applied!

Another way is to use the **Add Node** option and then select the DSC configuration.

Other solutions

Another big player in the orchestration market is Puppet. Until very recently, the support for Azure in Puppet was very limited, but that is changing very fast. The Puppet module `puppetlabs/azure_arm` is still in a somewhat early stage, but Puppetlabs/Azure provides you with everything you'll need. Both modules needs `azure-cli` to work. The integration in their commercial Puppet Enterprise Product is amazingly good. Azure has a virtual machine extension available for virtual machines that will become Puppet nodes.

More information can be found at:

`https://puppet.com/products/managed-technology/microsoft-windows-azure.`

The Chef software provides an automation and orchestration platform that has been around for a long time. Development started in 2009! The user writes "recipes" that describe how Chef manages the "kitchen" using tools such as a knife. In Chef, many terminologies come from the kitchen. Chef integrates very well with Azure, especially if you use Chef Automate from the Azure marketplace. There is also a virtual machine extension available. Chef is meant for big environments and has a relatively high learning curve, but it's worth trying it at least.

More information can be found at: `https://www.chef.io/partners/azure/`.

Summary

I started this chapter with a little introduction to orchestration, why you want to use orchestration, and the different approaches: imperative versus declarative.

After that I covered Ansible, Salt, and PowerShell DSC platforms. Many details were covered about the following:

- How to install the platform
- Working with resources at the OS level
- Integration with Azure

Ansible is by far the most complete solution, and maybe the one with the lowest learning curve. However, all of the solutions are very powerful and there are always ways around the limitations. And for all orchestration platforms, the future is promising in terms of even more features and capabilities.

Creating Linux virtual machines is not the only way to create a workload in Azure; you can also use container virtualization to deploy a platform for your application. In the next chapter, we're going to cover container technologies.

Questions

For this chapter, let's skip the normal questions. Fire up some virtual machines and choose the orchestration platform of your choice. Configure the network security groups to allow HTTP traffic.

Try to configure the following resources with Ansible, SaltStack, or PowerShell DSC:

1. Create a user and make it a member of the group wheel (RH-based distributions) or `sudo` (Ubuntu).
2. Install an Apache web server, serve content from `/wwwdata`, and secure it with AppArmor (Ubuntu) or SELinux (RH-based distributions) and serve a nice `index.html` page on this web server,
3. Restrict SSH to your IP address. HTTP ports must be open to the whole world. You can use systemd methods by providing override files or FirewallD.
4. Deploy a new virtual machine of the distribution and version of your choice.
5. Create a new `/etc/hosts` file using variables. If you use PowerShell DSC, you'll need PowerShell as well for this task. For experts: use the hostnames and IP addresses of other machines in your resource group.

Further reading

I really hope that you enjoyed the introduction to the orchestration platforms. It's only a fast introduction to make you curious to learn more. All the websites of the orchestration tools mentioned in this chapter are great resources and a pleasure to read.

Some extra resources to mention:

- **PowerShell DSC**: The book, *Pro PowerShell Desired State Configuration: An In-Depth Guide to Windows PowerShell DSC* by Ravikanth Chaganti, published by Apress, and the videos of Prajeesh Prathap that are published at Packt Publishing are a must. The *Hey, Scripting Guy!* blog (`https://blogs.technet.microsoft.com/heyscriptingguy`) is always a very good place to start if you want tutorials about PowerShell and PowerShell DSC.

- **Ansible**: I do think that *Learn Ansible* by Russ McKendrick and other titles by the same author about Ansible deserve a lot of credit. If you are too lazy to read the book, try it, dive further into the Ansible documentation, don't read it! But if you do, you'll become a master. For the lazier people: there is a nice tutorial available at `https://github.com/leucos/ansible-tuto`.

- **SaltStack**: There are, so far as I know, no recent books about SaltStack. That doesn't mean that the old books are completely useless. *Learning SaltStack* (the second edition) is a good and solid read. Yes, I already mentioned the websites of the orchestration tools, but did I mention the blog of SaltStack? On `https://saltstack.com/blog/`, you'll not only find marketing and social-related stuff, but also cool tutorials.

Container Virtualization in Azure

In the `Chapter 2`, *Getting Started with the Azure Cloud*, of this book, we started our journey in Azure with the creation of our first workload in Azure: the deployment of a Linux virtual machine. After that, we covered many aspects of the Linux operating system.

In `Chapter 7`, *Deploying Your Virtual Machines*, we explored several options to deploy your virtual machine, and in the previous chapter, it was all about what to do afterwards in terms of configuration management, using orchestration tooling.

Orchestration is more and more a part of a sort of a movement called DevOps. DevOps is about breaking down the classic silos in an organization. The different teams involved in developing, testing, and deploying products must communicate and work together. DevOps is a combination of cultural philosophies, practices, and tools. And DevOps is a way to make deployments incremental, frequent, and routine events while constraining the impact of failure.

Virtual machines are not the only way to deploy workloads: you can also deploy your workload with something called containers. It makes it possible, together with orchestration, to fulfill the wishes of DevOps.

A container is not the Holy Grail, it doesn't fix all your problems, but if the following is true, container technology is a great way to deploy workloads:

- There is a need for applications that often need updates with new features, preferably without downtime, driven by business needs.
- System engineers and developers can work together to reply to business needs and have enough understanding and knowledge of both sites (without being a specialist on both), including a culture of continual experimenting and learning.

- There is room for failure, in order to make the application better.
- The application is not a single point of failure.
- The application is not a critical application in terms of availability and security.

Maybe one little other thing: if you have many different types of applications and there is almost no code shared between the applications, container technology is still an option, but it's possible that virtual machines are a better solution in this scenario.

In this chapter, I'll cover a little bit of history of container technology to have a better understanding where it comes from. After that, we'll explore some of the solutions available today: systemd-nspawn, Rkt, and Docker. There are more container virtualization implementations available, even some of the earliest implementations such as LXC. In fact, that doesn't matter: if you understand the ideas and concepts behind it, it's easy to implement others. That's why we start covering systemd-nspawn and that the biggest part of this chapter is about the most widely used one, Docker.

History of containers

Containers are very popular nowadays. But they are not new, they didn't come out of the blue. It's even not easy to point to an exact time when they started. As explained earlier, I don't want to give you a lesson in the facts of history, but history can give you a better understanding of the technology and even give you a clue about why or when you should use it in your organization.

So instead of focusing on an exact timeline, I'll only cover the important steps, implementations of technologies that are important to understand container technology as it is today.

Chroot environment

In Linux, there is a root filesystem, as covered in `Chapter 5`, *Advanced Linux Administration*, and everything is mounted to that filesystem. It is the root filesystem as known as, visible to process 1 and all the child processes.

A process running in chroot experiences it's own root filesystem, fully separated from the system-wide root `fs`. chroot is often implemented to limit the impact of a process on the filesystem. (S)FTP servers are most often run in so called **chroot jails**. When the services get compromised, the damage is only local to the FS represented in the chroot jail. It is also often used in development. Install a minimal Linux filesystem, including a shell and some libraries in a separate directory, install your application in the same directory, and execute the following:

```
chroot /<directory>
```

This method was often used as a test environment, before containers become popular for development.

The `chroot` system-call was introduced into Version 7 Unix in 1979 and introduced into BSD Unix in 1982. Linux has had this system-call implemented since the early days of its existence.

OpenVZ

In 2005, a company called Virtuozzo, almost at the same time that Solaris started their container technology, started the OpenVZ project.

They took the principle of the chroot environment and applied it to other resources. A process can have its own:

- Root filesystem
- Users and groups
- Devices
- Process tree
- Network
- Interprocess communication objects

At that time, OpenVZ was seen as a lightweight alternative for virtualization based on hypervisor and also as a solid platform for developers. It still exists and you can use it on top of every Linux operating system, running in the cloud or not.

Using OpenVZ is more similar to using a virtual machine: create an image with a base installation of your favorite distribution and, if you want, after that you can use orchestration to install the application and maintain everything.

LXC

Engineers at Google started in 2006 working on a feature in the Linux kernel called **cgroups** (**control groups**) to enable resource control on resources such a CPU, memory, disk I/O and network for collections of processes (resource groups).

A related feature of the Linux kernel is the concept of **namespace isolation**: the possibility to isolate resource groups, so that they cannot see resources in other groups. So cgroups became a namespace itself.

In 2008, cgroups was merged into the Linux kernel and new namespace was introduced, the user namespace. Both technologies were then enabled for a new step in containers: LXC.

Other available namespaces are: pid, mount, network, uts (own domain name), and ipc.

There is no need any longer to keep on par with Linux kernel development: every component needed is available and there is much better resource management.

Currently, Canonical is developing a new project, LXD. Their website states the following:

LXD builds on top of LXC, to provide a new, better user experience. Under the hood, LXD uses LXC through liblxc and its Go binding to create and manage the containers.

It's basically an alternative to LXC's tools and distribution template system with the added features that come from being controllable over the network.

Systemd-nspawn

Systemd comes with a container solution. It started as an experiment around 2013, but in 2015 the main developer Lennart Poettering considered it as ready for production. It is in fact the base for another solution: Rkt.

Systemd-nspawn is not very well known, but it is a powerful solution that is available on every modern Linux system. It is built on top of the kernel namespaces and systemd for management. It's a sort of chroot on steroids.

Containers can be created using package managers such as yum and by extracting raw cloud images (several distributions provides such images, for instance https://cloud.centos.org/centos/7/images and https://cloud-images.ubuntu.com/). You can even use Docker images!

If you want to learn more about the underlying technologies of containers, systemd-nspawn is a good start. Here, every component is visible and can be configured manually if you want. The downside of systemd-nspawn is that you have to do everything on your own: from creating the image, orchestration, to high availability: all possible, but you have to build it.

As stated, there are multiple ways to create a container. As an example, I'll cover two of them: debootstrap and yum.

Creating a container with debootstrap

The debootstrap utility is a tool which will install a Debian or Ubuntu base system into a subdirectory of another, already installed system. It is available in the repositories of SUSE, Debian, and Ubuntu; on CentOS or other Red Hat-based distributions, you'll need to pull it from the EPEL repository.

As an example, let's bootstrap Debian on a CentOS machine to create a template for our systemd containers.

For the purposes of this chapter, if you are running it on CentOS, you have to change the security label for systemd-nspawn:

```
semanage fcontext -a -t virtd_lxc_exec_t /usr/bin/systemd-nspawn
 restorecon -v /usr/bin/systemd-nspawn
```

First, install debootstrap:

```
sudo yum install epel-release
```

```
sudo yum install debootstrap
```

Create a subdirectory:

```
sudo mkdir -p /var/lib/machines/releases/stretch
```

```
sudo -s
```

```
cd /var/lib/machines/releases
```

And bootstrap, for instance, from the US mirror of Debian:

```
debootstrap --arch amd64 stretch stretch \
   http://ftp.us.debian.org/debian
```

Creating a container with yum

Yum is available in every repository and can be used to create a container with a Red Hat based distribution.

Create a directory in which to install CentOS and that will be used for our template:

```
sudo mkdir -p /var/lib/machines/releases/centos7

sudo -s

cd /var/lib/machines/releases/centos7
```

First, you have to download the `centos-release` rpm package from `http://mirror.centos.org/centos-7/7/os/x86_64/Packages/`.

Initialize the `rpm` database and install this package:

```
rpm --rebuilddb --root=/var/lib/machines/releases/centos7

rpm --root=/var/lib/machines/releases/centos7 \
   -ivh --nodeps centos-release*rpm
```

Now, you are ready to install at least the bare minimum:

```
yum --installroot=/var/lib/machines/releases/centos7 \
   groups install  'Minimal Install'
```

After the installation of the packages, a complete root-filesystem is available, providing everything that is needed to boot the container. You can also use this root-filesystem as a template; in that scenario, some work must be done, to make sure that every container is unique.

systemd-firstboot

systemd-firstboot is a nice way to configure a few things if you start the container for the first time. You can configure the following parameters:

- The system locale (--locale=)
- The system keyboard map (--keymap=)
- The system time zone (--timezone=)
- The system hostname (--hostname=)
- The machine ID of the system (--machine-id=)
- The root user's password (--root-password=)

You can also use the -prompt parameter to ask for this parameters at first boot.

Execute chroot into the container directory. Let's take our CentOS image as an example:

```
chroot /var/lib/containers/releases/centos7

passwd root
```

Fire-up the image:

```
systemd-nspawn --boot -D centos7
```

Open the systemd-firstboot unit, /usr/lib/systemd/system/systemd-firstboot.service and modify it:

```
[Unit]
Description=First Boot Wizard
Documentation=man:systemd-firstboot(1)
DefaultDependencies=no
Conflicts=shutdown.target
After=systemd-readahead-collect.service systemd-readahead-replay.service
systemd-remount-fs.service
Before=systemd-sysusers.service sysinit.target shutdown.target
ConditionPathIsReadWrite=/etc
ConditionFirstBoot=yes

[Service]
Type=oneshot
RemainAfterExit=yes
ExecStart=/usr/bin/systemd-firstboot --locale=en_US-utf8 --root-
password=welk0mITG! --timezone=Europe/Amsterdam
```

```
StandardOutput=tty
StandardInput=tty
StandardError=tty
```

Enable the service:

```
systemctl enable systemd-firstboot
```

Clean up the settings:

```
rm /etc/\
  {machine-id,localtime,hostname,shadow,locale.conf,securetty}
```

Exit the chroot environment with *Ctrl + D*.

Deploying the first container

If you are using the BTRFS filesystem and the template directory is a subvolume, you can use the --template parameter of systemd-nspawn. It will create a new subvolume, otherwise:

```
cd /var/lib/machines/releases
```

```
cp -rf centos7/ /var/lib/machines/centos01
```

Time to boot our first container:

```
systemd-nspawn --boot -D centos01
```

Try to log in and kill it with *Ctrl +]]]*.

From now on, you can manage the containers with the machinectl command:

```
machinectl start <machine name>
```

Log in with the following:

```
machinectl login <machine name>
```

There are many other parameters of machinectl worth investigating! If you get a permission denied, think about SELinux troubleshooting! Also, journalctl has a parameter -M to see the logging within the container, or use the following:

```
journalctl _PID=<pid of container> -a
```

If you execute `hostnamectl` in the container, you'll see something similar to the following:

```
[root@centos01 ~]# hostnamectl
      Static hostname: n/a
   Transient hostname: centos01
            Icon name: computer-container
              Chassis: container
           Machine ID: 75a8d3f58d9b47ce9e15f3f8e6aecae4
              Boot ID: e7374a2812ab4a64920accabb3753f7f
        Virtualization: systemd-nspawn
      Operating System: CentOS Linux 7 (Core)
          CPE OS Name: cpe:/o:centos:centos:7
                Kernel: Linux 3.10.0-862.3.3.el7.x86_64
          Architecture: x86-64
```

The kernel is the one of the host!

Enabling a container at boot time

To make a container available at boot time, enable the target `machines.target`:

```
sudo systemctl enable machines.target
```

Now create an nspawn file, for instance, for our container:
`/etc/systemd/nspawn/centos01.nspawn`. The filename must be the same as the
container:

```
[Exec]
PrivateUsers=pick

[Network]
Zone=web
Port=tcp:80

[Files]
PrivateUsersChown=yes
```

`[Network]` also sets up port forwarding from TCP port `80` in the container to port `80` on
the host. You have to configure an IP address on the network interface in the container and
on the host on the virtual Ethernet interface in the subnet to make it work.

Now enable the virtual machine:

```
sudo machinectl enable centos01
```

Rkt

Container Linux, formerly known as CoreOS, was developed in 2013 as a very small Linux distribution optimized as a host for running containers. They started with using Docker, but in 2014 they switched to their own container technology, Rkt, which is heavily dependent on systemd-nspawn. In January 2018, the company behind Container Linux was acquired by Red Hat.

While it is perfectly possible to install Rkt on other distributions (for more information, visit `https://coreos.com/rkt/docs/latest/distributions.html`), in this section I'm going to use Container Linux. You can simply deploy via the latest stable version via the Azure Portal or use the Azure CLI/PowerShell method.

In the Azure Marketplace, Container Linux is still available under the old name CoreOS at the time of writing. This will change in the near future.

Getting started with Rkt

The virtual machine is ready to go, just log in and the most important utility is available at your service is **rkt**. There is no daemon involved!

Execute the following:

```
rkt version
```

This will enable you to find out a little bit more about rkt:

```
linvirt@rkt01 ~ $ rkt version
rkt Version: 1.30.0
appc Version: 0.8.11
Go Version: go1.9.6
Go OS/Arch: linux/amd64
Features: -TPM +SDJOURNAL
```

Like systemd-nspawn, there is no such a thing as a repository with images. If you need images, create your own. Besides creating your own, it's very happy running containers from others, such as Docker. The developers even created a website, https://quay.io/, to make conversions very easy. Let's use that website to create our first container. Execute the following:

```
sudo rkt run --interactive quay.io/coreos/alpine-sh
```

Your first App Container Image (ACI) is downloaded and running. To import Docker containers directly, you can use the following:

```
sudo rkt run --interactive docker://ubuntu
```

Sometimes, the signature is not found (for instance, if you are using a Docker repository). If you get an error about the signatures, add the parameters --insecure-options=image.

The Alpine ACI is running now; exit it with *Ctrl+]]]*. Back in the Container Linux environment, you can list the stored images:

```
sudo rkt list
```

The output should be something similar to this:

```
linvirt@rkt01 ~ $ sudo rkt list
UUID          APP          IMAGE NAME                          STATE
98db8f3d      alpine-sh    quay.io/coreos/alpine-sh:latest exited
```

If you are looking in the available help, using rkt help, the list parameter refers to something called **pod**. Time for a more detailed explanation. Rkt is using App Containers (appc), available in an image format ACI. This ACI is a tarball containing the root filesystem and a manifest file. A pod contains one or more appcs with some additional metadata for the complete pod.

In the feature, maybe Rkt is going to switch to the OCI format, an open standard from the Open Container Initiative (part of the Linux Foundation). At least, there is a lot of work going on to fully support this format. The status of this work can be found on https://github.com/rkt/rkt/projects/4.

To find more about the status of the pod, you'll need the UUID as provided in the output of the `rkt list` command:

```
linvirt@rkt01 ~ $ sudo rkt status 98db8f3d
state=exited
created=2018-07-28 10:39:37 +0000 UTC
started=2018-07-28 10:39:37 +0000 UTC
networks=default:ip4=172.16.28.2
pid=1394
exited=true
```

The list of stored images can be found using the following:

```
sudo rkt image list
```

```
linvirt@rkt01 ~ $ sudo rkt image list
ID                        NAME
sha512-6426eb927234       coreos.com/rkt/stage1-coreos:1.30.0
sha512-2222d0a86708       quay.io/coreos/alpine-sh:latest
```

To run the container again, you'll need the NAME or ID:

```
sudo rkt run <ID>
```

If you want to enter the container:

```
sudo rkt run --interactive
```

Another interesting parameter is `--exec` to execute a command in the container and get the output in your current. An image such as Alpine doesn't provide a running application, just a shell. If you really want it running in the background, you can use the following:

```
sudo systemd-run --slice=machine rkt run <id> --interactive
```

There is also a command `rkt` run-prepared, which makes running a pod more interactively easier, and on top of that you can mount volumes and set up a container network. In this book, I will not cover working with prepared pods or multiple container; in the next chapter, it will be more clear why.

A little bit of Shell scripting can help to execute commands. For instance, create an alias to stop all pods:

```
alias podstop="for pod in \
  $(sudo rkt list --no-legend | awk '{print $1}'); \
  do rkt stop $pod; done"
```

Creating Rkt images with acbuild

To be able to work with Rkt images, we'll need extra software to install.

The utility acbuild can be used to create images. The tool is unsupported, but stable. Download the latest build from https://github.com/containers/build/releases and extract the archive:

```
mkdir ~/bin

cd /tmp

wget https://github.com/containers/build/releases/download\
  /v0.4.0/acbuild-v0.4.0.tar.gz

tar xf acbuild-v0.4.0.tar.gz -C ~/bin
```

Remove the ~/.bash_profile and create a new one:

```
# /etc/skel/.bash_profile

# This file is sourced by bash for login shells. The following line
# runs your .bashrc and is recommended by the bash info pages.
if [[ -f ~/.bashrc ]] ; then
  . ~/.bashrc
fi

export PATH=$PATH:$HOME/bin
```

Then, create a /etc/profile.d/acbuild.sh:

```
export PATH=$PATH:/home/<username>/bin
```

Let's build a new image, and use Ubuntu as a base. First, become root:

```
sudo -i
```

Start the build, using the Ubuntu as a base dependency:

```
acbuild --debug begin docker://ubuntu
```

Set the name of the container and some additional information:

```
acbuild --debug set-name test/apache2

acbuild --debug label add arch amd64

acbuild --debug label add os linux
```

Update the Ubuntu image:

```
acbuild --debug run -- apt update

acbuild --debug run -- apt upgrade
```

Install Apache:

```
acbuild --debug run -- apt install apache2
```

Open port 80:

```
acbuild --debug port add http tcp 80
```

Apache must be started in the foreground:

```
acbuild --debug set-exec -- /usr/sbin/apachectl -e info -DFOREGROUND
```

Save the results and quit the `acbuild` environment:

```
acbuild --debug write --overwrite apache2-linux-amd64.aci

acbuild --debug end
```

Finally, run the container:

```
rkt run apache2-linux-amd64.aci --insecure-options=image
```

Check the status:

```
rkt status $(rkt list | awk '/apache2/ {print $1}')
```

The output should be similar to the following:

```
rkt01 linvirt # rkt status $(rkt list | awk '/apache2/ {print $1}')
state=running
created=2018-07-29 12:05:07 +0000 UTC
started=2018-07-29 12:05:07 +0000 UTC
networks=default:ip4=172.16.28.2
pid=5084
exited=false
```

You can also execute a simple test with the following:

```
curl <ip address>
```

Exit the container with *Ctrl+]]]* and execute it using `systemd-run`:

```
rkt image list
```

```
systemd-run --slice=machine rkt run <image id> --net=host
```

The parameter `--net=host` makes port `80` available on the host. Execute `curl` again, but now with `127.0.0.1` as the IP address!

Creating Rkt images with Buildah

The `acbuild` utility works well, but is unsupported and there is a new tool on the horizon: Buildah (`https://github.com/projectatomic/buildah`). It's under heavy development, but stable enough to use.

At the moment, it is not possible to install it in Linux container. There are several reasons for this: one is that the tool itself cannot be run in a container, another one is that you have a physical or virtual machine dedicated to development. After the development phase, you can push it to a production environment.

Installation of Buildah is, thanks to the heavy development, not always that easy as it should be. I strongly suggest using a Fedora 28 server for it. If you want a virtual machine in Azure, the publisher `tunnelbiz.com` provides one. This virtual machine comes with a small additional cost.

At the moment, Buildah is not working if SELinux is configured in the enforcing state. You have to set the state to permissive.

Install the necessary dependencies:

```
sudo dnf -y install make golang bats ostree btrfs-progs-devel \
    device-mapper-devel glib2-devel gpgme-devel \
    libassuan-devel libseccomp-devel ostree-devel \
    git bzip2 go-md2man runc containers-common jq
```

Install an older version of Buildah with the following:

```
sudo dnf -y install buildah
```

Or install the latest version, cloned from GitHub:

```
mkdir ~/buildah

cd ~/buildah

export GOPATH=$(pwd)

git clone https://github.com/projectatomic/buildah \
    ./src/github.com/projectatomic/buildah
```

Then, compile it:

```
cd ./src/github.com/projectatomic/buildah

make

sudo make install
```

You also need a convertor from Docker to ACI format (as long as OCI is not fully implemented in Rkt):

```
git clone git://github.com/appc/docker2aci

cd docker2aci

./build.sh

sudo cp bin/docker2aci /usr/local/bin/
```

Like acbuild, Buildah must be executed as root:

```
sudo -i
```

Let's create a script, using the exact equivalents of acbuild:

```
#!/bin/bash -x
container=$(buildah from ${1:-ubuntu})

buildah config --arch amd64 $container
buildah config --os linux $container
buildah run $container -- apt update
buildah run $container -- apt upgrade
buildah run $container -- apt install apache2
buildah config --cmd "/usr/sbin/apachectl -e info -DFOREGROUND" \
   $container
buildah config --port 80 $container
buildah commit $container ${2:-test/apache2}
```

View the images:

```
buildah images
```

The output should be similar to the following:

```
[root@fedora01 linvirt]# buildah images
IMAGE ID            IMAGE NAME
735f80812f90        docker.io/library/ubuntu:latest
8be34820f18d        localhost/test/apache2:latest
```

You can push the image to a remote repository but, for now, export it to a local archive:

```
buildah push <image id> oci:apache2:latest

tar cvf apache2.oci -C apache2 .
```

And convert it:

```
docker2aci --image apache2:latest apache2.oci
```

If this fails with an error message Image not found, fix it using the following procedure:

```
cd apache2/

mkdir -p refs/

jq -j '.manifests[] | (tostring + "\u0000")' index.json |\
   xargs -0 -n1 sh -c 'tag=$(echo $0 |\
   jq .annotations[\"org.opencontainers.image.ref.name\"] -r); echo \
   $0 > refs/$tag'
```

And create the OCI file again.

Docker

In March 2010 Solomon Hykes started the development of Docker. It started in France as an internal project of the company dotCloud. Thanks to a the public release on a big Python conference in 2013 and the interest of Red Hat, Docker really took off. In the last quarter of that same year, the name of the company was changed to Docker Inc. At the time of writing, Docker is by far the biggest player in container virtualization.

Docker was originally built on top of LXC but after a while, LXC was replaced with their own libcontainer library.

The architecture of Docker is quite complex: it consists of a client, Docker, and a daemon, `dockerd`. Another daemon, `containerd`, is an abstraction layer for OS and type of container technology that is being used. You can interact with containerd using the (docker-) containerd-ctr utility. The `containerd` daemon is responsible for the following:

- The registry (where you can store images)
- The image (building, metadata, and so on)
- Networking
- Volumes (to store persistent data)
- Signing (trust on content)

At the end, containerd communicates with RunC, which is responsible for the following:

- Life cycle management
- Runtime information
- Running commands within the container
- Generating the specs (image ID, tags, and so on)

Docker is available in a **Community Edition** (**CE**) and **Enterprise Edition** (**EE**). The EE version add on top of Docker support, but also an integrated security framework, certified plugins, and support for RBAC/AD/LDAP.

Docker installation

There are multiple ways to install and use Docker CE in Azure. You can install a Linux distribution of your choice and install Docker on top of it. There are several virtual machines available in the Azure Marketplace, such as the Docker on Ubuntu Server that was created by Canonical and Microsoft together. Another interesting choice is RancherOS, which is a very minimal Linux distribution that is especially created to run Docker. And last but not least, there is the Docker for Azure template that is provided by Docker on `https://docs.docker.com/docker-for-azure`.

For the purposes of this chapter, the Docker on Ubuntu Server virtual machine is absolutely not a bad idea; it saves a lot of work! But there are several reasons not to use this virtual machine:

- It really can help to understand things better if you configure everything yourself.
- The software used is relatively old.
- The Docker VM extension that is used to create the virtual machine is deprecated and not in active development any longer.

The Docker for Azure template also installs and configures Docker Swarm, a Docker-native clustering system; that's something for our next chapter.

The Docker website provides excellent documentation about how to install Docker manually. One of the methods is using an installation script. Please notice that this script is convenient for lab environments, but not for production environments.

It installs the latest version of Docker, coming from the Edge channel, not from Stable. In theory, this can be a little bit unstable.

However, for the purposes of this chapter, it's a good way to getting started. To get things up and running very fast, let's use a technique learned in `Chapter 7`, *Deploying Your Virtual Machines*.

Start with creating a new resource group, for instance, `Docker_LOA`:

```
az group create --name Docker_LOA --location westus
```

Create a cloud-init configuration file; in my example, the file is named `docker.txt` with the following content:

```
#cloud-config
package_upgrade: true
write_files:
- content: |
    [Service]
    ExecStart=/usr/bin/dockerd
  path: /etc/systemd/system/docker.service.d/docker.conf
- content: |
    {
        "hosts": ["fd://","tcp://127.0.0.1:2375"]
    }
  path: /etc/docker/daemon.json
runcmd:
  - curl -sSL https://get.docker.com/ | sh
 - usermod -aG docker <ssh user>
```

Don't forget to replace `<ssh user>` with the login name of the account you're using executing the `az` command.

Create the virtual machine, with the distribution of your choice:

```
az vm create --name UbuntuDocker --resource-group Docker_LOA \
  --image UbuntuLTS --generate-ssh-keys\
  --custom-data docker.txt
```

When the virtual machine is ready, log in and execute the following:

```
sudo systemctl status docker
```

If you get a message `Warning: docker.service changed on disk.` Run `systemctl daemon-reload` to reload `docker.service`, be patient, `cloud-init` is still busy.

Execute the following to receive even more information about the Docker daemon:

```
docker info
```

It's time to download our first container and run it:

```
docker run hello-world
```

```
frederik@Ubuntu01:~$ docker run hello-world
Unable to find image 'hello-world:latest' locally
latest: Pulling from library/hello-world
9db2ca6ccae0: Pull complete
Digest: sha256:4b8ff392a12ed9ea17784bd3c9a8b1fa3299cac44aca35a85c90c5e3c7afacdc
Status: Downloaded newer image for hello-world:latest

Hello from Docker!
This message shows that your installation appears to be working correctly.

To generate this message, Docker took the following steps:
 1. The Docker client contacted the Docker daemon.
 2. The Docker daemon pulled the "hello-world" image from the Docker Hub.
    (amd64)
 3. The Docker daemon created a new container from that image which runs the
    executable that produces the output you are currently reading.
 4. The Docker daemon streamed that output to the Docker client, which sent it
    to your terminal.

To try something more ambitious, you can run an Ubuntu container with:
 $ docker run -it ubuntu bash
```

A docker container is an executed image. To list the available images on your system, execute the following:

```
docker image ls
```

```
frederik@Ubuntu01:~$ docker image ls
REPOSITORY          TAG          IMAGE ID          CREATED
SIZE
hello-world         latest       2cb0d9787c4d      12 days ago
1.85kB              _
```

If you run it again, it will not download an image, but just run it.

Let's download another image:

```
docker run ubuntu
```

After that, list all containers, even the ones that are not running:

```
docker ps -a
```

All containers have the status exited. If you want to keep the container running, you have to add the -dt parameters to the run command.

```
docker run -dt ubuntu bash
```

Verify that it is running by viewing the process list again:

```
docker ps
```

Using the container ID or name, you can execute a command in a container and receive the standard output in your Terminal:

```
docker exec <id> <command>
```

For instance, you can execute the following command:

```
docker exec <id> cat /etc/os-release
```

Attach to the container to verify whether the content is as expected:

```
docker attach <id>
```

And deattach using *Ctrl + P, Ctrl + Q*.

Building Docker images

A Docker image contains layers. For every command you run to add a component to the container, a layer is added. Each container is an image with read-only layers and a writable layer on top of a that. The first layer is the boot filesystem, the second is called base; it contains an operating system. You can pull that from the the Docker Registry (more about the Registry later on) or build it yourself.

If you want to build it yourself, you can do that in a similar way as we saw earlier on with systemd-nspawn containers. For instance, by using debootstrap. First, become root:

```
sudo -i
```

Download and extract Debian Stretch:

```
debootstrap --arch amd64 stretch stretch \
  http://ftp.us.debian.org/debian
```

Create a tarball and import it directly into Docker:

```
tar -C stretch -c . | docker import - stretch
```

Verify:

```
docker images
```

Docker also provides a very minimal base, called scratch.
A Docker image is built from a Dockerfile. Create a working directory:

```
mkdir ~/my-app
```

Then create a Dockerfile. The first line in this file adds the base image as a layer:

```
FROM stretch
```

The second layer contains Debian updates:

```
RUN apt-get --yes update
```

The third layer contains the Apache installation:

```
RUN apt-get --yes install apache2
```

Add the latest layer and run Apache in this read/write layer:

```
CMD /usr/sbin/apachectl -e info -DFOREGROUND
```

Open port 80:

```
EXPOSE 80
```

Save the file and build the container:

```
docker build -t apache_image .
```

If everything went well, the output should show something similar to the following:

```
Successfully built 059e5c8a6315
Successfully tagged apache_image:latest
```

You can test drive:

```
docker run -d <ID>
```

Review the history of the build:

```
docker history <ID>
```

```
root@UbuntuDocker:~/my-app# docker history 059e5c8a6315
IMAGE            CREATED           CREATED BY
059e5c8a6315     6 minutes ago     /bin/sh -c #(nop)  EXPOSE 80
aed0499b4b1c     6 minutes ago     /bin/sh -c #(nop)  CMD ["/usr/sbin/apachectl…
ea4250e29eb1     6 minutes ago     /bin/sh -c apt-get --yes install apache2
7662e8ae8d6d     8 minutes ago     /bin/sh -c apt-get --yes update
af1570b472a2     21 minutes ago
```

Execute docker ps to get the ID of the container and use that to collect information about the container:

```
docker inspect <ID> | less
```

In the output, you can find very interesting information, including the IP address of the container:

```
"Gateway": "172.17.0.1",
"GlobalIPv6Address": "",
"GlobalIPv6PrefixLen": 0,
"IPAddress": "172.17.0.2",
"IPPrefixLen": 16,
"IPv6Gateway": "",
"MacAddress": "02:42:ac:11:00:02",
"Networks": {
```

Use curl to see whether the web server is really running:

```
curl <ip address>
```

Stop the container with the following:

```
docker stop <ID>
```

And run it again:

```
docker run -d <ID> -p 8080:80
```

This makes the website available on localhost port 8080.

You can also use acbuild to build Docker containers.

Docker Machine

There is another way to create Docker containers: Docker Machine. This is a tool that creates virtual machines, installs the Docker Engine and manages them. Like Buildah, it's something you should run on a development machine, physical or not, and execute everything remotely.

Switch back to the Ubuntu machine, where we installed Docker. Install the dependency:

```
sudo apt-install sshfs
```

Download Docker Machine:

```
base=https://github.com/docker/machine/releases/download/v0.14.0 \
  & curl -L $base/docker-machine-$(uname -s)-$(uname -m) \
  >/tmp/docker-machine
```

And install it:

```
sudo install /tmp/docker-machine /usr/local/bin/docker-machine
```

Autocompletion can be very useful:

```
base=https://raw.githubusercontent.com/docker/machine/v0.14.0
for i in docker-machine-prompt.bash docker-machine-wrapper.bash \
  docker-machine.bash
do
  sudo wget "$base/contrib/completion/bash/${i}" \
    -P /etc/bash_completion.d
done
```

Log out and log in again. Verify the version:

```
docker-machine version
```

Using Azure as an driver, you can now deploy a virtual machine:

```
docker-machine create -d azure \
  --azure-subscription-id <subscription id> \
  --azure-ssh-user <username> --azure-open-port 80 \
  --azure-size <size> \
  --name <vm name>
```

Similar to the az login command from the Azure CLI and the Login-AzureRmAccount in PowerShell, you'll be prompted to authenticate via `http://microsoft.com/devicelogin`.

To tell Docker to use the remote environment instead of running containers locally, execute the following:

```
docker-machine env <vm name>

eval $(docker-machine env <vm name>)
```

To verify, execute the following:

```
docker info
```

Among other information, the output shows you that you are using a specific virtual machine running in Azure:

```
Kernel Version: 4.13.0-1018-azure
Operating System: Ubuntu 16.04.4 LTS
OSType: linux
Architecture: x86_64
CPUs: 2
Total Memory: 6.785GiB
Name: ubuntu02
ID: DB54:7BWP:WJER:RZVI:3PHM:7A4N:NAOJ:X
Docker Root Dir: /var/lib/docker
Debug Mode (client): false
Debug Mode (server): false
Registry: https://index.docker.io/v1/
Labels:
 provider=azure
Experimental: false
Insecure Registries:
 127.0.0.0/8
Live Restore Enabled: false
```

And for Docker Machine, execute the following:

```
docker-machine ls
```

The output should be similar to the following:

```
frederik@UbuntuDocker:~$ docker-machine ls
NAME        ACTIVE    DRIVER    STATE      URL
ubuntu02    *         azure_    Running    tcp://104.42.45.213:2376
```

Let's try it:

```
docker run -d -p 80:80 --restart=always nginx
```

Find the IP address of the virtual machine:

```
docker-machine ip <vm name>
```

And use that IP address in a browser to verify that nginx is running.

Docker Machine provides also the possibility to copy files into the virtual machine with the parameter scp or even mount it locally, for instance:

```
mkdir -m 777 /mnt/test
```

```
docker-machine mount <vm name>:/home/<username> /mnt/test
```

Use docker ps to find the running instances, stop, and remove them, to be ready for the next utility.

Docker Compose

Docker Compose is a tool to create a multiple container application, for instance, a web application that needs a web server and a database.

Check for the latest release of Docker Compose on `https://github.com/docker/compose/releases` and install it, replacing the version number in the command with the latest release:

```
sudo curl -L https://github.com/docker/compose/releases/download/1.22.0\
  /docker-compose-$(uname -s)-$(uname -m) \
  -o /usr/local/bin/docker-compose
```

```
sudo chmod +x /usr/local/bin/docker-compose
```

Verify the installation:

```
docker-compose version
```

```
frederik@UbuntuDocker:~$ docker-compose version
docker-compose version 1.22.0, build f46880fe
docker-py version: 3.4.1
CPython version: 3.6.6
OpenSSL version: OpenSSL 1.1.0f  25 May 2017
```

Create a file named `docker-compose.yml` with the following content:

```
wordpress:
  image: wordpress
  links:
    - db:mysql
  ports:
    - 80:80

db:
  image: mariadb
  environment:
    MYSQL_ROOT_PASSWORD: <password>
```

While still being connected to the Azure environment, using Docker Machine, execute the following:

```
docker-compose up -d
```

If the build is successful, two containers are running, which you can verify using docker ps and opening a browser to the correct IP address (`docker-machine ip <vm name>`). The WordPress installer is waiting for you.

Azure container instances

Now we are able to run a container in a virtual machine, we can go one step further: we can use the Azure Container Instances service to run it without managing servers.

You can do that using the Azure Portal: in the left navigation bar, select All Services and search for Container instances:

In the Container image field, fill in nginx:latest. In the next screen, expose port 80 and choose a DNS label:

You can also create containers with the command line using azure-cli:

```
az container create --resource-group <resource group> --name nginx \
    --image nginx:latest --dns-name-label nginx-loa --ports 80
```

You can also use PowerShell:

```
New-AzureRmContainerGroup -ResourceGroupName <resource group> `
  -Name nginx -Image nginx:latest r -OsType Linux `
  -DnsNameLabel nginx-loa2
```

Please note that the DNS label must be unique in your region.

In the output of the commands, the IP address is visible:

```
"ipAddress": {
  "additionalProperties": {},
  "dnsNameLabel": "nginx-loa",
  "fqdn": "nginx-loa.westus.azurecontainer.io",
  "ip": "40.112.132.135",
  "ports": [
    {
      "additionalProperties": {},
      "port": 80,
      "protocol": "TCP"
    }
  ]
},
```

You should be able to access the web server on FQDN and IP address. Query again with the following:

```
az container list
```

Alternatively, execute the following:

```
PS /> Get-AzureRmContainerGroup | Format-List
```

Docker registry

Every time we executed docker run or docker pull (download only), images were fetched from the internet. Where did they come from?

```
docker info | grep Registry
```

The output of the command above gives you the answer: `https://index.docker.io/v1/`. This URL is the official Docker Hub. The Docker Hub, or Docker Store, has also a nice web interface available via `https://hub.docker.com`, an online repository of private and public available Docker images.

The docker search command is available to search this repository. To limit the output of this command, you can add filters:

```
docker search --filter "is-official=true" nginx
```

```
frederik@UbuntuDocker:~/build$ docker search --filter "is-official=true" nginx --no-trunc
NAME              DESCRIPTION                                                      STARS
nginx             Official build of Nginx.                                         9130
kong              Open-source Microservice & API Management layer built on top of NGINX.  209
```

Optionally, add the --no-trunc parameter to see the complete description of the image. In the output, there is also a star rating that can help to select the best available image.

If you create your own account on the website of the Docker Hub, you can use docker push to upload your images to the registry. It is free of charge!

Log in with the following:

```
docker login -u <username> -p <password>
```

Build the image:

```
docker build -t <accountname>/<image>:versiontag .
```

You can also tag the image afterwards:

```
docker tag <tag id> <accountname>/<image>:versiontag
```

For versioning, it is a good idea to use a string such as v1.8.1.2018, which means the first version released on August 1, 2018. If you don't add the version, it is tagged as the latest version.

You can't see the tags using the docker search command. You'll need the web interface or query the Docker API using curl (a tool to transfer data to and from a server) and jq (a tool similar to sed but specifically for JSON data):

```
curl https://registry.hub.docker.com/v2/repositories/library/\
  <image name>/tags/'|jq '."results"[]["name"]
```

Azure container registry

Instead of the service of Docker Inc., you can also use the private Azure Container Registry. This service is not free of charge! Using the Azure service has the advantage that you have all the features of Blob storage (reliability, availability, replication, and so on) and can keep all the traffic within Azure, which makes this registry feature-wise, performance-wise, and cost-wise an interesting option.

The easiest way to create it is by using the Azure Portal. In the left navigation bar, select All Services and search for Container Registry. Click on Add. Don't forget to enable the option Admin User:

If the registry is ready, there will be a popup that the job is finished and you're able to go to the resource:

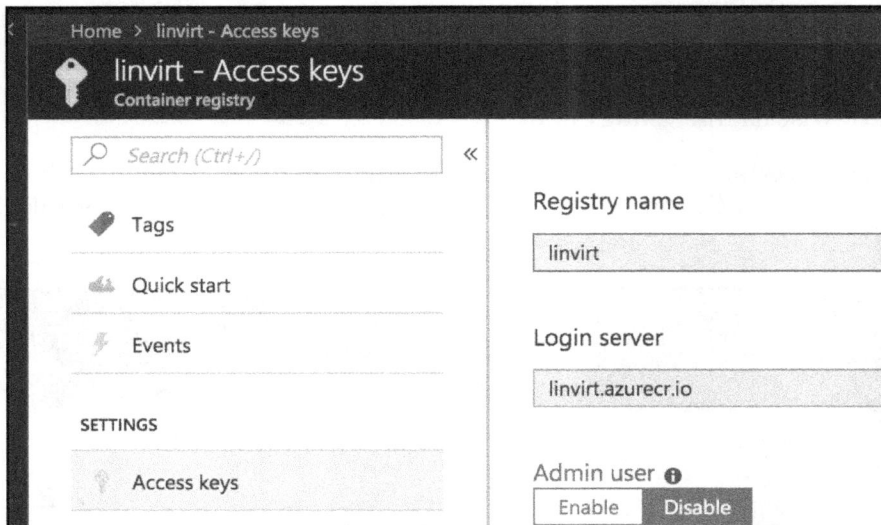

Now you know the login server and your username, which is the same as the registry name. Select Enable and you'll see the provided passwords.

Use this information to log in to the repository, the same way you did with the Docker Hub.

After pushing an image, it will be available under the repositories. From there, you can deploy it to the Azure Container Instance Service and run it.

Containers and storage

The last part of this chapter is about containers and storage. Every build tool that can create images provides the option to add data to your container.

You should use this feature only to provide configuration files. Data for applications should be hosted, as much as possible, outside the container: if you want to quickly update/remove/replace/scale, and so on, your container, it's almost impossible if the data is within the container.

There are often multiple ways to do this: you can use your local storage, or mounts on the host, and so on. Here is just one example in Rkt:

```
rkt run --volume data,kind=host,source=/directory>,readOnly=false \
    <container>
```

This will make /srv/data on the localhost available on /var/data.

For Docker, there are solutions such as `https://github.com/ContainX/docker-volume-netshare`.

If you are using Docker and want to use the Microsoft Azure File Storage, you can use Cloudstor, a plugin that can access it. More information is available at `https://docs.docker.com/docker-for-azure/persistent-data-volumes/`.

Using the Microsoft Azure File Storage solution is maybe not the cheapest solution, but this way you get all the availability and backup options you need.

If you're going to use Kubernetes, it's a whole other story. We'll cover that in the next chapter.

Summary

In this chapter, another way of deploying your workload in Azure was discussed. After an introduction into the history, ideas, and concepts of container virtualization, we went into some of the available options. Together with older implementations such as LXC, they are all great and rock solid implementations to host containers: systemd-nspawn, Rkt, and Docker

We not only saw how to run existing images, pulled from repositories, but also how to create your own image. Maybe the greatest news is that there is a tool called Buildah, which is able to create an image using the OCI standard of the Open Container Initiative that can be used for Docker, but also for Rkt.

The biggest part of this chapter was about Docker. This is by far the most widely implemented container solution today. And talking about implementations, there are really many methods to implement/deploy Docker:

- Deploying it manually in a virtual machine
- Deploying a ready-to-go virtual machine from the marketplace
- Docker machine
- Azure container instances

And last but not least, working with the Docker Hub Registry and the Azure Container Registry was discussed. Don't forget that you can use them with Rkt as well!

We ended the chapter with a few words about containers and storage, already referring to the next chapter, Working with the Azure Container Service; by using Kubernetes, we get even more exciting possibilities with containers.

Questions

1. What are the reasons for using containers?
2. And when are containers not the solution for your needs?
3. If you need something like a virtual private server, do you want a virtual machine, or is there a container virtualization solution available that is maybe a good idea?
4. Why shouldn't it be difficult to migrate from one solution, let's say Docker, to another, for example Rkt?
5. What is the usage for a development machine?
6. Why is using Buildah such a good idea, even if it is under heavy development?
7. Why shouldn't you store application data in a container?

Further reading

Reading further is not a very easy topic in the area of container virtualization. For systemd-nspawn, it's relatively easy: the man pages are an easy read. Maybe a suggestion that is relevant for systemd-nspawn, Rkt, and even Docker: Red Hat provides on their website a document called The Resource Management Guide (`https://access.redhat.com/documentation/en-us/red_hat_enterprise_linux/7/html/resource_management_guide/`) with good information about cgroups.

The documentation for Rkt is not always up to date. Double-check it with their GitHub project: `https://github.com/rkt/rkt/`. It's the same for Container Linux, check out also their GitHub project on `https://github.com/coreos/docs/`. There is a book from Matt Bailey about Container Linux: CoreOS in Action, that is a must-have if you are going to play with Container Linux and Rkt: it really provides everything you'll need BUT a second edition is needed: fleet is replaced with Kubernetes.

What a big difference for Docker: so many blogs, so many books, videos, and so on. At the top of my list is Docker Deep Dive by Nigel Poulton: excellent explanations, good hands-on exercises! The second one is Deployment with Docker from Srdjan Grubor, maybe not a deep-dive but very practical: you can really see that it is written by someone with a lot of field experience and I do think he had some troubleshooting to do during his field work

10
Working with Azure Kubernetes Service

In the previous chapter, we explored the world of container virtualization, especially Docker containers. In this chapter, it's all about managing containerized workloads using **Azure Kubernetes Service** (**AKS**).

This chapter is different from all the other chapters in this book. Until now, in every chapter, it was about infrastructure and providing a platform: the classic system administrator working in the cloud. Even the `Chapter 9`, *Container Virtualization in Azure* has more about questions such as "How can we install Docker?" and "How do we get the container up and running?" The questions I'll answer in this chapter are the following:

- How can we deploy and manage our workload, during the development phase and afterwards?
- How can we scale up/down?
- What are the availability options?

Kubernetes provides an important answer to many of these questions. It is a solution that automates the deployment, management, scaling, networking, and availability of container-based applications.

Kubernetes was originally designed by Google and is now maintained by the Cloud Native Computing Foundation (`https://www.cncf.io`). Microsoft is a big partner of this foundation and is an important distributor to the Kubernetes projects in terms of money and code. Actually, one of the co founders of Kubernetes, Brendan Burns, is working for Microsoft and leads the teams that works on container orchestration within Microsoft. On top of that, Microsoft started several open source projects with additional tooling for Kubernetes.

Because Microsoft is so heavily involved in Kubernetes, it is able to implement a version of Kubernetes in Azure that is fully upstream-compatible. This is also important for developers so they can use a local Kubernetes installation to develop software, and when the development is done, release it to the Azure Cloud.

AKS provides a fully managed container as a service solution for Kubernetes. This means that you don't have to think about the configuration, management, and upgrades of the Kubernetes software. The control plane is managed by Azure.

AKS makes it easy to deploy and manage Kubernetes within Azure: it can handle the complete maintenance process from provisioning, to keeping your applications up to date, and upscaling it to your needs.

Even the process of upgrading your Kubernetes cluster, without any downtime, can be done with AKS.

And last but not least, monitoring is available for every part of your Kubernetes cluster.

Technical requirements

As stated in the introduction of this chapter, this chapter is different from all the other chapters and this affects also the technical requirements. Until now, the technical requirements were easy, you just needed a bunch of virtual machines.

This chapter needs a DevOps environment. Maybe even an environment where not only developers and operators are in the same team, working closely together, but someone who is doing both.

Another choice has to be made: where do we develop? Locally or in the Azure Cloud? Both are possible and it shouldn't make any difference! Cost-wise, it's maybe better to do it on a workstation. In this chapter, I sort of assume that you're doing it locally. So you'll need a workstation (or virtual machine). We need the following:

- Azure CLI and/or PowerShell.
- Docker and build tools.
- Kubernetes.
- Some essential developer tools such as Git.
- Some other tools such as Helma, covered later on.

- A good **integrated development environment** (**IDE**). I prefer Microsoft Studio Code with the Microsoft extensions for Docker and Kubernetes (only if a graphical interface is available, otherwise Vim or Emacs).
- Optionally, an orchestration tool such as Ansible. Please have a look at the Ansible `azure_rm_aks` and `8ks_raw` modules.

Installing dependencies

I am going to use Ubuntu 18.04 LTS Desktop edition. But you can do it on a Ubuntu 18.04 LTS server in an Azure virtual machine as well. With all the knowledge you've gained in the other chapters, it's easy to translate it into other Linux distributions, macOS, and even Windows. Most of this section is a recap of `Chapter 2`, *Getting Started with the Azure Cloud*:

1. First, upgrade Ubuntu:

   ```
   sudo apt update & sudo apt upgrade
   ```

2. Install the developer tools, including some other dependencies and `openssh`:

   ```
   sudo apt install build-essential git curl openssh-server \
     ebtables ethtool socat
   ```

3. First, I am going to install the Azure CLI:

   ```
   sudo apt-add-repository \
     https://packages.microsoft.com/repos/azure-cli

   curl -L https://packages.microsoft.com/keys/microsoft.asc \
     | sudo apt-key add -

   sudo apt update

   sudo apt install azure-cli
   ```

4. To install PowerShell and Visual Studio Code Editor, I am using snaps, universal software packages similar to the Portable Apps for Windows:

   ```
   sudo snap install --classic powershell

   sudo snap install --classic vscode
   ```

5. Install the Azure cmdlet for Azure:

```
sudo pwsh -Command "Install-Module PowerShellGet -Force"

sudo pwsh -Command "Install-Module -Name AzureRM.Netcore \
  -AllowClobber"

sudo chown -R $USER ~/.local/
```

6. Install Docker:

```
curl -sSL https://get.docker.com/ | sudo sh

sudo usermod -aG docker $USER
```

7. Stop Docker for now:

```
sudo systemctl stop docker.service
```

Minikube

Minikube is a tool that makes it easy to run Kubernetes locally. You can use Minikube as a test and development environment and deploy your workload afterwards in Azure. First, we'll need to install the kubectl command. To do so, we're going to use the Azure CLI. To have the correct permissions, you'll have to execute the commands as root:

```
sudo -i

az login

az aks install-cli
```

A command-line tool for one of the components of Kubernetes is also needed:

```
cd /tmp

wget https://github.com/kubernetes-incubator/\
  cri-tools/releases/download/v1.11.1/\
  crictl-v1.11.1-linux-amd64.tar.gz

sudo tar xf crictl-v1.11.1-linux-amd64.tar.gz -C /usr/local/bin/
```

The latest step involves installing Minikube:

```
curl -Lo minikube \
  https://storage.googleapis.com/minikube/releases/v0.28.2/\
  minikube-linux-amd64 & chmod +x minikube & \
  sudo mv minikube /usr/local/bin
```

Check for the latest releases on: https://github.com/kubernetes/minikube/releases.

Make the hostname minikube available on the system:

```
echo "127.0.0.53 minikube" >> /etc/hosts
```

After setting some variables in /etc/profile.d/kubernetes.sh, start the Minikube for the first time:

```
source /etc/profile.d/kubernetes.sh
```

```
sudo -E minikube start --vm-driver=none
```

It will download all the necessary components and start a local Kubernetes cluster. Together with Minikube, the kubectl utility is installed to administer Kubernetes.

Now verify the installation, by asking for the version information:

```
kubectl version
```

> This is completely outside the scope of this book, but I personally like to use the ZSH shell with a nice customization called spaceship. The prompt gives you more insight into where you are and what you are doing, while working with AKS.
>
> Here is the quick installation:
>
> ```
> sudo apt install zsh npm fonts-powerline
> zsh # and create a .zshrc file with option 0
> npm install spaceship-prompt
> chsh -s /bin/zsh
> ```

To enable autocompletion in Bash, execute the following:

```
kubectl completion bash > ~/.kube/completion.bash.inc

printf "
 # Kubectl shell completion
 source '$HOME/.kube/completion.bash.inc'
 " >> $HOME/.bash_profile

source $HOME/.bash_profile
```

For ZSH, execute the following:

```
sudo -i

kubectl completion zsh > "${fpath[1]}/_kubectl"

exit

source <(kubectl completion zsh)
```

> If you are using `kubectl` and you get error messages similar to **Error from server (NotAcceptable): unknown (get nodes)**, downgrade your client, using `https://dl.k8s.io/v1.10.6/kubernetes-client-linux-amd64.tar.gz`.

Starting to use AKS

With Minikube installed, it's time to set up and explore the Kubernetes environment in Azure:

1. Create a cluster
2. Find information about the cluster
3. Deploy a simple workload
4. The Kubernetes components behind the workload

Creating a cluster with the Azure CLI

In Kubernetes, you're going to work with clusters. A cluster contains a master or control plane that is in control of everything and one or more worker nodes. In Azure, you don't have to care about the master, only about the nodes.

It's a good idea to make a new resource group for the purposes of this chapter:

```
az group create --location westus --name MyKubernetes
```

In this resource group, we will deploy our cluster:

```
az aks create --resource-group MyKubernetes \
  --name Cluster01 \
  --node-count 1 --generate-ssh-keys
```

This command can take up to 10 minutes. As soon as you get your prompt back, verify it with the following:

```
az aks list
```

In the output, you'll find a lot of information, such as the full qualified domain name, the name of the cluster, and so on:

```
"location": "westus",
"name": "Cluster01",
"networkProfile": {
  "dnsServiceIp": "10.0.0.10",
  "dockerBridgeCidr": "172.17.0.1/16",
  "networkPlugin": "kubenet",
  "networkPolicy": null,
  "podCidr": "10.244.0.0/16",
  "serviceCidr": "10.0.0.0/16"
},
"nodeResourceGroup": "MC_MyKubernetes_Cluster01_westus",
```

There is a web interface available, called Kubernetes dashboard, to access the cluster. To make it available, execute the following:

```
az aks browse --name Cluster01 --resource-group MyKubernetes
```

Point your browser to `http://127.0.0.1:8001`:

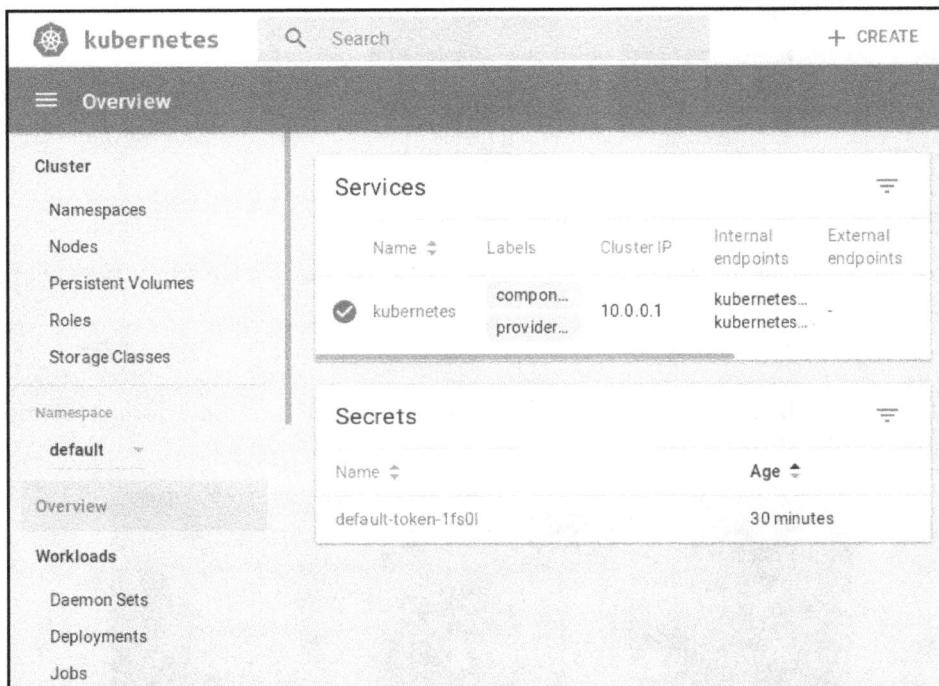

The `az` utility is tunneling the portal to your localhost. Press *Ctrl + C* to exit the tunnel.

To be able to use the `kubectl` utility, we need to merge the configuration into the local configuration file:

```
az aks get-credentials --resource-group MyKubernetes \
  --name Cluster01
```

Thanks to my fancy Command Prompt, you can see that I switched from my local Kubernetes cluster to the cluster in Azure. To see the available clusters, execute the following:

```
kubectl config get-contexts
```

```
→ kubectl config get-contexts
CURRENT    NAME        CLUSTER     AUTHINFO
*          Cluster01   Cluster01   clusterUser_MyKubernetes_Cluster01
           minikube    minikube    minikube
```

You can switch to the other cluster using `kubectl config use-context <cluster>`.

You can also find information about your cluster using `kubectl`:

```
kubectl cluster-info
```

```
→ kubectl cluster-info
Kubernetes master is running at https://cluster01-mykubernetes-88525b-08335046.h
estus.azmk8s.io:443
Heapster is running at https://cluster01-mykubernetes-88525b-08335046.hcp.westus
k8s.io:443/api/v1/namespaces/kube-system/services/heapster/proxy
KubeDNS is running at https://cluster01-mykubernetes-88525b-08335046.hcp.westus.
8s.io:443/api/v1/namespaces/kube-system/services/kube-dns:dns/proxy
kubernetes-dashboard is running at https://cluster01-mykubernetes-88525b-0833504
p.westus.azmk8s.io:443/api/v1/namespaces/kube-system/services/kubernetes-dashboa
roxy

To further debug and diagnose cluster problems, use 'kubectl cluster-info dump'.
```

We asked for one node:

```
kubectl get nodes
```

```
→ kubectl get nodes
NAME                         STATUS    ROLES    AGE    VERSION
aks-nodepool1-18722659-1     Ready     agent    7m     v1.8.14
```

Creating a cluster with PowerShell

You can create the Kubernetes cluster in PowerShell as well.

Create a new resource group:

```
New-AzureRmResourceGroup -Location westus -Name MyKubernetes
```

List the Kubernetes cluster:

```
Get-AzureRmAks
```

After that, you have to install the `kubectl` utility manually (`https://kubernetes.io/docs/tasks/tools/install-kubectl`).

Start the dashboard:

```
Start-AzureRmAksDashboard -ResourceGroupName MyKubernetes `
    -Name Cluster01
```

You can stop it using `Stop-AzureRmAksDashboard`. Import and merge the configuration for `kubectl`:

```
Import-AzureRmAksCredential -ResourceGroupName MyKubernetes `
    -Name Cluster01
```

First deployment in AKS

With a very simple command, we're going to deploy a Docker container in AKS:

```
kubectl run nginx --image=nginx --port=80
```

And within seconds, there is a message: `deployment.apps/nginx created`.

Verify using the following:

```
kubectl get deployment
```

```
➜ kubectl get deployment
NAME      DESIRED   CURRENT   UP-TO-DATE   AVAILABLE   AGE
nginx     1         1         1            1           35m
```

When we executed the `run` command, the Docker container was deployed into the cluster. Or more specifically, a pod was created with the container running in it. A pod is a group of container(s) with shared resources such as storage and network. It's created by a specification for how to run the containers. To see the created pod, execute the following:

```
kubectl get pods
```

```
→ kubectl get pods
NAME                      READY     STATUS    RESTARTS   AGE
nginx-1423793266-7tncg    1/1       Running   0          13m
```

pod come and go; they are created dynamically while scaling up/down, and so on. Using the describe command, you can find all kind of information about the pod:

```
kubectl explain pods/<pod name>
```

Let's delete the pod:

```
kubectl delete pod <pod name>
```

Execute kubectl get pods again; a new one is available.

Creating services

But, actually, you shouldn't care about the pod: the service is important. A service is an object that makes the application accessible to the outside world. Behind the service, there are one or more pod. The service keeps tracks of the pod, their IP addresses, and so on:

```
kubectl get services
```

```
→ kubectl get services
NAME         TYPE        CLUSTER-IP   EXTERNAL-IP   PORT(S)    AGE
kubernetes   ClusterIP   10.0.0.1     <none>        443/TCP    1h
```

Only one service is found, the CLUSTER-IP. A little bit more details can be found using the following:

```
kubectl describe services/kubernetes
```

Let's get rid of our first deployment:

```
kubectl delete deployment nginx
```

And create a new one:

```
kubectl run nginx --image=nginx
```

Please notice that we didn't expose the ports. List the `pod` using `kubectl get pods`. To make the resource accessible, we add a service of the type `LoadBalancer`:

```
kubectl expose pod <pod name> --port=80 --target-port=80 \
  --type=LoadBalancer
```

```
→ kubectl get service
NAME                    TYPE          CLUSTER-IP     EXTERNAL-IP       PORT(S)
kubernetes              ClusterIP     10.0.0.1       <none>            443/TCP
nginx-7c87f569d-vbh7q   LoadBalancer  10.0.135.39    40.118.186.145    80:32161/TCP
```

Use the `EXTERNAL-IP` address in your browser, it will show you the welcome page of nginx.

Multicontainer pods

Having multiple containers in one `pod` is, in an ideal world, not a good idea. A container should be able to do one task; the `pod` is nothing more than the smallest unit possible to make that happen. A `pod` is also an abstraction layer used by Kubernetes to maintain the container.

But their use cases are based on the fact that a `pod` provides shared resources for the container(s) within the `pod`:

- Containers with helper applications such as logging and monitoring
- Reverse proxies

Until now, we used the `--image` parameter to create a simple `pod`. For a more complex `pod`, we need to make a specification in YAML format. Create a file called `myweb.yaml` with the following content:

```
apiVersion: v1
kind: Pod
metadata:
  name: myweb
spec:

  restartPolicy: Never

  volumes:
  - name: logger
    emptyDir: {}
```

```
containers:
- name: nginx
  image: nginx
  volumeMounts:
  - name: logger
    mountPath: /var/log/nginx
    readOnly: false
- name: logmachine
  image: ubuntu
  volumeMounts:
  - name: logger
    mountPath: /var/log/nginxmachine
```

In this file, a shared volume is created, called `journal`. The `emptydir` directive makes sure that the volume is created while creating the `pod`.

To verify, execute the following:

```
kubectl exec myweb -c nginx findmnt | grep logger
```

This command executes in the `pod myweb`; on the container nginx, use the `findmnt` command.

> This is by no means usable as a cluster solution. You should probably mount one of the containers the filesystem as read-only, using the `mountOptions` flag.

Working with Helm

Helm (`https://helm.sh` and `https://github.com/helm`) is the package manager for Kubernetes. You can compare it with `apt` and `yum` for Linux. It helps to manage Kubernetes using charts, which define, install, and upgrade the application you want to deploy on Kubernetes.

There are many charts available in their GitHub repository and Microsoft, who is one of the biggest contributors of this project, also provides a repository with examples.

Installing Helm

If you are on a Ubuntu system, you have two choices—you can install Helm with a `snap` package or just download the binary from `https://github.com/kubernetes/helm/releases`. Using the binary works for every Linux distribution and the `snap` repository doesn't always have the latest version. So let's use that method:

```
cd /tmp

wget https://storage.googleapis.com/kubernetes-helm/\
  helm-v2.9.1-linux-amd64.tar.gz

sudo tar xf helm-v2.9.1-linux-amd64.tar.gz --strip=1 -C \
  /usr/local/bin linux-amd64/helm
```

Always check for the latest release on the website and change the command accordingly.

macOS users can use Brew (`https://brew.sh/`):

```
brew install kubernetes-helm
```

The client is installed and with this client, we can deploy the server part, Tiller, into our Kubernetes cluster:

```
helm init
```

Verify the versions:

```
helm version
```

The output should be similar to the following:

```
→ helm version
Client: &version.Version{SemVer:"v2.9.1", GitCommit:"20adb27c7c586846
64e7390ebe710", GitTreeState:"clean"}
Server: &version.Version{SemVer:"v2.9.1", GitCommit:"20adb27c7c586846
64e7390ebe710", GitTreeState:"clean"}
```

To enable Helm to get access to the Kubernetes cluster, a service account must be created with a corresponding role:

```
kubectl create serviceaccount \
  --namespace kube-system tiller

kubectl create clusterrolebinding tiller-cluster-rule \
```

```
--clusterrole=cluster-admin \
--serviceaccount=kube-system:tiller
```

Reconfigure Helm:

```
helm init --service-account tiller --upgrade
```

Helm repository management

There are already two repositories added during the installation:

- https://kubernetes-charts.storage.googleapis.com/
- http://127.0.0.1:8879/charts

Let's add the repository from Microsoft:

```
helm repo add azure \
   https://kubernetescharts.blob.core.windows.net/azure
```

Check the available repositories:

```
helm repo list
```

The output should be similar to the following:

```
→ helm repo list
NAME      URL
stable    https://kubernetes-charts.storage.googleapis.com
local     http://127.0.0.1:8879/charts
azure     https://kubernetescharts.blob.core.windows.net/azure
```

To update the repository information, execute the following:

```
helm repo update
```

You can also remove repositories using the remove parameter.

Installing applications with Helm

Let's see what is available in the repositories:

```
helm search wordpress
```

```
➜ helm search wordpress
NAME                    CHART VERSION    APP VERSION    DESCRIPTION
azure/wordpress         0.10.0           4.9.4          Web publishi
stable/wordpress        2.1.4            4.9.7          Web publishi
```

If you want information about the chart, how to use it, the available parameters, and so on, you can use the `helm inspect` command. For now, we're just going to deploy it:

```
helm install stable/wordpress
```

Have a good look at the notes in the output, they provide you with the necessary information to access the WordPress instance.

Verify the status:

```
helm ls
```

```
➜ helm ls
NAME             REVISION    UPDATED                      STATUS
coy-aardwolf     1           Wed Aug  1 00:37:48 2018     DEPLOYED
```

Review the previous output of the installation process:

```
helm status <NAME>
```

And, of course, `kubectl` will also show you the following results:

```
➜ kubectl get deployment
NAME                      DESIRED    CURRENT    UP-TO-DATE    AVAILABLE    AGE
coy-aardwolf-wordpress    1          1          1             1            35m
```

```
➜ kubectl get service
NAME                      TYPE            CLUSTER-IP      EXTERNAL-IP       PORT(S)                       AGE
coy-aardwolf-mariadb      ClusterIP       10.0.16.176     <none>            3306/TCP                      5m
coy-aardwolf-wordpress    LoadBalancer    10.0.239.129    104.42.183.133    80:30608/TCP,443:31070/TCP    5m
kubernetes                ClusterIP       10.0.0.1        <none>            443/TCP                       3h
```

Let's remove our deployment (the name can be found using `helm ls`):

```
helm delete <NAME>
```

To customize the application, execute the following:

```
helm inspect stable/wordpress
```

Then, search for the settings of WordPress:

```
## Bitnami WordPress image version
## ref: https://hub.docker.com/r/bitnami/wordpress/tags/
##
image:
  registry: docker.io
  repository: bitnami/wordpress
  tag: 4.9.7-debian-9
  ## Specify a imagePullPolicy
  ## Defaults to 'Always' if image tag is 'latest', else set to 'I
  ## ref: http://kubernetes.io/docs/user-guide/images/#pre-pulling
  ##
  pullPolicy: IfNotPresent
  ## Optionally specify an array of imagePullSecrets.
  ## Secrets must be manually created in the namespace.
  ## ref: https://kubernetes.io/docs/tasks/configure-pod-container
  ##
  # pullSecrets:
  #   - myRegistrKeySecretName

## User of the application
## ref: https://github.com/bitnami/bitnami-docker-wordpress#enviro
##
wordpressUsername: user
```

Create a YAML file, for instance, `custom.yaml`, with the following content:

```
image:
  registry: docker.io
  repository: bitnami/wordpress
  tag: 4-ol-7

wordpressUsername: student01
wordpressEmail: student01@example.com
wordpressFirstName: John
wordpressLastName: Doe
wordpressBlogName: Linux on Azure!
```

Then, deploy the WordPress application:

```
helm install stable/wordpress -f custom.yaml
```

You can verify the results using the kubectl command. First, get the pod name:

```
kubectl get pod
```

After that, execute the following:

```
kubectl describe pod <podname>
```

For instance, in the **Events** section, you'll see that the image docker.io/bitnami/wordpress:4-ol-7 is pulled.

Clean up everything:

```
helm delete stable/wordpress

kubectl scale sts --all --replicas=0

kubectl delete pod --all

kubectl delete sts --all --cascade=false
```

Don't bother about the statefulsets (sts); they were created by this application to have an ordered deployment and shared persistent storage.

Creating Helm charts

There are many charts available, but it is also possible to create your own.

First, create a working directory and make it ready for use:

```
helm create myhelm

cd myhelm
```

Some files and directories are created:

- Chart.yaml file: This file contains basic information about the chart
- values.yaml file: Default configuration value
- charts directory: Dependency charts
- templates directory: Used to create manifest files for Kubernetes

Additionally, you can add a LICENSE file, a READM.md file, and a file with requirements, requirements.yaml.

Let's modify Chart.yaml a little bit:

```
apiVersion: v1
appVersion: 1.15.2
description: My First Nginx Helm
name: myhelm
version: 0.1.0
maintainers:
- name: John Doe
    email: jdoe@example.com
    url: http://packtpub.com
```

The file is more or less self-explanatory: the maintainers are optional; the appVersion refers to the version of, in this example, nginx.

Verify the configuration with the following:

helm lint

Take some time to investigate the files in the template directory and the value.yaml file. Of course, there is a reason why I used nginx as an example, because the files that are created by helm create also use nginx as an example.

First, execute a dry run:

helm install --dry-run --debug ../myhelm

This way, you can see the manifest that will be used to deploy the application. After that, you're ready to install it:

helm install ../myhelm

After the installation, I realized that looking at the dry run, there is something that is not OK: the version of nginx is nginx:stable, which is version 1.14.0. Open the values.yaml file and change tag: stable to tag: 1.15.2.

Use helm ls to find the name and update it:

helm upgrade <name> ../myhelm

A new pod will be created; the old one will be deleted. There is even a rollback option!

Working with Draft

Helm is typically something you're going to use as a developer on applications that are more or less production-ready and should be maintained. It's also most likely that you hosted the code on a version control system such as GitHub.

This is where Draft (`https://github.com/Azure/draft`) comes in. It tries to streamline the process, starting with your code, into the Kubernetes cluster.

The tool is in heavy development. With Draft, this means that it's not only getting more stable, but also that there are still languages and features coming to this tool and that it is possible that there are little changes in the syntax to come.

In daily life, Draft is something you maybe want on your local Minikube, but that's your choice. If the development phase turns into something that seems to be usable, you can still use Draft, but it's more likely that you switch to Helm only.

To find out which programming languages are supported, you can execute the following after the installation:

```
draft pack list
```

Installing Draft

To be able to use Draft, Helm must be installed and configured.

Get your copy from `https://github.com/Azure/draft/releases`:

```
cd /tmp

wget https://azuredraft.blob.core.windows.net/draft/\
  draft-v0.15.0-linux-amd64.tar.gz

sudo tar xf draft-v0.15.0-linux-amd64.tar.gz --strip=1 \
  -C /usr/local/bin linux-amd64/draft
```

Always check for the latest release on the website and change the command accordingly.

macOS users can install it with Brew:

```
brew tap azure/draft & brew install draft
```

You can see that the developers who work on Helm are also involved with the development of Draft. In both cases, many of them are Microsoft developers. Similar to Helm, after installing the client, you have to initialize Draft:

```
draft init
```

This will install some default plugins and setup the repositories you can use within Draft.

Check the version with the following:

```
draft version
```

At the time of writing, it's version 0.15.0:

```
→ draft version
&version.Version{SemVer:"v0.15.0", GitCommit:"9d73889a1318
```

The last step involves configuring a Docker repository, Docker Hub, or Azure. For the purposes of this book, I am using Azure.

Configure the repository:

```
draft config set registry <ACR login server>
```

Log in to the registry:

```
az acr login --name <ACR Registry Name>
```

And create a trust between Draft and the Azure Container Registry (ACR):

```
export AKS_SP_ID=$(az aks show \
  --resource-group <resource group> \
  --name <Kubernetes Cluster> \
  --query "servicePrincipalProfile.clientId" -o tsv)

export ACR_RESOURCE_ID=$(az acr show \
  --resource-group <resource group>\
  --name <ACR Name> --query "id" -o tsv)

az role assignment create --assignee $AKS_SP_ID --scope $ACR_RESOURCE_ID --role contributor
```

Using Draft

Let's develop some code. Create a directory called `mynode` and, in this directory, create a file called `mynode.js` with the following code:

```
var http = require('http');

var server = http.createServer(function(req, res) {
res.writeHead(200);
res.end('Hi all!');
});
server.listen(8080);
```

This is a simple web server that serves a page saying `Hi All!` We're in the very early stage of our development process. To create a `package.json`, execute the following:

```
npm init
```

And fill up the information:

```
name: (mynode)
version: (1.0.0) 0.0.1
description: My first Node App
entry point: (mynode.js)
test command: node mynode.js
git repository:
keywords: webapp
author: John Doe
license: (ISC)
```

Now we are ready to execute Draft:

```
draft create
```

```
✦ ⇒ draft create
--> Draft detected JavaScript (100.000000%)
--> Ready to sail
```

This will create a Dockerfile and all the information for Helm.

The last line in the output, "Ready to sail" actually means that you ready to execute:

```
draft up
```

```
✦ ➜ draft up
Draft Up Started: 'mynode': 01CKTRRQJS57FV02WPAPJFK24A
mynode: Building Docker Image: SUCCESS ⚓ (1.0008s)
mynode: Pushing Docker Image: SUCCESS ⚓ (275.2875s)
mynode: Releasing Application: SUCCESS ⚓ (6.5091s)
Inspect the logs with `draft logs 01CKTRRQJS57FV02WPAPJFK24A`
```

This will build the image and release the application.

Executing `helm ls` will show the `mynode` application:

```
NAME      REVISION     UPDATED                    STATUS      CHART
mynode    1            Wed Aug  1 05:10:27 2018   DEPLOYED    javascript-v0.1.0
```

Use `kubectl get services` to show the service:

```
✦ ➜ kubectl get services
NAME                 TYPE         CLUSTER-IP     EXTERNAL-IP    PORT(S)
kubernetes           ClusterIP    10.0.0.1       <none>         443/TCP
mynode-javascript    ClusterIP    10.0.156.106   <none>         8080/TCP
```

Everything seems to be OK here, but `kubectl get pod` tells us otherwise:

```
✦ ➜ kubectl get pod
NAME                                    READY    STATUS
mynode-javascript-576bcfffbc-sd5dv      0/1      Error
```

The `draft logs` command doesn't show any error. So let's find out what Kubernetes thinks:

```
kubectl logs <Pod Name>
```

It states `npm ERR! missing script: start`. On purpose, I made a mistake in the `package.json` file. Change the content, modifying the values as per the following example:

```
{
  "name": "mynode",
```

```
    "version": "0.0.2",
    "description": "My first Node App",
    "main": "mynode.js",
    "scripts": {
      "start": "node mynode.js",
      "test": "echo \"Error: no test specified\" & exit 1"
    },
    "keywords": [
      "webapp"
    ],
    "author": "John Doe",
    "license": "ISC"
}
```

Update the application by executing the following again:

```
draft update
```

Connect to the application:

```
draft connect
```

```
→  draft connect
Connect to javascript:8080 on localhost:39053
[javascript]:
[javascript]: > mynode@0.0.2 start /usr/src/app
[javascript]: > node mynode.js
[javascript]:
```

Open another Terminal:

```
curl localhost:39053
```

And, the output must be Hi All!

Press *Ctrl* + *C* in the Terminal running draft connect and remove the deployment:

```
draft delete
```

Check the cluster resources with kubectl get all and clean up, if needed.

Managing Kubernetes

We created a Kubernetes cluster, we learned about the `kubectl` utility and about some of the tools available to develop and maintain your applications in the Kubernetes cluster.

So, if you look back at my three questions in the introduction of this chapter, I've answered the first question. In this section, I am going to answer the other two questions and also cover how to update the Kubernetes version.

Updating applications

Earlier on, we used Helm and Draft to manage our application, doing all the hard work. But you can also update the workload with the help of `kubectl`.

Normally, your cluster is empty now, let's quickly deploy our nginx `pod` again:

```
kubectl run nginx --image=nginx
```

Have a good look at the deployment:

```
→ kubectl get deployment
NAME       DESIRED    CURRENT    UP-TO-DATE    AVAILABLE    AGE
nginx      1          1          1             1            19m
```

This actually tells us that we wanted one instance, there is one running, that one is up to date (the number of instances that were updated to match the desired), and it is available. The version of nginx running is not the latest one, so I want to update it to version 1.15.2. Execute the following:

```
kubectl edit deployment/nginx
```

Change the image: `nginx:1.15.2`:

```
spec:
  containers:
  - image: nginx:1.15.2
```

Check the rollout status:

```
kubectl rollout status deployment nginx

kubectl rollout history deployment nginx
```

Or, even better, use the following:

```
kubectl describe deployment nginx
```

```
→ kubectl describe deployment/nginx
Name:                    nginx
Namespace:               default
CreationTimestamp:       Thu, 02 Aug 2018 08:40:53 +0200
Labels:                  run=nginx
Annotations:             deployment.kubernetes.io/revision=2
                         kubernetes.io/change-cause=kubectl edit deployment/nginx
  --record=true
Selector:                run=nginx
Replicas:                1 desired | 1 updated | 1 total | 1 available | 0 unavai
lable
StrategyType:            RollingUpdate
MinReadySeconds:         0
RollingUpdateStrategy:   25% max unavailable, 25% max surge
Pod Template:
  Labels:  run=nginx
  Containers:
   nginx:
    Image:          nginx:1.15.2
```

Another way to do it is the following:

```
kubectl set image deployment nginx nginx=nginx:1.15.2 --record
```

Scaling applications

Go back to `kubectl get deployment`:

```
→ kubectl get deployment
NAME     DESIRED   CURRENT   UP-TO-DATE   AVAILABLE   AGE
nginx    1         1         1            1           19m
```

At the moment, there is one `pod` running, but to handle all the load coming in, you may need more instances and to load balance the traffic. To do so, you'll need replicas to define a specified number of `pod` replicas that are running at any given time.

The desired (configured) state at this moment is 1. The current situation is 1 and there is 1 available.

To scale up to three instances, execute the following:

```
kubectl scale deployment nginx --replicas=3
```

Run `kubectl get deployments` again; after that, look into the available `pods`:

```
kubectl get pods -o wide
```

```
→ kubectl get pods -o wide
NAME                      READY   STATUS    RESTARTS   AGE    IP
NODE
nginx-59f57bcfc8-kjzhz    1/1     Running   0          2m     10.244.0.11
aks-nodepool1-18722659-0
nginx-59f57bcfc8-kslkr    1/1     Running   0          34m    10.244.0.9
aks-nodepool1-18722659-0
nginx-59f57bcfc8-rknh5    1/1     Running   0          2m     10.244.0.10
aks-nodepool1-18722659-0
```

Create a load balancer service:

```
kubectl expose deployment nginx --type=LoadBalancer \
  --name=nginx-lb --port 80
```

```
kubectl get services
```

Now, every HTTP request is taken by the load balancer and traffic is spread over the instances.

You can also use autoscaling. First, install the Metric Server:

```
git clone https://github.com/kubernetes-incubator/metrics-server.git
```

```
kubectl create -f metrics-server/deploy/1.8+/
```

Configure autoscaling: if the load is above 50 percent, an extra instance is created, with a maximum of 10:

```
kubectl autoscale deployment nginx --cpu-percent=50 --min=3 --max=10
```

Of course, in this scenario, it makes sense to have at least two nodes available in your cluster:

```
az aks scale --name Cluster01 \
  --resource-group MyKubernetes \
  --node-count 2
```

```
kubectl get nodes
```

Note, this process will take about 10 minutes. To view the status of autoscaling, execute the following:

```
kubectl get hpa
```

Upgrading Kubernetes

Having multiple nodes available is also needed if you want to upgrade the Kubernetes control plane without downtime.

First, view the current version:

```
az aks list --query "[].kubernetesVersion"
```

```
➜ az aks list --query "[].kubernetesVersion"
[
  "1.9.9"
]
```

Ask for the available versions in your location:

```
az aks get-versions --location westus --output table | egrep "^1.9.9"
```

```
➜ az aks get-versions --location westus --output table | egrep "^1.9.9"
1.9.9               1.10.3, 1.10.5, 1.10.6
```

We can upgrade to version 1.10.6:

```
az aks upgrade --resource-group MyKubernetes
  --name Cluster01 \
  --kubernetes-version 1.10.6 --yes --no-wait
```

Adding the `--no-wait` parameter has the effect that you'll get your prompt back almost directly.

This way, after about three minutes, you can start playing with the `kubectl` to get the status of the nodes and `pod` (use the `-o` wide parameter!) and find out that a new node is created with the newest version. The workload are recreated on that node, the other node is getting updated, after that the last one remaining is emptied and upgraded.

Persistent storage

In the previous chapter, I already stated that there are multiple ways to use persistent storage in your container and I referred also to this chapter.

Kubernetes can configure persistent storage, but you have to provide it, for instance via a NFS container or by implementing StorSimple iSCSI Virtual Array (especially useful if you need read/write access from multiple containers). Even if you are using Azure storage there are many choices to make. Do you want to use disks, or the Azure File Storage? Do you want to create them on the fly (dynamic) or use existing ones (static)? Most of these questions are answered based on costs and the need for services such as replication, backup, and snapshots.

In this section, I want to cover the dynamic options; orchestration-wise, it's a better choice because you can do everything within Kubernetes (or tooling around it).

For both Azure File Storage or using disks, you'll need a storage account in the same resource group as Kubernetes:

```
az storage account create --resource-group MyKubernetes \
  --name k8linvirt --sku Standard_LRS
```

Please revisit `Chapter 2`, *Getting Started with the Azure Cloud* for the syntax of the preceding command. Remember that the name must be unique.

Azure Disk for Kubernetes

Create a YAML file to create the storage class. This makes it possible to automatically provision the storage:

```
kind: StorageClass
apiVersion: storage.k8s.io/v1
metadata:
  name: storageforapp
provisioner: kubernetes.io/azure-disk
parameters:
 skuName: Standard_LRS
 location: westus
 kind: shared
```

Apply it with the following:

```
kubectl -f storageclass.yaml
```

Replace the filename with the name of the file you just created.

Another YAML file is needed to claim the persistent volume, or in other words, create it:

```
kind: PersistentVolumeClaim
apiVersion: v1
metadata:
  name: claimstorageforapp
  annotations:
    volume.beta.kubernetes.io/storage-class: storageforapp
spec:
  accessModes:
  - ReadWriteOnce
  resources:
    requests:
      storage: 5Gi
```

Please note that the match is made in the annotations. Apply this file as well. Verify the result with the following:

```
kubectl get sc
```

```
→ kubectl get sc

NAME                PROVISIONER                  AGE
default (default)   kubernetes.io/azure-disk     6h
managed-premium     kubernetes.io/azure-disk     6h
storageforapp       kubernetes.io/azure-disk     4m
```

To use the storage in a `pod`, you can use it in a similar way to the following example:

```
kind: Pod
apiVersion: v1
metadata:
  name: my-web
spec:
  containers:
    - name: nginx
      image: nginx
      volumeMounts:
      - mountPath: "/var/www/html"
        name: volume
```

```
volumes:
  - name: volume
    persistentVolumeClaim:
      claimName: claimstorageforapp
```

Azure File for Kubernetes

The configuration for Azure File is not that different. The YAML file to create the storage class is as follows:

```
kind: StorageClass
apiVersion: storage.k8s.io/v1
metadata:
  name: azurefile
provisioner: kubernetes.io/azure-file
parameters:
  skuName: Standard_LRS
```

To claim it, execute the following:

```
apiVersion: v1
kind: PersistentVolumeClaim
metadata:
  name: azurefile
spec:
  accessModes:
    - ReadWriteMany
  storageClassName: azurefile
  resources:
    requests:
      storage: 5Gi
```

The result is as follows:

```
→ kubectl get sc
NAME                 PROVISIONER                  AGE
azurefile            kubernetes.io/azure-file     5s
default (default)    kubernetes.io/azure-disk     6h
managed-premium      kubernetes.io/azure-disk     6h
storageforapp        kubernetes.io/azure-disk     13m
```

The specification in the pod remains the same.

Summary

This chapter was all about Kubernetes. I started this chapter by describing a possible work environment as a developer: a good workstation with tooling to start local development, even with Kubernetes locally installed. I used Ubuntu Desktop as an example, but in fact it doesn't really matter, as long you are happy with your development environment.

With everything in place locally, I covered the configuration of the Kubernetes cluster in Azure, using the Azure CLI and PowerShell.

Deployment of workloads in Azure can be as simple as executing `kubectl run`, but more complex scenarios were also explored: multi-container applications.

As a developer, two tools are available to help to streamline your development process: Draft and Helm. Draft is used for the initial development phase, probably on your local Minikube, and Helm is used afterwards to install and maintain the application.

Kubernetes is a tool to manage your containers and make it easy to deploy, maintain, and update your workloads. Scalability is one of the advantages of using Kubernetes; it's even possible to automatically scale depending on the needed CPU and memory resources.

The last section of this chapter covered the use of persistent storage in Kubernetes, actually providing you with a much better way than storing the data in the container or attaching storage directly to the container.

In the next and final chapter, we're going back to the Ops part of DevOps, that is, troubleshooting and monitoring your workloads, workloads as in virtual machines with Linux installed, containers, and AKS.

Questions

1. What would be a good reason to install Minikube locally?
2. How can you switch between the local Minikube and the remote cluster in Azure?
3. What is a `pod`?
4. What would be a good reason to create a multiple container `pod`?
5. What are the methods to deploy your application in Kubernetes?
6. What are the methods to update your application in Kubernetes?
7. Do you need to create extra nodes in Kubernetes if you want to upgrade the control plane?

8. Can you think of any reason why you would want an iSCSI solution?
9. And as an exercise: recreate the multi-container `pod`, using persistent storage.

Further reading

The goal of this chapter was to provide you a practical approach to get your workload running in the Azure Cloud. I hope it's the beginning of a journey into the world of Kubernetes. There is so much more to discover!

Nigel Poulton, the author who has already created a great book about Docker, has also written a book about Kubernetes, *The Kubernetes Book*. It's a good starting point if you are really new to Kubernetes. Gigi Sayfan has written *Mastering Kubernetes*. Make sure you buy the second edition! Not only because the first edition was not that good, but just because it's a must have and provides much more information then the first edition.

As a developer, you should give *Kubernetes for Developers* a try: Joseph Heck can tell you much more about the development life cycle using Kubernetes, using examples in Node.js and Python. In the last chapter of his book, he mentions emerging projects such as Helm and Brigade. I hope this will be explored in more detail in a later edition, or maybe even in another book.

Talking about Brigade, `https://brigade.sh` is described on its own website as *a tool for running scriptable, automated tasks in the cloud — as part of your Kubernetes cluster*. It's far beyond the scope of this book and it's more or less in the early stages of development. As a developer, you should invest some time in reading more about it and try it.

Last but not least, I want to mention Open Service Broker for Azure (OSBA; `https://osba.sh`). It didn't make it into this chapter, because it's not completely production ready at the time of writing. OSBA is a open standard to communicate with external services such as databases and storage. It's another solution providing data to and storing data from your container.

11
Troubleshooting and Monitoring Your Workloads

Troubleshooting and logging are strongly related; that's where you start when you experience problems.

Troubleshooting problems and fixing the problems found in a cloud environment can be different than troubleshooting in more classic deployments. This chapter explains the differences, the challenges, and the new possibilities of troubleshooting Linux workloads in the Azure environment.

Technical requirements

For this chapter, you'll need one or two virtual machines running a Linux distribution. You can use the smallest size if you want. The audit daemon must be installed and, for the purpose of having something to analyze, it's a good idea to install Apache and a MySQL/MariaDB server.

Here is an example in CentOS:

```
sudo yum groups install "Basic Web Server"
sudo yum install mariadb mariadb-server
sudo yum install setroubleshoot
sudo systemctl enable --now apache2
sudo systemctl enable --now mariadb
```

In this chapter, the Azure management and operations management suite are covered. The agent that is needed to collect information from the virtual machine is not supported in every Linux distribution; please visit `https://docs.microsoft.com/en-us/azure/virtual-machines/extensions/oms-linux` before making a decision about which distribution you want to use in this chapter.

Accessing your system

Troubleshooting workloads in Azure is not always that different from troubleshooting in other environments. In this section, there are some tips and tricks that hopefully will help you in your daily job.

No remote access

You played with firewall rules or access control lists and now you are not able to log in remotely.

The first thing you can try is to run a command in the virtual machine. Go in the Azure portal to your virtual machine and select **Run command**:

Run Command uses the VM agent to let you run a script inside this virtual machine. This can be helpful for troubleshooting and recovery, and for general machine and application maintenance. Select a command below to see details.

NAME	DESCRIPTION
RunShellScript	Executes a Linux shell script
ifconfig	List network configuration

Or use the command-line, for instance:

```
az vm run-command invoke --name <vm name> \
  --command-id RunShellScript \
  --scripts hostnamectl \
  --resource-group <resource group>
```

As you can see, it's not necessary for a script; every Linux command will work. PowerShell is also an option, but instead of providing remote commands, you have to create a local script:

```
Invoke-AzureRmVMRunCommand `
  -VMName <vm name> -ResourceGroupName ResourceGroup `
  -CommandId RunShellScript `
  -ScriptPath '/<path-to>/<script>' | Format-Wide
```

If you are doing it via the command line or via the Azure portal, in both scenarios, it only works if the Microsoft Azure Linux guest agent is still running and reachable.

> PowerShell versions, released before July 27, 2018, return empty. A workaround is adding the -Debug parameter.

Another option is to use the serial console; you can find this option in the **SUPPORT + TROUBLESHOOTING** section on the page of the virtual machine:

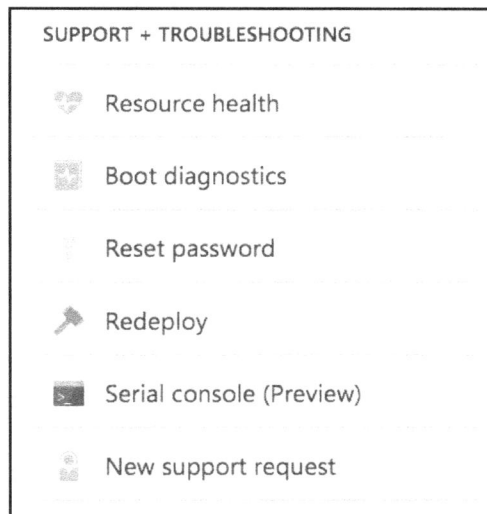

This only works if you have a user that is configured with a password. If you deployed your virtual machine with SSH keys, then you are lucky: the **Reset password** option in the same section will do the job:

This option is using the VMAccess extension (`https://github.com/Azure/azure-linux-extensions/tree/master/VMAccess`). Like the **Run command** option discussed before, it needs the Azure Agent.

The console always works!

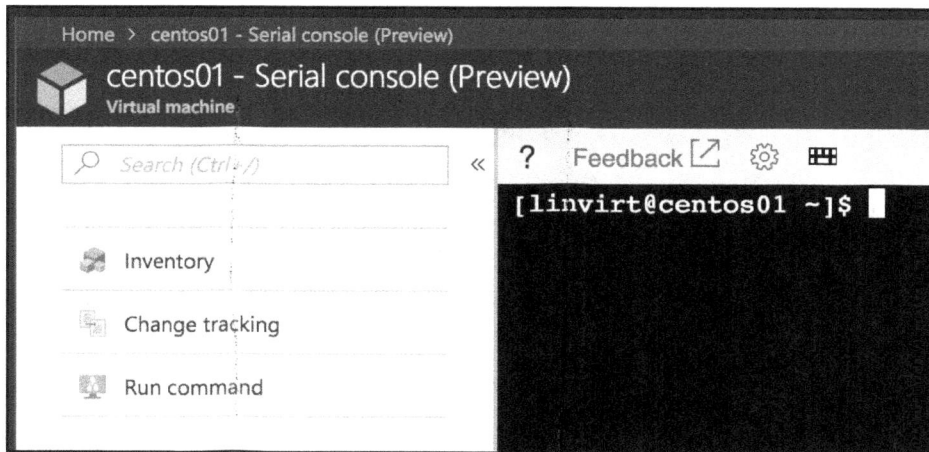

Knocking on the port

One of the possible reasons that you don't have remote access, can be network-related. In the `Chapter 5`, *Advanced Linux Administration*, the `ip` command was briefly introduced in the *Networking* section. You can use this command to verify the IP address and the route table. And, don't forget to verify the DNS configuration in `/etc/resolv.conf`, using `host` or `dig`.

On the Azure site, the network and the Network Security Groups must be checked, as covered in `Chapter 3`, *Basic Linux Administration*. In the virtual machine, you can use the `ss` command, such as `ip`, a part of the `iproute2` package. To list the UPD (`-u`) and TCP (`p`) ports in listening state, together with the process ID (`-p`) that opened the port:

```
[linvirt@centos01 ~]$ ss -tulpn
Netid State      Recv-Q Send-Q Local Address:Port          Peer Address:Port
udp   UNCONN     0      0              *:56610                    *:*
udp   UNCONN     0      0      127.0.0.1:323                      *:*
udp   UNCONN     0      0              *:68                       *:*
udp   UNCONN     0      0              *:111                      *:*
udp   UNCONN     0      0              *:680                      *:*
udp   UNCONN     0      0            ::1:323                    :::*
udp   UNCONN     0      0            :::111                     :::*
udp   UNCONN     0      0            :::680                     :::*
tcp   LISTEN     0      50             *:3306                     *:*
tcp   LISTEN     0      10     127.0.0.1:29131                    *:*
tcp   LISTEN     0      128            *:111                      *:*
tcp   LISTEN     0      128            *:22                       *:*
tcp   LISTEN     0      100    127.0.0.1:25                       *:*
tcp   LISTEN     0      128          :::111                     :::*
tcp   LISTEN     0      128          :::80                      :::*
tcp   LISTEN     0      128          :::22                      :::*
tcp   LISTEN     0      100          ::1:25                     :::*
```

A quick check on the firewall rules can be done with `firewall-cmd --list-all --zone=public`; if you have multiple zones and interfaces, you need to execute this for every zone. To include the rules created by the Azure fabric, `iptables-save` can help:

```
[linvirt@centos01 ~]$ sudo iptables-save
# Generated by iptables-save v1.4.21 on Mon Aug  6 05:04:46 2018
*security
:INPUT ACCEPT [25620:47224378]
:FORWARD ACCEPT [0:0]
:OUTPUT ACCEPT [25059:6565020]
-A OUTPUT -d 168.63.129.16/32 -p tcp -m owner --uid-owner 0 -j ACCEPT
-A OUTPUT -d 168.63.129.16/32 -p tcp -m conntrack --ctstate INVALID,NEW -j DROP
COMMIT
# Completed on Mon Aug  6 05:04:46 2018
```

Unfortunately, there is no comment available to see all the access rules at once configured at the systemd unit level. Don't forget to verify them as discussed in `Chapter 6`, *Managing Linux Security and Identities*.

Boot diagnostics

You created your virtual machine, probably orchestrated, most likely your own virtual machine, and it doesn't boot.

When you create a virtual machine, there is an option to enable boot diagnostics (in the **Monitoring** section). You can also enable it afterwards, using PowerShell:

```
Set-AzureRMVMBootDiagnostics -VM <VM Name> `
 -Enable -ResourceGroupName <resource group> `
 -StorageAccountName "<storage account>"
```

You'll need a storage account to be able to store the data. List the storage accounts that are already available with the `Get-AzureRmStorageAccount` cmdlet and, if needed, create one with `Set-AzureRmStorageAccount`.

In put in Azure CLI, execute:

```
az vm boot-diagnostics enable --name <vm name>\
  --resource-group <resource group> \
  --storage <url>
```

The difference is that you don't need the name of the storage account, but the name of the storage blob, which can be found with the `az storage account list` command, as a property of the storage account.

To receive the bootlog, execute the following:

```
Get-AzureRmVMBootDiagnosticsData -Name <virtual machine> `
  -Linux -ResourceGroupName <resource group> `
  -LocalPath <local directory>
```

Or in Azure CLI:

```
az vm boot-diagnostics get-boot-log \
  --name <virtual machine> \
  --resource-group <resource group>
```

Strangely enough, you get more in PowerShell; there are even screenshots provided. The output is also automatically stored in a file; in Azure CLI, it's a good idea to pipe it through less or redirect it to a file.

Logging in Linux

In earlier chapters, we already encountered the `journalctl` command. In this chapter, I'll discuss this command in much more detail.

In Linux distributions, such as the latest versions of RHEL/CentOS, Debian, Ubuntu and SUSE, that uses systemd as their init system, the `systemd-journald` daemon is used for logging. This daemon collects the standard output of a unit, syslog message, and, if the application support it: direct messages from the application to systemd.

The logs are collected in a database that can be queried with `journalctl`.

Working with journalctl

If you execute `systemctl status <unit>`, you already see the last entries of the logging. To see the full log, `journalctl` is the tool that you need. There is a difference with `systemctl`: you can view the status on other hosts, using the `-H` parameter. You can't use the `journalctl` to connect to other hosts. Both utilities have the parameter `-M` to connect to `systemd-nspawn` and `Rkt` containers.

To view the entries in the journal database, execute this:

```
sudo journalctl --unit <unit>
```

By default, the log is paged with `less`. If you want another pager, for instance `more`, then you can configure that via the `/etc/enviroment` file. Add a line:

```
SYSTEMD_PAGER=/usr/bin/more
```

Here is an example of the output:

```
Jul 16 14:04:10 ubuntu-vm sshd[6629]: Failed password for root from
122.226.181.
```

- The first column is the timestamp. In the database itself, it's defined in EPOCH time, so if you change your timezone, no problem: it will be translated.
- The second column is the hostname, as shown with the `hostnamectl` command.
- The third column contains an identifier and the process ID.
- The fourth column is the message.

Instead of a unit, you can also choose the following:

- `--dmesg`: Kernel messages, replacement for the old `dmesg` command
- `--identifier`: Identifier string
- `--boot`: Messages during the current boot process; you can also select previous boots if the database is persistent across reboots

Filters

Of course, you can `grep` in the standard output, but `journalctl` has some parameters that really help to filter out the information you want:

- `--priority`: Filter on `alert`, `crit`, `debug`, `emerg`, `err`, `info`, `notice`, and `warning`. The classification of these priorities is the same as in the syslog protocol specification.
- `--since` and `--until`: Filter on timestamp. See `man systemd.time` to see all the possibilities.
- `--lines`: Number of lines, similar to `tail`.
- `--follow`: Behavior similar to `tail -f`.
- `--reverse`: Last line first.
- `--output`: Changes the output format to formats such as JSON, or to add more verbosity to the output.
- `--catalog`: Add explanation to the message if available.

All the filters can be combined with one another, for instance:

```
sudo journalctl -u sshd --since yesterday --until 10:00 \
  --priority err
```

Filtering based on fields

There is also the possibility to filter on fields. Type this:

```
sudo journactl _
```

Now press *Ctrl + I* twice; you see all the available fields. The same principle applies with the other filters: you can combine them:

```
sudo journalctl _UID=1000 _PID=1850
```

You can even combine them with the normal filters:

```
sudo journalctl _KERNEL_DEVICE=+scsi:5:0:0:0 -o verbose
```

Database persistence

By default, the logging database is not persistent. To make it persistent, you have to edit the configuration file `/etc/systemd/journald.conf`. Change the line `#Storage=auto` into this:

```
Storage=persistent
```

Restart the `systemd-journald` daemon with force:

```
sudo systemctl force-reload systemd-journald
```

To view the recorded boots:

```
sudo journalctl --list-boots
```

You can add the boot ID as a filter, using the `--boot` parameter, for instance:

```
journalctl --priority err --boot <boot id>
```

By this means, the output of the `hostnamectl` shows the current boot ID.

The journal database is not dependent on the daemon. You can view it using the `--directory` and `--file` parameters.

Syslog protocol

Logging in Linux and other members of the Unix family was done by an implementation of the syslog protocol. It is still in use to send logging to remove services.

What is important to understand from this protocol is that it is using facilities and severity. Both are standardized in rfc5424 (`https://tools.ietf.org/html/rfc5424`). A facility is used to specify the type of program that is logging the message, for instance the kernel or cron. The severity label is there to describe the impact, such as informational or critical.

The programmers' man page for syslog (**man 3 syslog**) also gives a good insight into these facilities and severities and how a program can use this protocol. The bad news about syslog is that it only works if the application supports it and the applications run long enough to provide this functionality. Journald is able to get everything regarding the output of a program.

Adding log entries

You can manually add entries to logging. For syslog, the `logger` command is available:

```
logger -p <facility.severity> "Message"
```

For the journald there is `systemd-cat`:

```
systemd-cat --identifier <identifier> --priority <severity> <command>
```

For instance:

```
systemd-cat --identifier CHANGE --priority info \
  echo "Start Configuration Change"
```

As an identifier, you can use free strings or the syslog facilities. Both `logger` and `systemd-cat` can be used to generate entries in your logging. You can use this if the application doesn't have syslog support; for instance, in an Apache configuration you can use this directive:

```
errorlog  "tee -a /var/log/www/error/log  | logger -p local6.info"
```

Or as a part of change management.

Integrating journald with RSYSLOG

To collect your data for your own monitoring service, your monitoring service needs syslog support. Good examples of these monitoring services are available as a ready-to-go virtual machine in Azure: **Splunk** and the **Elastic Stack**.

RSYSLOG is the most commonly used syslog protocol implementation nowadays. It's already installed by default in the Ubuntu, SUSE, and Red Hat-based distributions.

RSYSLOG can work very well together with the journal database, using the `imjournal` module. In Red Hat and SUSE-based distributions this is already configured; in Ubuntu, you have to make a modification to the `/etc/rsyslog.conf`:

```
# module(load="imuxsock")

module(load="imjournal")
```

After the modification, restart RSYSLOG:

```
sudo systemctl restart rsyslog
```

Using the settings in `/etc/rsyslog.d/50-default.conf`, it logs to plain-text files.

To send everything coming from the local syslog to a remote syslog server, you have to add to this file:

```
*. *   @<remote server>:514
```

> This is the name of the file in Ubuntu. In other distributions use `/etc/rsyslog.conf`.

Use `@@` if you want TCP instead of the UDP protocol.

Other log files

You can find log files of applications that don't support syslog or `systemd-journald` in the `/var/log` directory structure. One important file to notice is the `/var/log/waagent.log` file that contains the logging from the Azure Linux VM agent, and there is the `/var/log/azure` directory that contains logging from other Azure agents (such as OMS) and virtual machine extensions.

Microsoft Log Analytics

Microsoft Log Analytics is a part of the operations management suite. It is a service in Azure that collects log data from multiple systems in a single data store in a central place. It consists of two important components:

- The Azure Log Analytics portal with alerting, reporting and analyzing features
- The OMS Agent to install on the virtual machine

There is also a mobile app available (in the iOS and Android store, you can find it under the name *Microsoft Operations Management Suite*) if you want to view the state of your workloads while you are on the way.

In this section, I'll only use the Azure Portal and PowerShell; the options in Azure CLI are very limited or sometimes even none existent.

Configuring the Log Analytics service

In the Azure portal, select from the left-hand bar **All Services** and search for **Log Analytics**. Select **Add** and create a new OMS workspace. At the time of writing, it is not available in all regions at the moment. Using the service is not limited to the region; if the virtual machine is in another region, you can still monitor it.

> This service is not free! Read `http://aka.ms/PricingTierWarning` for more details.

Another way to create the service is with PowerShell:

```
New-AzureRmOperationalInsightsWorkspace `
  -Location 'West Europe' `
  -Name <OMS name> -ResourceGroupName <resource group> `
  -Sku pernode
```

After the creation of the service, there is a popup that gives you the possibility to navigate to the newly created resource. Alternatively, you can search again in **All Services**.

Please note at the top-right of the resource pane, the OMS and the workspace ID; you'll need this information later on. Navigate to **Advanced settings** to find the workspace key.

In PowerShell you can collect this information using the following:

```
Get-AzureRmOperationalInsightsWorkspace
```

To receive the workspace ID, also known as `CustomerID` and to receive the shared keys use the following command:

```
Get-AzureRmOperationalInsightsWorkspaceSharedKeys `
  -ResourceGroupName <resource group> -Name <OMS name>
```

Installing the OMS agent

Before installing the OMS agent, make sure that the audit package (in Ubuntu: `auditd`) is installed.

To install the OMS Agent in the Linux VM, you have two possibilities: use the virtual machine extension `OMSAgentforLinux` or download and install it in Linux.

It is not possible to install the agent via the portal. But it can be done afterward with PowerShell. First set some variables to make scripting easier:

```
$rg = "<resource group>"
$loc = "<vm location>"
$omsName = "<OMS Name>"
$vm = "<vm name>"
```

You need the workspace ID and key. The `Set-AzureRmVMExtension` cmdlet needs the keys in JSON format, so a conversion is needed:

```
$omsID = $(Get-AzureRmOperationalInsightsWorkspace `
 -ResourceGroupName $rg -Name $omsName.CustomerId)

$omsKey = $(Get-AzureRmOperationalInsightsWorkspaceSharedKeys `
 -ResourceGroupName $rg -Name $omsName).PrimarySharedKey

$PublicSettings = New-Object psobject | Add-Member `
 -PassThru NoteProperty workspaceId $omsId | ConvertTo-Json

$PrivateSettings = New-Object psobject | Add-Member `
 -PassThru NoteProperty workspaceKey $omsKey | ConvertTo-Json
```

Now you can add the extension to the virtual machine:

```
Set-AzureRmVMExtension -ExtensionName "OMS" `
  -ResourceGroupName $rg -VMName $vm `
  -Publisher "Microsoft.EnterpriseCloud.Monitoring"
```

```
-ExtensionType "OmsAgentForLinux" -TypeHandlerVersion 1.0 `
-SettingString $PublicSettings
-ProtectedSettingString $PrivateSettings -Location $loc
```

The previous procedure is pretty complex and takes more time. The download method is easier, but you have to log in as the guest. Of course, both methods can be automated/orchestrated:

```
cd /tmp

wget \
  https://raw.githubusercontent.com/Microsoft/OMS-Agent-for-Linux\
  /master installer/scripts/onboard_agent.sh

sudo -s

sh onboard_agent.sh -w <OMS id> -s <OMS key> -d \
  opinsights.azure.com
```

If you have problems during the installation of the agent, look in the configuration files `/var/log/waagent.log` and `/var/log/azure/Microsoft.EnterpriseCloud.Monitoring.OmsAgentForLinux/*/extension.log`

The installation of the extensions also configured a file for `rsyslog`, `/etc/rsyslogd.d/95-omsagent.conf`:

```
kern.warning @127.0.0.1:25224
user.warning @127.0.0.1:25224
daemon.warning @127.0.0.1:25224
auth.warning @127.0.0.1:25224
syslog.warning @127.0.0.1:25224
uucp.warning @127.0.0.1:25224
authpriv.warning @127.0.0.1:25224
ftp.warning @127.0.0.1:25224
cron.warning @127.0.0.1:25224
local0.warning @127.0.0.1:25224
local1.warning @127.0.0.1:25224
local2.warning @127.0.0.1:25224
local3.warning @127.0.0.1:25224
local4.warning @127.0.0.1:25224
local5.warning @127.0.0.1:25224
local6.warning @127.0.0.1:25224
local7.warning @127.0.0.1:25224
```

It basically means that the syslog messages (`facility.priority`) are sent to the OMS agent.

At the bottom pane of the new resource, there is a section entitled **Get started with Log Analytics**:

Get started with Log Analytics

Log Analytics collects data from a variety of sources and uses a powerful query language to give you insights into the operation of your applications and resources. Use Azure Monitor to access the complete set of tools for monitoring all of your Azure resources

Learn more

Transitioning from OMS Portal - FAQ's
Documentation site
Community

1 Connect a data source

Select one or more data sources to connect to the workspace

Azure virtual machines (VMs)
Windows, Linux and other sources
Azure Activity logs

2 Configure monitoring solutions

Add monitoring solutions that provide insights for applications and services in your environment

View solutions

Click on **Azure virtual machines (VMs)**. You'll see the virtual machines that are available in this workspace:

NAME	OMS CONNECTION	OS
centos01	This workspace	Linux
centos02	Not connected	Linux

We finished the first step mentioned in the pane: **Connect a data source**.

Getting the data

In the **Advanced settings** section of this resource, you can add performance and syslog data sources. You can access all the data via the log search, using a special query language. If you are new to this language, you should visit https://docs.loganalytics.io/docs/Learn/Getting-Started/Getting-started-with-queries and https://docs.loganalytics.io/index.

For now, just execute the query:

```
search *
```

To see whether there is data available, limit the search to one virtual machine:

```
search * | where Computer == "centos01"
```

Or to get all the syslog messages, as a test, you can reboot your virtual machine, or play with this:

```
logger -t <facility>. <priority> "message"
```

Execute the following query in syslog to view the results:

```
Syslog | sort
```

There are also many examples available under the button **Saved searches**.

Solutions, management providers for monitoring, can be very interesting add-ons to make it even easier. In the resource pane, click on **View solutions**:

Get started with Log Analytics

Log Analytics collects data from a variety of sources and uses a powerful query language to give you insights into the operation of your applications and resources. Use Azure Monitor to access the complete set of tools for monitoring all of your Azure resources

Learn more

Transitioning from OMS Portal - FAQ's
Documentation site
Community

1 Connect a data source

Select one or more data sources to connect to the workspace

Azure virtual machines (VMs)
Windows, Linux and other sources
Azure Activity logs

2 Configure monitoring solutions

Add monitoring solutions that provide insights for applications and services in your environment

View solutions

Click **Add**:

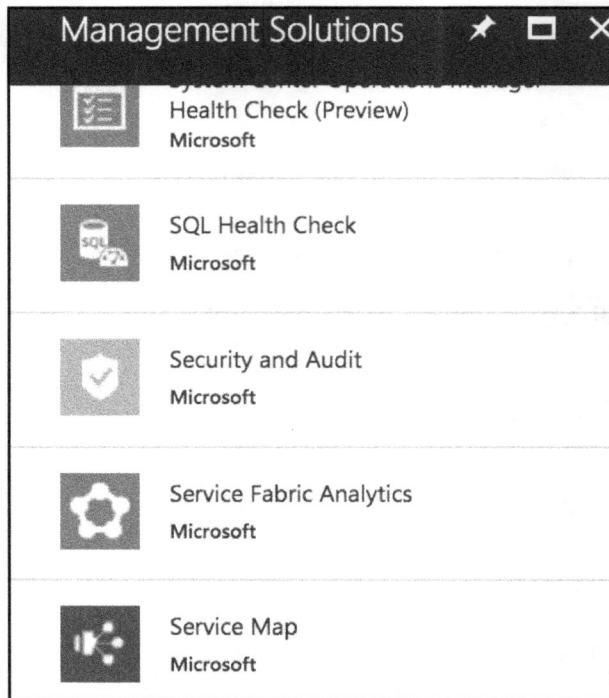

Service Map is a must-have. It gives a great overview of your resources and provides an easy interface to logs, performance counters, and so on. After installing the service map, you have to install an agent in the Linux machine:

```
cd /tmp

wget --content-disposition https://aka.ms/dependencyagentlinux \
  -O InstallDependencyAgent-Linux64.bin

sudo sh InstallDependencyAgent-Linux64.bin -s
```

After the installation, select **Solutions** on the OMS pane:

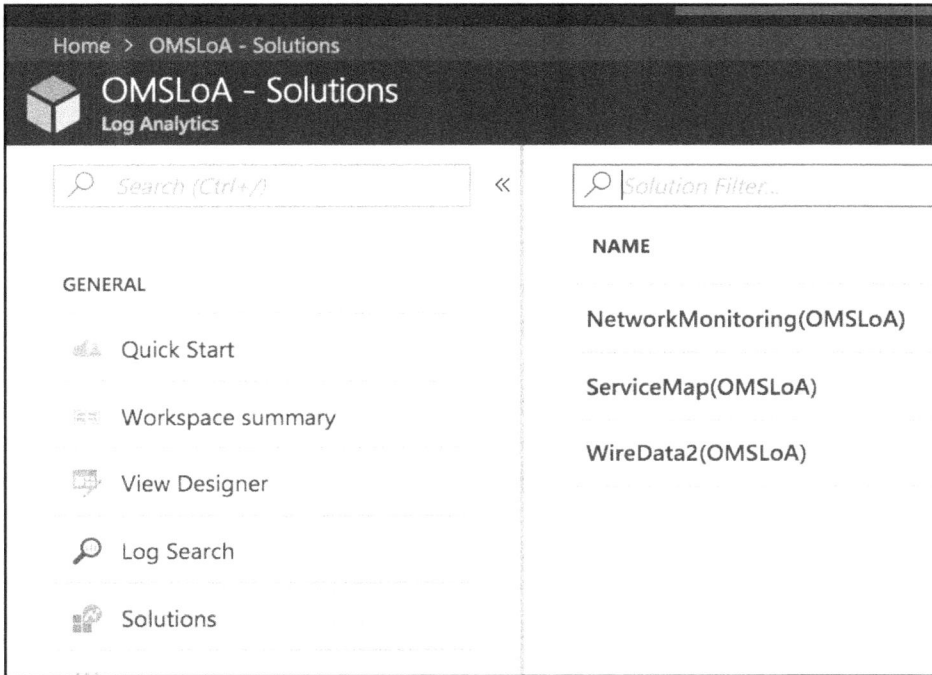

Now, click on **Summary**:

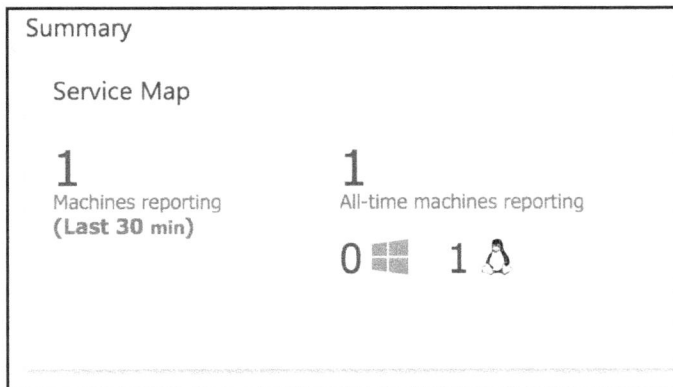

Monitor your applications, view the log files, and so on:

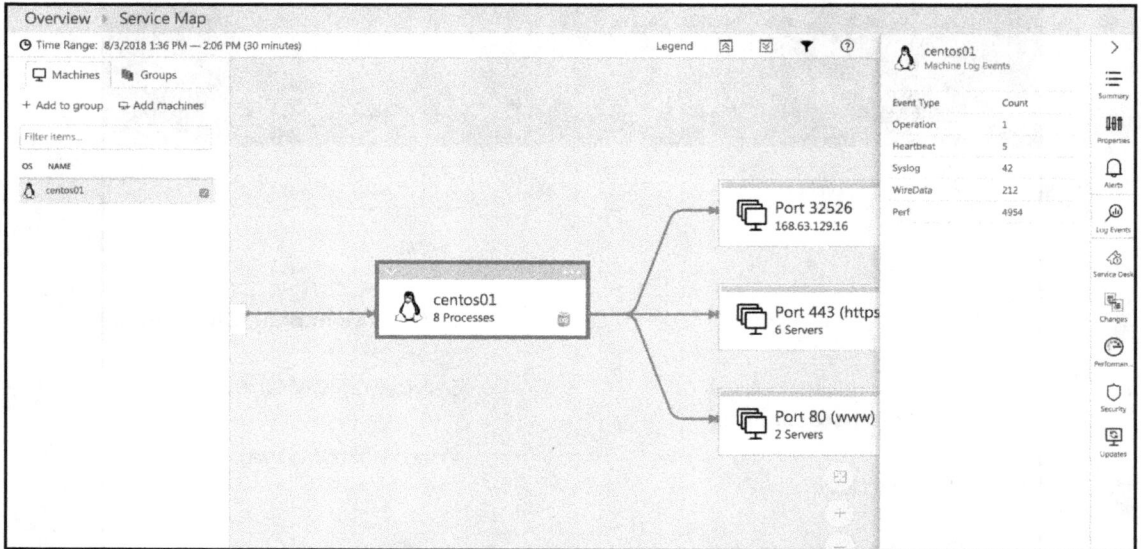

Log Analytics and Kubernetes

Thanks to `https://github.com/Microsoft/OMS-docker`, it is possible to have an OMS agent in Kubernetes. Download from the Kubernetes folder the necessary files:

```
wget
https://raw.githubusercontent.com/Microsoft/OMS-docker/master/Kubernetes/\
    omsagent-ds-secrets.yaml
```

```
wget
https://raw.githubusercontent.com/Microsoft/OMS-docker/master/Kubernetes/om
sagent.yaml
```

```
wget
https://raw.githubusercontent.com/Microsoft/OMS-docker/master/Kubernetes/se
cret-gen.sh
```

```
wget
https://raw.githubusercontent.com/Microsoft/OMS-docker/master/Kubernetes/\
    secret-template.sh
```

Execute the following command:

```
sh secret-gen.sh
```

Provide the OMS workspace ID and the primary key, and the script will generate a secret YAML.

Create the secrets pod:

```
kubectl create -f omsagentsecret.yaml
```

Now create the agent pod:

```
kubectl create -f omsagent-ds-secrets.yaml
```

Or you can do it the easy way with `helm`:

```
helm install --name omsagent --set omsagent.secret.wsid=<Workspace ID>,\
   omsagent.secret.key=<key> stable/msoms
```

Log Analytics for your network

Another solution in the OMS suite is Traffic Analytics. It visualizes network traffic from and to your workloads, including open ports. It is able to generate alerts for security threads; for instance, if an application tries to reach a network, where it's not allowed to so. And, it provides in detail monitoring options with log export options available.

If you want to use Traffic Analytics, first you have to create a network watcher to every region you want to analyze:

```
New-AzureRmNetworkWatcher -Name <name> `
  -ResourceGroupName <resource group> -Location <location>
```

After that, you have to reregister the network provider and add Microsoft Insight, so the network watcher can hook into it:

```
Register-AzureRmResourceProvider -ProviderNamespace `
  "Microsoft.Network"

Register-AzureRmResourceProvider -ProviderNamespace Microsoft.Insights
```

You can't use this solution with other providers, such as the `Microsoft.ClassicNetwork`.

The next step involves **network security group** (**NSG**) flow logging on an NSG. At the moment of writing, this is only possible using the Azure Portal. In the left-hand bar of the Azure Portal, select **Monitor | Network watcher** and then select **NSG flow logs**. Now you are able to select the NSG that you want to enable an **NSG flow log** for.

Enable it, select a storage account, and select your OMS workspace.

> In the third quarter of 2018, the cmdlet `Set-AzureRmNetworkWatcherConfigFlowLog` will be available.

It will take some time before the information is coming in and collected. After about 30 minutes, the first information should be visible: Select **Monitor** in the left-hand bar of the Azure portal, go to the **Network watcher**, and then **Traffic Analytics**. Or, start from your OMS workspace:

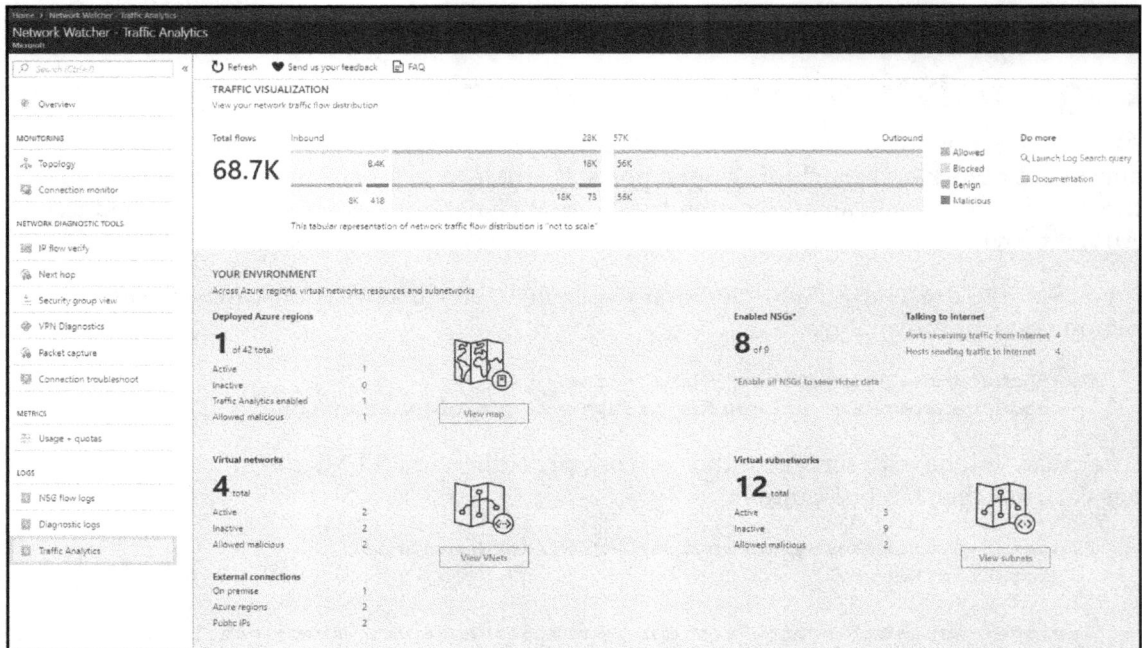

Performance monitoring

In the Azure Management and Operations Management Suite, there are many options available for monitoring. For instance, the performance counters gives you much insight about your workload. There are also application-specific options available.

Even if you don't use OMS, Azure can provide you all kinds of metrics per virtual machine, but not in one central place. Just navigate to your virtual machine. In the **Overview** pane, you can see performance data for CPU, memory, and storage. Detailed information is available in the section **Metrics** under **Monitoring**. There are all kinds of data available, such as CPU, storage, and networking:

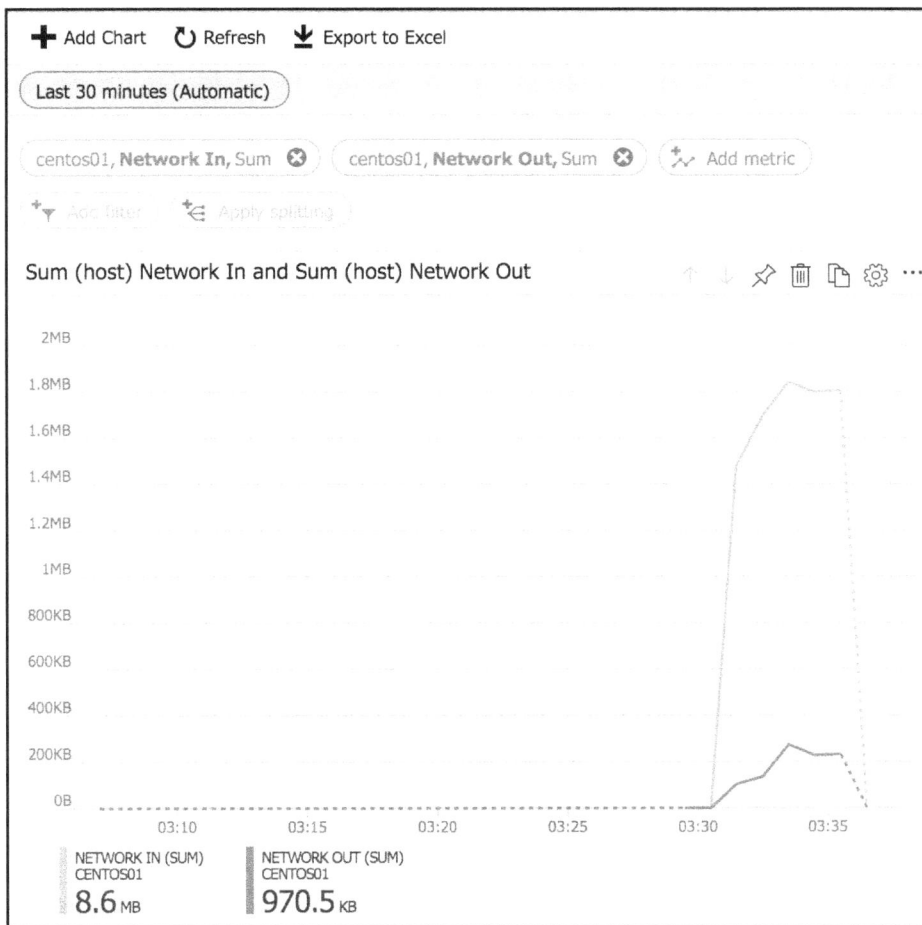

The problem with many of these solutions is that they are application specific, or you are looking into the end-results, without knowing what the cause is. If you need information about the general performance of the resources utilized by the virtual machine(s), use the information provided by Azure. If you need information on the webserver or database you're running, look and see if there is an Azure solution. But in many scenarios, it is very helpful if you can do performance troubleshooting in the virtual machine as well. In a way, we're going to start where the *Process Management* section in the Chapter 3, *Basic Linux Administration* left off.

Before we start, there are multiple ways and methods to do performance troubleshooting. Can the author of this book provide you the only method you should use, or tell you the one tool you'll need? No, unfortunately not! But, what I can do is make you aware of the tools available and cover at least the basic usage. For more specific needs, you can always dive into the man-pages. In this section, we're especially looking into what the load is and who is causing it.

And one last thing: this section is called *Performance Monitoring*, but it's maybe not the perfect title. It's balancing on the edge between monitoring, troubleshooting, and analyzing. However, isn't that often the case in the daily life of every system engineer?

> Not all the tools mentioned are by default available in the Red Hat/CentOS repository. You'll need to configure the epel repository: yum install epel-release.

Displaying Linux processes with top

If you look into a topic as performance monitoring and Linux, top is always mentioned. It is the number one tool command to quickly get an idea of what is running on the system.

You can display many things at the top and it comes with a good man page explaining all the options. Let's focus on the most important ones, starting at the top of the screen:

```
top - 13:54:12 up 26 min,  2 users,  load average: 0.00, 0.15, 0.45
Tasks: 123 total,   1 running, 122 sleeping,   0 stopped,   0 zombie
%Cpu(s):  2.0 us,  0.3 sy,  0.0 ni, 97.7 id,  0.0 wa,  0.0 hi,  0.0 si,  0.0 st
KiB Mem :   931964 total,   281300 free,   209140 used,   441524 buff/cache
KiB Swap:        0 total,        0 free,        0 used.   513504 avail Mem
```

- **Wait IO** (wa): If this value is continuously above 10%, this means that the underlying storage is slowing down the server. It displays the amount of time the CPU spends waiting on the storage system to process a request. In Azure, you can see this often on machines running on HDDs, instead of the standard SSDs. Using multiple HDDs in a raid configuration can help, but it's better to migrate to SSD. If that is not enough, there are premium SSD solutions available as well.
- **User space CPU** (us): CPU utilization by applications; please notice that CPU is summed across all CPUs.
- **System CPU** (sy): The amount of time the CPU spends doing on kernel tasks.
- Swap: Memory paged out caused by having not enough memory for your applications, should be zero most of the time.

The bottom of the top screen also has some interesting columns:

PID	USER	PR	NI	VIRT	RES	SHR	S	%CPU	%MEM	TIME+	COMMAND
3061	root	20	0	396264	26968	5644	S	3.0	2.9	0:46.28	python
1	root	20	0	128016	6236	3724	S	0.0	0.7	0:08.43	systemd
2	root	20	0	0	0	0	S	0.0	0.0	0:00.00	kthreadd
3	root	20	0	0	0	0	S	0.0	0.0	0:00.30	ksoftirqd/0
5	root	0	-20	0	0	0	S	0.0	0.0	0:00.00	kworker/0:+
6	root	20	0	0	0	0	S	0.0	0.0	0:00.67	kworker/u2+
7	root	rt	0	0	0	0	S	0.0	0.0	0:00.00	migration/0
8	root	20	0	0	0	0	S	0.0	0.0	0:00.00	rcu_bh

Personally, I wouldn't advise you to worry about the priority and nice values this day. The effect on the performance is minimal. The first interesting field is **VIRT**: **Virtual Memory** represents how much memory the program is able to access at the present moment. It includes memory shared with other applications, video memory, files that are read into memory by the application and so on. It also includes idle, swapped memory, and residential memory. Residential memory is the memory that is physically in use by this process. **SHR** is the amount of memory that is shared between applications. This information can actually help to have an idea about the amount of swap you should configure on your system: take the top five processes, summarize VIRT and subtract **RES** and **SHR**. It's not perfect, but it's a good indicator.

The last column I want to cover is the status:

- D is uninterruptible sleep, most of the time caused by waiting on storage or network IO.
- R is running—consuming CPU.
- S is sleeping—waiting on IO, no CPU usage. Waiting for a trigger by a user or other process.

- T is stopped by the job control signal, most of the time because the user pressed *Ctrl + Z*.
- Z is zombie—the parent process died, it's labeled as a zombie by the kernel, while the kernel is busy cleaning up. On physical machines, it can also be an indication of failing CPUs (caused by temperature or crappy bios); in that scenario, you can see many zombies. In Azure, that is not going to happen. Zombies don't hurt, so don't kill them; the kernel takes care of this.

Top alternatives

There are many top alike utilities, such as **htop**, which looks fancier and is easier to configure.

Very similar but even more interesting is **atop**. It offers accounting of all processes and their resource usage, even for the processes that died between atop's screen updates. This comprehensive accounting is very helpful for understanding problems by individually short-lived processes. Atop is also able to gather information about running containers, networking, and storage.

Another one is **nmon**, which is similar to atop, but is more focused on statistics and gives more detailed information, especially for memory and storage:

```
nmon-16g────[H for help]───Hostname=centos01────Refresh= 2secs ──14:32.19─
┌ CPU Utilisation Stats ┐
ALL    3.5    0.0    0.0    96.0    0.0    0.0    0.0    0.0    0.0    0.0
CPU  User%  Nice%   Sys%  Idle%  Wait% HWirq% SWirq% Steal% Guest% GuestNice%
 1     3.5    0.0    0.0    96.0    0.0    0.0    0.0    0.0    0.0    0.0
┌ Memory and Swap ┐
PageSize:4KB    RAM-Memory  Swap-Space        High-Memory     Low-Memory
Total (MB)        910.1        0.0          - not in use    - not in use
Free  (MB)        154.5        0.0
Free Percent       17.0%       0.0%
Linux Kernel Internal Memory (MB)
                       Cached=    455.5    Active=    404.0
Buffers=    2.0 Swapcached=        0.0  Inactive =   179.9
Dirty  =    0.0 Writeback =        0.0  Mapped   =    24.7
Slab   =   94.9 Commit_AS =      730.4  PageTables=    7.3
┌ Virtual Memory ┐
nr_dirty    =        9 pgpgin    =        0              High Normal    DMA
nr_writeback=        0 pgpgout   =       60  alloc          0      0      0
nr_unstable =        0 pgpswpin  =        0  refill         0      0      0
nr_table_pgs=     1876 pgpswpout =        0  steal          0      0      0
nr_mapped   =     6325 pgfree    =       75  scan_kswapd    0      0      0
nr_slab     =       -1 pgactivate =       0  scan_direct    0      0      0
                        pgdeactivate=       0
allocstall  =        0 pgfault   =     1416  kswapd_steal   =      0
```

`nmon` can also be used to collect data:

```
nmon -f -s 60 -c 30
```

The preceding command collects every minute thirty rounds of information in a comma-separated file format that is easy to parse in a spreadsheet. On the developers website of IBM, `https://www.ibm.com/developerworks/community/wikis/home?lang=en#!/wiki/Power+Systems/page/nmon_analyser`, you can find an Excel spreadsheet, which makes this a very easy job. It even offers some extra data-analyzing options.

Glances is also gaining a lot of popularity lately:

```
centos01 (CentOS Linux 7.5.1804 64bit / Linux 3.10.0-862.3.3.el7.x86_64)            Uptime: 15:16:36

CPU  [  8.0%]   CPU       8.0%      MEM      60.9%     SWAP      0.0%      LOAD     1-core
MEM  [ 60.9%]   user:     5.2%      total:   910M      total:    0        1 min:   0.07
SWAP [  0.0%]   system:   2.3%      used:    555M      used:     0        5 min:   0.06
                idle:     92.6%     free:    356M      free:     0        15 min:  0.05

NETWORK      Rx/s    Tx/s    TASKS 124 (215 thr), 2 run, 122 slp, 0 oth sorted automatically
eth0         442Kb   215Kb
lo           0b      0b      CPU%  MEM%    PID USER      NI S Command
                            3.8   1.6    2795 linvirt    0 R /usr/bin/python /usr/bin/glances
DISK I/O     R/s     W/s     2.6   2.7    3061 root       0 S python -u bin/WALinuxAgent-2.2.30
fd0          0       0       0.3   0.2     510 root       0 S /usr/lib/systemd/systemd-logind
sda1         0       0       0.3   0.4    1274 postfix    0 S cleanup -z -t unix -u
sda2         0       21K     0.3   0.6       1 root       0 S /usr/lib/systemd/systemd --switch
sdb1         0       0       0.3   0.4     350 root       0 S /usr/lib/systemd/systemd-journald
                            0.0   0.2     795 root       0 S /sbin/dhclient -q -lf /var/lib/dh
FILE SYS     Used    Total   0.0   0.2     372 root       0 S /usr/sbin/lvmetad -f
/ (sda2)     4.38G   29.5G   0.0   0.0      28 root       5 S ksmd
/boot        105M    497M    0.0   0.0   47876 root       0 S kworker/u256:1
_resource    16.0M   3.87G   0.0   0.0     277 root     -20 S xfs-cil/sda2
                            0.0   0.0     278 root     -20 S xfs-reclaim/sda
```

It is the most advanced one. It offers all the features of the alternatives, and, on top of it, you can use it remotely. Execute on the server:

```
glances --username <username> --password <password> --server
```

Execute on the client too:

```
glances --client @<ip address>
```

By default, port `61209` is used. If you use the `--webserver` parameter instead of `--server`, you even don't need a client. A complete web interface is available on port `61208`!

Glances is able to export logs in many formats and can be queried using an API. Experimental support for the SNMP protocol is on the way as well.

Sysstat – a collection of performance-monitoring tools

The `sysstat` package contains utilities for performance monitoring. The most important ones in Azure are `sar`, `iostat`, and `pidstat`. If you are also using Azure File storage, `cifsiostat` can become handy as well.

`sar` is the main utility. The main syntax is this:

```
sar -<resource> interval count
```

For instance, to report CPU statistics five times with an interval of one second:

```
sar -u 1 5
```

To monitor cores one and two:

```
sar -P 1 2 1 5
```

(If you want to monitor all the cores individually you can use the keyword: `ALL`.)

Here are some other important resources:

- `-r`: Memory
- `-s`: Swap
- `-d`: Disk
- `-n <type>`, network types, such as these:
  - `DEV`: Displays network devices EDEV
  - `NFS`: Displays NFS client activities
  - `SOCK`: Displays sockets in use for IPv4
  - `IP`: Displays IPv4 network traffic
  - `TCP`: Displays TCPv4 network traffic
  - `UDP`: Displays UDPv4 network traffic
  - `ALL` types: This displays all of the preceding information

`pidstat` can collect CPU data from a specific process, by their process ID, in the next screenshot, two samples show every five seconds. It can do the same for memory and disk:

```
[linvirt@centos01 ~]$ pidstat -p 53287 2 5
Linux 3.10.0-862.3.3.el7.x86_64 (centos01)        08/05/2018        _x86_64_        (1 CPU)

03:15:12 PM   UID       PID    %usr %system  %guest    %CPU   CPU  Command
03:15:14 PM     0     53287    7.11    0.00    0.00    7.11     0  sysbench
03:15:16 PM     0     53287    8.04    0.50    0.00    8.54     0  sysbench
03:15:18 PM     0     53287    5.56    0.00    0.00    5.56     0  sysbench
03:15:20 PM     0     53287    7.50    0.00    0.00    7.50     0  sysbench
03:15:22 PM     0     53287    8.04    0.00    0.00    8.04     0  sysbench
Average:        0     53287    7.25    0.10    0.00    7.35     -  sysbench
```

`iostat` is the utility, as you can already assume from the name, it can measure IO but it also creates reports for CPU usage:

```
[linvirt@centos01 ~]$ iostat -dh 1 /dev/sda 1
Linux 3.10.0-862.3.3.el7.x86_64 (centos01)        08/05/2018        _x86_64_        (1 CPU)

Device:          tps   kB_read/s   kB_wrtn/s    kB_read    kB_wrtn
sda
               19.72      744.20     1530.29    4880180   10035037
```

`tps` means number of transfers per second issued to the device is a function of track seek time. The `kb_read/s` and `kB_wrtn/s` is the amount of KB per second measured during one second; the last column is the total amount where the first report contains statistics for the time since system startup.

During the installation of the `sysstat` package, a cronjob was installed in the file `/etc/cron.d/sysstat`.

> In modern Linux systems, both systemd-timers and the old method using cron are available. `sysstat` is still using crons. To check whether the cron is available and running, go to here: `systemctl | grep cron`. This can help.

The cron runs every 10 minutes the `sa1` command that collects system activity daily and stores it in a binary database. Once a day, the `sa2` command is executed to generate a report. The data is stored in the `/var/log/sa` directory. You can query that database with `sadf`:

```
[root@centos01 sa]# sadf -s 15:20:00 -e 15:40:00 /var/log/sa/sa03
localhost.localdomain    598    2018-08-03 15:30:01 UTC all    %user    2.61
localhost.localdomain    598    2018-08-03 15:30:01 UTC all    %nice    0.00
localhost.localdomain    598    2018-08-03 15:30:01 UTC all    %system 0.67
localhost.localdomain    598    2018-08-03 15:30:01 UTC all    %iowait 0.00
localhost.localdomain    598    2018-08-03 15:30:01 UTC all    %steal   0.00
localhost.localdomain    598    2018-08-03 15:30:01 UTC all    %idle   96.72
```

This screenshot shows the data from the August 3, between `15:20:00` and `15:40:00`. By default, it's displaying CPU stats, but you can customize it using the same parameters as `sar`, for instance:

```
adf /var/log/sa/sa03 -- -n DEV
```

This displays the network stats of every network interface on the August 3.

dstat

`sysstat` is available for historical reports, `dstat` is for real-time supports. Where top is the monitoring version of `ps`, `dstat` is the monitoring version of `sar`:

```
[root@centos01 sa]# dstat
You did not select any stats, using -cdngy by default.
----total-cpu-usage---- -dsk/total- -net/total- ---paging-- ---system--
usr sys idl wai hiq siq| read  writ| recv  send|  in   out | int   csw
 10   2  75  14   0   0|1205k 2727k|   0     0 |   0     0 |  41   315
  1   0  99   0   0   0|   0     0 | 330B  962B|   0     0 |  22   131
  0   1  99   0   0   0|   0     0 |  66B  350B|   0     0 |  22   120
  0   1  99   0   0   0|  32k  510k|  66B  350B|   0     0 |  29   180
  7   1  92   0   0   0|   0   164k|  88k   15k|   0     0 |  62   281
  0   0 100   0   0   0|   0     0 |  66B  358B|   0     0 |  23   130
  0   0 100   0   0   0|   0     0 |  66B  350B|   0     0 |  21   119
  7   2  91   0   0   0|   0    60k|  94k   17k|   0     0 |  72   441
  1   0  99   0   0   0|   0     0 |  66B  358B|   0     0 |  26   124
  0   0 100   0   0   0|   0     0 |  66B  350B|   0     0 |  22   148
```

If you don't want to see it all at once, add the following parameter(s), such as these:

- c: CPU
- d: Disk
- n: Network
- g: Paging
- s: Swap
- m: Memory

Network stats with iproute2

Earlier in this chapter, we talked about ip. This command also provides an option to get statistics for the network interface:

```
ip -s link show dev eth0
```

```
[root@centos01 sa]# ip -s link show dev eth0
2: eth0: <BROADCAST,MULTICAST,UP,LOWER_UP> mtu 1500 qdisc mq state UP mode DEFAULT group defaul
t qlen 1000
    link/ether 00:0d:3a:36:76:21 brd ff:ff:ff:ff:ff:ff
    RX: bytes  packets  errors  dropped overrun mcast
    450592991  442379   0       0       0       1
    TX: bytes  packets  errors  dropped carrier collsns
    70900598   225254   0       0       0       0
```

It parses information from the directory /proc/net. Another utility that can parse this information is ss. A simple summary can be requested with this:

```
ss -s
```

Using the -t parameter not only shows you the ports in listening state, but also the incoming and outgoing traffic on this specific interface.

If you need more details, the `iproute2` package provides you with another utility: `nstat`. Using the `-d` parameter, you can even run it in on interval mode:

```
[root@centos01 sa]# nstat
#kernel
IpInReceives            682          0.0
IpInDelivers            682          0.0
IpOutRequests           905          0.0
TcpActiveOpens          113          0.0
TcpEstabResets          3            0.0
TcpInSegs               568          0.0
TcpOutSegs              847          0.0
TcpOutRsts              3            0.0
UdpInDatagrams          114          0.0
UdpOutDatagrams         112          0.0
TcpExtTW                4            0.0
TcpExtTCPHPHits         57           0.0
TcpExtTCPPureAcks       146          0.0
TcpExtTCPHPAcks         60           0.0
TcpExtTCPAbortOnClose   3            0.0
TcpExtTCPRcvCoalesce    3            0.0
TcpExtTCPAutoCorking    18           0.0
TcpExtTCPOrigDataSent   443          0.0
IpExtInOctets           1189603      0.0
IpExtOutOctets          241424       0.0
IpExtInNoECTPkts        1413         0.0
```

That's already much more than the simple summary of `ss`. But the `iproute2` package has more to offer: `lnstat`.

This is the command:

```
lnstat -d
```

This shows you everything it can display or monitor. It's pretty low-level, but the author of this book solved already some firewall performance-related issues, using `lnstat -f /proc/net/stat/nf_conntrack`, while monitoring the drops counter.

Network monitoring with IPTraf-NG

Yes, you can get network details from tools such as `nmon`, but if you want details, IPTraf-NG is a very nice tool to do real-time monitoring. It is a console-based network-monitoring utility that collects all the network data and is able to break down the information in size or TCP/UDP. A few basic filters are included as well.

Everything is in a menu-driven interface, so there are no parameters that you have to remember:

tcpdump

Of course, `tcpdump`, is not a performance-monitoring solution. This utility is a great tool to monitor, capture, and analyze network traffic.

To view network traffic on all the network interfaces, execute the following:

```
tcpdump -i any
```

Or on a specific interface, try this:

```
tcpdump -i eth0
```

In general, it's a good idea not to resolve the hostnames:

```
tcpdump -n -i eth0
```

You can add different levels of verbosity, by multiplying the parameter v, with the maximum verbosity of three:

```
tcpdump -n -i eth0 -vvv
```

You can filter the traffic based on source and destination IP:

```
tcpdump host <ip address> -n -i eth0
```

Or based on source or destination IP:

```
tcpdump src <source ip address -n -i eth0
```

```
tcpdump dst <destination ip address> -n -i eth0
```

Filtering on a specific port is also possible:

```
tcpdump port 22
```

```
tcpdump src port 22
```

```
tcpdump not port 22
```

All parameters can be combined:

```
tcpdump -n dst net <subnet> and not port ssh -c 5
```

The parameter -c was added, so only five packets were captured. You can save the captured data to a file:

```
tcpdump -v -x -XX -w /tmp/capture.log
```

Two parameters were added to increase the compatibility with other analyzers that can read the format of tcpdump:

- -XX: Print the data of each packet in hex and ASCII format
- -x: Add headers to every packet

To read the data with a complete timestamp in human readable format, use this code:

```
tcpdump -tttt -r /tmp/capture.log
```

> **TIP**
>
> Another great network analyzer is Wireshark. It's a graphical tool available for many operating systems. This analyzer can import the captured data of `tcpdump`. It comes with a great search filter and analyzing tools for many different network protocols and services.
>
> It makes sense to make the capture in your virtual machine and download it to your workstation to analyze the data further in Wireshark.

Summary

In this chapter, we covered several topics regarding troubleshooting, logging, monitoring, and even analyzing. Starting with getting access to a virtual machine, we investigated logging in Linux, locally and remotely.

There is a thin line between performance monitoring and performance troubleshooting. There are many, many different utilities available to find out what the cause is of your performance issues. Each has a different goal, but there is also much overlap. I covered the most popular utilities in Linux and some of the options available in Linux.

In the first chapter, I showed you that Azure is a very open source friendly environment and that Microsoft puts a lot of effort to make Azure an open, standard cloud solution with interoperability in mind. In this chapter, I showed you that Microsoft not only puts a lot of effort in supporting Linux while deploying your application but also in supporting it in the Azure management and operations management suite.

Questions

1. Why should you have at least one user with a password in a virtual machine?
2. What is the purpose of the `systemd-journald` daemon?
3. What are syslog facilities?
4. Which priorities are available in syslog?
5. How can you add entries in the log and why should you do that?
6. Which services are available to view metrics in Azure?

7. Why is `top` only useful to have a first look into performance-related problems, and which utility or utilities can fix that?
8. What is the difference between the `sysstat` utilities and `dstat`?
9. Why should you install Wireshark on your workstation?

Further reading

My first steps into the performance and troubleshooting world, already many years ago, were started by documents written by Sander van Vugt. Many of this information and more survived in a video course: *Red Hat Performance Troubleshooting and Optimization* (`https://www.sandervanvugt.com/`).

Another big source of information is the website of Brendan D Gregg (`http://www.brendangregg.com`), where he shares an unbelievably big list of his documentation, slides, videos and so on. On top of that, there are some some nice utilities! He was the one who taught me in 2015 that it is important how to identify the problem:

- What makes you think that there is a problem?
- Was there a time that there wasn't a problem?
- Has something changed recently?
- Try to find technical descriptions: such as latency, run-time error and so on.
- Is it only the application, or are other resources affected as well?
- Come up with an exact description of the environment.

You also have to consider the following:

- Who is causing the load (which process, IP address and so on)?
- Why was the load called?
- Which resource(s) is/are used by the load?
- Does the load change? If so, how is it changing over time?

Last, but not least, the *Red Hat Enterprise Linux Troubleshooting Guide* by Benjamin Cane. I know, some parts of the book are outdated, as it was printed in 2015. And, for sure, I definitely hope for a second edition, but, especially if you are more or less new to Linux, buy this book.

Assessments

Chapter 1: Exploring the Azure Cloud

1. You can virtualize compute, network, and storage. Of course, at the end of the day you'll still need hardware somewhere in the world to run the hypervisors, and possibly a cloud platform on top of that.
2. In hardware virtualization, everything is transformed into software. In container virtualization, only processes are isolated. You're still using the same kernel and hardware as the host.
3. It depends; do you develop your application on the same platform? PaaS is the service type for you, otherwise use IaaS. SaaS provides an application, it's not a hosting platform.
4. It depends; Azure is compliant with and helps you to comply with legal rules and security/privacy policies. Plus, there is the concept of different regions: if there are concerns about having data in other parts of the world. But there are always exceptions, most of the time company policies or governmental rulings.
5. In question 4, you can see that regions play a role in possible legal issues. On top of that, it is very important for scalability, performance, and redundancy.
6. Central Identity Management, not only in Azure but also in a hybrid environment for your own data center.

Chapter 2: Getting Started with the Azure Cloud

1. It helps with automation. Besides that, the web-based portal changes frequently, and the command-line interface is much more stabilized. In my opinion, it also gives you a better understanding of the underlying technology, caused by a more or less strict workflow.
2. It provides access to store data. You'll need one for boot diagnostics and data for the Azure Cloud Shell. More details in Chapter 4, *Managing Azure*.
3. The storage account must be unique in Azure.

4. An offer is a group of related images offered by a publisher, such as UbuntuServer. An image is a specific image.

5. A stopped virtual machine is halted at the OS level. A dynamically allocated public IP address will not be released and the virtual machine still costs money.

6. Not sending the username and password over the internet.

7. Both a public and private key will be created (if they are still necessary) and stored in your home directory (~/.ssh); the public key will be stored in the virtual machine as well.

Chapter 3: Basic Linux Administration

1. `for user in lisa john karel carola; useradd $user; done`

2. `passwd <user>`

3. `getent <user>`

4. `groupadd finance; groupadd staff`

5. `groupmems -g <group> -a <user>`, alternatively: `usermod -aG <group> <user>`

6. **mkdir -m 2770 /home/{staff,finance}**
   chown -R .staff /home/staff
   chown -R .finance /home/finance

7. `setfacl -m g:staff:rx /home/finance; setfacl -d -m g:staff:rx /home/finance`

8. The sgid bit on the directory (mode 2770) and the default acl (`setfacl -d`) will take care of that.

Chapter 4: Managing Azure

1. Virtual networks with a
   - Resource Group
   - Vnet
   - Configured subnet
   - Network security group
   - Public IP address
   - Network interface

2. A storage account to storage diagnostic data and have access to other data store services.

3. Sometimes (for instance, for a storage account), the name must be unique. A prefix combined with a random generated number is a nice way make the name recognizable and unique.

4. To define the network that can be used within a virtual network.

5. To create one or more subnets within the virtual network that can be isolated or routed to each other, without going outside the virtual network.

6. A network security group provides access control lists for the network and provides port-forwarding to the virtual machines or containers.

7. Traffic from the virtual machine to the internet is done via Source Network Address Translation (SNAT). This means that the IP address of the originating packet is replaced with the public IP address.

8. A dynamically allocated public IP address will be released when the virtual machine is deallocated. When the virtual machine starts again, it will get another IP address.

Chapter 5: Advanced Linux Administration

1. The Linux kernel.

2. Systemd-udevd.

3. `ls /sys/class/net` and `ip link show`.

4. The Azure agent for Linux.

5. ls `/sys/class/net` and `lsblk`. The `lsscsi` command can be helpful as well.

6. It is a good idea to use RAID0 to improve performance and allow improved throughput compared to using just a single disk.

7. At the filesystem level using BTRFS or ZFS, or at the block level using Linux Software Raid (`mdadm`) or LVM (not covered in this chapter).

8. Create the raid, format it, and make a mount point:

```
mdadm --create /dev/md127 --level 0 --raid-devices 3 \
    /dev/sd{c,d,e}
mkfs.xfs -L myraid /dev/md127

mkdir /mnt/myraid
```

Create a unit file, /etc/systemd/system/mnt-myraid.mount:

```
[Unit]
Description = myRaid volume

[Mount]
Where = /mnt/myraid
What = /dev/md127
Type = xfs

[Install]
WantedBy = local-fs.mount
```

Start and enable it at boot:

```
systemctl enable --now mnt-myraid.mount
```

Chapter 6: Managing Linux Security and Identities

1. Using the firewall-cmd file or by deploying XML files in the /etc/firewalld directory.
2. Otherwise it's runtime only and not persistent across reboots.
3. In Linux, you can restrict access using ACLs in Systemd. Some applications also provides other Host Allow/Deny options. In Azure, you have the network security groups and the Azure Firewall service.
4. DAC restricts access based on users/groups and permissions on files. MAC further restricts access based on classification labels for each resource object.
5. If you gain access illegally to an application or system, in DAC, there is no way to prevent further access, especially for files with the same user/group owner and files with permissions for others. MAC frameworks utilitizing the Linux Security Modules to fix this problem are as follows:
   - SELinux: Red Hat-based distributions and SUSE
   - AppArmor: Ubuntu and SUSE
   - The lesser known Tomoyo: SUSE, not covered in this book

6. Besides the fact that SELinux can protect more resource objects, AppArmor protects per application, while SELinux protects the whole system:
   - Kerberos client for authorization
   - SSSD: A backend that is responsible for the configuration and utilization of features such as using and caching credentials
   - Samba libraries to be compatible with Windows features/options
   - Some utilities to join and manage the domain, such as `realm`, `adcli`, and the `net` command

Chapter 7: Deploying Your Virtual Machines

1. To get a reproducible environment quickly up and running.
2. Besides the answer to the previous question, a standardized working environment makes team-based application-development possible.
3. Scripting is very flexible and it's somewhat easier to make it exactly the way you want it. But you have to create everything yourself. In automation, the hard work is already done and it's often a little bit more platform agnostic.
4. The Azure Resource Manager is the most important one. For initial configuration, the Cloud-Init and the Custom Script Extension are available.
5. Vagrant deploys a workload in Azure; Packer creates a custom image that you can deploy.
6. For multiple reasons; the most important ones are as follows:
   - Security
   - To much customization needed on a standard image
   - Not dependent on the offerings of a third party
   - Capture an existing virtual machine
   - Convert a snapshot to an image
   - Build a custom VHD and upload it
   - Packer

Chapter 8: Exploring Continuous Configuration Automation

Example scripts are available on GitHub.

Chapter 9: Container Virtualization in Azure

1. Many similar applications with the same needs, such as OS dependencies and software installed. On top of that, you need availability and scalability.
2. Exactly the opposite. If there are many different workloads, it's often not worth the effort. Another reason is security: containers are much harder to protect.
3. In general, a virtual machine is the solution here, but LXC is a very usable solution. It's somewhere between a virtual machine and a container in terms of creating and managing it.
4. Tools such as Buildah make it possible to create virtual machines that can be used in every solution. Rkt also supports the Docker format. The Open Container Initiative is working very hard to create standards to make it even easier.
5. Development can be pretty expensive if you do everything in the cloud. Developing locally and then pushing to a remote environment is a very good solution.
6. It's container-platform-agnostic, and the acbuild tool for Rkt is not maintained any longer. In the opinion of the author, it's easier to use than other tools and you don't need a Docker daemon running.
7. It makes availability and scalability almost impossible. Besides that, containers are not always easy to back up.

Chapter 10: Working with the Azure Kubernetes Service

1. Develop locally, deploy remotely.
2. `kubectl config use-context <cluster>`.
3. A pod is a group of containers with shared resources, such as storage and network.
4. A pod shares resources between the containers within the pod, this can be useful for containers with helper applications such as logging and monitoring and reverse proxies:
   - Using the `kubectl --image` command
   - Using a specification file in YAML format
   - Helm

5. There are multiple methods available. In this chapter, Draft was covered during the early stages of development, and then Helm afterwards.

6. You don't need to do that yourself. It will be done automatically by Azure.

7. If you want access to a filesystem read/write at the same time from multiple containers, you'll need a clustered filesystem and iSCSI.

8. Example code is provided on GitHub.

Chapter 11: Troubleshooting and Monitoring Your Workloads

1. To be able to log in into the virtual machine console, you'll need a username and password. If the Azure Agent is not reachable, you can't reset the credentials or create a password for users that are normally able to log in via SSH.

2. To collect all the standard output, syslog messages, and related messages from the kernel, systemd processes, and the units.

3. Syslog is using the following list of severities (per application):
   - Alert: action must be taken immediately
   - Critical: critical conditions
   - Error: error conditions
   - Warning: warning conditions
   - Notice: normal but significant condition
   - Informational: informational messages
   - Debug: debug-level messages

4. Use `logger` or `systemd-cat`. You can use that if an application or script doesn't have syslog support. Another option is to add logging entries as a part of your change-management.

5. Per virtual machine metrics and the Microsoft Operations Management Suite.

6. There are several shortcomings in the `top` utility: for instance, you can't see short-lived processes. The `atop` and `dstat` utilities are solutions to this problem.

7. sysstat utilities provides historical data; dstat provides real-time monitoring.

8. It makes the collection of data coming from `tcpdump` easier to read and it has great analysis potential.

Other Books You May Enjoy

If you enjoyed this book, you may be interested in these other books by Packt:

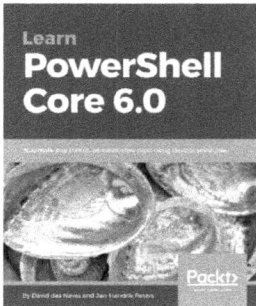

Learn PowerShell Core 6.0
David das Neves, Jan-Hendrik Peters

ISBN: 978-1-78883-898-6

- Get to grips with PowerShell Core 6.0
- Explore basic and advanced PowerShell scripting techniques
- Get to grips with Windows PowerShell Security
- Work with centralization and DevOps with PowerShell
- Implement PowerShell in your organization through real-life examples
- Learn to create GUIs and use DSC in production

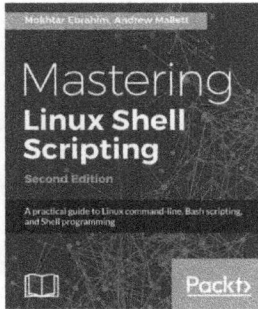

Mastering Linux Shell Scripting - Second Edition
Mokhtar Ebrahim, Andrew Mallett

ISBN: 978-1-78899-055-4

- Make, execute, and debug your first Bash script
- Create interactive scripts that prompt for user input
- Foster menu structures for operators with little command-line experience
- Develop scripts that dynamically edit web configuration files to produce a new virtual host
- Write scripts that use AWK to search and reports on log files
- Draft effective scripts using functions as building blocks, reducing maintenance and build time
- Make informed choices by comparing different script languages such as Python with BASH

Leave a review - let other readers know what you think

Please share your thoughts on this book with others by leaving a review on the site that you bought it from. If you purchased the book from Amazon, please leave us an honest review on this book's Amazon page. This is vital so that other potential readers can see and use your unbiased opinion to make purchasing decisions, we can understand what our customers think about our products, and our authors can see your feedback on the title that they have worked with Packt to create. It will only take a few minutes of your time, but is valuable to other potential customers, our authors, and Packt. Thank you!

Index

R

Raid
about 142, 143
reference 142
Read The Fine Manual (RTFM) 53
RedDog Front-End (RDFE) 13
Resource Group
reference 27
resources, PowerShell desired state configuration
(DSC)
nxArchive 261
nxEnvironment 261
nxFile 261
nxFileLine 261
nxGroup 261
nxPackage 261
nxScript 261
nxService 261
nxUser 261
reference 261
rfc5424
reference 348
Rkt
about 276
images, creating with acbuild 279, 280, 281
images, creating with Buildah 281, 282, 283
implementing 276, 277, 278, 279
reference 276, 277
role based access control (RBAC) 171
rpm query
parameters 112
RPM software manager 112, 113, 114
RSYSLOG
journald, integrating 349

S

SaltStack
about 246
authorization 248, 249
execution modules, using 249
grains 251
installation 247
integration, with Azure 253, 254, 256
reference 252, 253

state conditions 252
states 250
templates 253
terminology 246
top file, creating 251
variables 253
SELinux
about 162
Boolean 169
configuration 163, 164
context on files 167, 168, 169
context on ports 164, 165, 167
reference 162
snapshots
custom images, creating 216, 217
SOA 10
Software Defined Networking (SDN) 9
software management
about 111
DPKG software manager 115, 116
RPM software manager 112, 113, 114
with apt 121, 122
with YUM 116, 117
with Zypp 118, 119, 120
Software-Defined Datacenter (SDDC) 9, 10
Software-Defined Storage (SDS) 9
Source Network Address Translation (SNAT) 100
Splunk 349
SSH private key
Linux virtual machine, logging into 37, 38
storage accounts
Blob storage 85
storage 85
StorageV2 85
storage services
Azure Files 85, 91
Azure Files, using 92, 93
Azure Queue storage 85
Blob storage 84, 94, 95, 97
Disk storage 85
managed disks 88, 90, 91
storage accounts 85, 86, 87
Table storage 85
types 84
storage

www.ingramcontent.com/pod-product-compliance
Lightning Source LLC
Chambersburg PA
CBHW081040220326
41598CB00038B/6944